THE DEVELOPMENT OF MENTAL PROCESSING: EFFICIENCY, WORKING MEMORY, AND THINKING

Andreas Demetriou
Constantinos Christou
George Spanoudis
Maria Platsidou

WITH COMMENTARY BY
Kurt W. Fischer
Theo L. Dawson

Willis F. Overton
Series Editor

MONOGRAPHS OF THE SOCIETY FOR RESEARCH IN CHILD DEVELOPMENT
Serial No. 268, Vol. 67, No. 1, 2002

Blackwell
Publishing

Boston, Massachusetts   Oxford, United Kingdom

THE DEVELOPMENT
OF MENTAL PROCESSING:
EFFICIENCY, WORKING MEMORY,
AND THINKING

CONTENTS

COMMENTARY

ABSTRACT

DEMETRIOU, ANDREAS; CHRISTOU, CONSTANTINOS; SPANOUDIS, GEORGE; and PLATSIDOU, MARIA. The Development of Mental Processing: Efficiency, Working Memory, and Thinking. *Monographs of the Society for Research in Child Development*, 2002, **67**(1, Serial No. 268).

This *Monograph* aims to contribute to the information processing, the differential, and the developmental modeling of the mind, and to work these into an integrated theory. Toward this aim, a longitudinal study is presented that investigates the relations between processing efficiency, working memory, and problem solving from the age of 8 years to to the age of 16 years. The study involved 113 participants, about equally drawn among 8-, 10-, 12-, and 14-year-olds at the first testing; these participants were tested two more times spaced one year apart. Participants were tested with a large array of tasks addressed to processing efficiency (i.e., speed of processing and inhibition), working memory (in terms of Baddeley's model, phonological storage, visual storage, and the central executive of working memory), and problem solving (quantitative, spatial, and verbal reasoning).

Confirmatory factor analysis validated the presence of each of the above dimensions and indicated that they are organized in a three-stratum hierarchy. The first stratum includes all of the individual dimensions mentioned above. These dimensions are organized, at the second stratum, in three constructs: processing efficiency, working memory, and problem solving. Finally, all second-order constructs are strongly related to a third-order general factor. This structure was stable in time.

Structural equation modeling indicated that the various dimensions are interrelated in a cascade fashion so that more fundamental dimensions are part of more complex dimensions. That is, speed of processing is the most important aspect of processing efficiency, and it perfectly relates to the condition of inhibition, indicating that the more efficient one is in stimulus encoding and identification, the more efficient one is in inhibition. In turn, processing efficiency is strongly related to the condition of executive processes in working memory, which, in turn, is related to the condition of the two modality-specific stores (phonological and visual). Finally, problem solving is related to processing efficiency and working memory, the central executive in particular.

All dimensions appear to change systematically with time. Growth modeling suggested that there are significant individual differences in attainment in each of the three aspects of the mind investigated. Moreover, each of the three aspects of the mind as well as their interrelations change differently during development. Mixture growth modeling suggested that there are four types of developing persons, each defined by a different combination of performance in these aspects of the mind. Some types are more efficient and stable developers than others. These analyses indicated that processing efficiency is a factor closely associated with developmental differences in problem solving, whereas working memory is associated with individual differences. Modeling by logistic equations uncovered the rates and form of change in the various dimensions and their reciprocal interactions during development. These findings are discussed from the point of view of information processing, differential, and developmental models of thinking, and an integrative model is proposed.

I. INTRODUCTION: THE INFORMATION PROCESSING, THE DIFFERENTIAL, AND THE DEVELOPMENTAL TRADITIONS IN THE STRUCTURE AND DEVELOPMENT OF THE MIND

For almost a century, scientific study of the human mind has been conducted from the perspective of three distinct epistemological traditions: the experimental, the differential, and the developmental. The experimental tradition has focused primarily on the more dynamic aspects of mental functioning to explain how information from the environment is recorded, processed, represented, and stored for the purpose of understanding and problem solving. In the experimental tradition, information processing models have dominated research and theorizing since the early 1950s. For example, Broadbent (1958) pioneered the assumption that humans are active processors of information who operate under limited processing resources, which frequently suffice for only a part of the information that may reach the senses. Fighter pilots, for example, frequently cannot make use of all of the information provided by the plane's instruments and this may be the cause of improper manipulations or even accidents. Thus, Broadbent considered selective attention to be a crucial mechanism in problem solving and decision making because it enables the thinker to focus the available limited processing resources on task-relevant information. G. A. Miller (1956), at about the same time, proposed that the capacity of the processing resources available to the normal human adult equals seven units or chunks of information, plus or minus two.

Thanks to these pioneers, today it is generally accepted that humans usually operate under conditions of uncertainty caused by conflicting, incongruent, or redundant information relative to a specific goal. Thus, to meet their goals, humans must be able to focus attention and process goal-relevant information efficiently, filtering out goal-irrelevant information. In effect, speed of processing, controlled attention, and working memory are considered to be important variables in understanding, learning, and problem solving (Deary, 2000; Lohman, 2000; MacLeod, 1991).

1

It may be noted that this tradition bases its models on evidence normally gathered under controlled laboratory situations where individuals are led to respond to very carefully manipulated stimulus conditions.

The differential tradition has primarily attempted to measure and explain individual differences in mental abilities. This tradition has been very successful in two respects: Psychometric research has uncovered a number of stable dimensions of ability and cognitive functioning that can be used to compare individuals, and it has advanced models about the organization of these dimensions. Most of the models that dominate psychometric theory and research today involve abilities or constructs organized in three hierarchical levels or strata (Carroll, 1993; Davidson & Downing, 2000; Gustafsson & Undheim, 1996; Jensen, 1998; Kaufman, 2000; Mackintosh, 2000; Sternberg, 1985; Sternberg 1975).

At the first or basic level there are many narrow task- or medium-specific abilities, such as reasoning in different contexts (e.g., mathematical reasoning, inductive reasoning, classificatory reasoning), speed of processing in different contexts (e.g., speed of reasoning, speed of perceptual recognition, reaction time), and different types of memory (e.g., memory span for words, numbers, and forms or locations), and so forth.

At the second level there is a set of broad abilities or modules of thought and problem solving that enable thinking and problem solving in a particular type or domain of information and problems. Spatial, verbal, and numerical reasoning abilities, frequently identified by tests of intelligence, are examples of abilities of this kind. The narrow or specific abilities or processes described above are considered to emanate from these broad abilities. In other words, the narrow or medium-specific abilities are instantiations of these broad abilities in different contexts or conditions.

Finally, at the third level there is an ability that is common to all abilities residing at the lower levels. This ability is known as *general intelligence* or *g*. In modern models of intelligence *g* is considered to include processes and functions that define processing efficiency and capacity (such as processing speed, selective attention, and working memory; Jensen, 1998; Kyllonen, 2002), general inferential processes (such as induction and deduction; Carroll, 1993), and even general self-awareness and self-regulation processes (Sternberg, 1985).

Also, the psychometric tradition has been very successful in the production of valid and reliable tests that can be used to measure an individual's relative standing on each of the dimensions (Kaufman, 2000). The Wechsler Intelligence Scale for Children (1991) test is one of the most well-known products of this tradition. In fact, the models of intelligence formulated in this tradition are based on the examination of large groups of individuals by these or similar tests and the careful examination of the

2

relations between performance on test items addressed to different abilities or cognitive processes.

The third epistemological tradition is the developmental. This tradition has focused primarily on the development of mental functions in order to specify both their quality and form at different phases of life, and to articulate mechanisms underlying their transformation with growth. Thus, this tradition has modeled the stages and the dynamics of the development of mental functions. Piaget's (1970, 2001) theory of cognitive development, which is certainly the first comprehensive and most researched model of the development of the human mind, postulated that the quality of understanding and problem solving is deeply different at the successive stages of cognitive development (i.e., the stages of sensorimotor, preoperational, concrete operational, and formal operational thought).

More recently, developmental theorists have attempted to explain cognitive growth along Piagetian stages by invoking various aspects of processing capacity as the causal factor of stage transitions (Case, 1985, 1992a; Halford, 1993; McLaughlin, 1963; Pascual-Leone, 1970, 1988). Moreover, there have been systematic attempts to understand individual differences in cognitive development (Case, Demetriou, Platsidou, & Kazi, 2001; Demetriou, 1998a, 1998b; Demetriou & Efklides, 1987; Demetriou, Efklides, & Platsidou, 1993; Shayer, Demetriou, & Prevez, 1988). In general, models of cognitive development are based on evidence about the performance of individuals of different ages on tasks of different kinds and complexity.

The summary above suggests that, despite large conceptual and methodological differences, the three traditions converge in their gross conception of the most important constructs in the architecture of the mind. At the same time, they diverge considerably in terms of the relative importance and exact role of the various constructs in the functioning and development of the mind and their dynamic interrelations. This *Monograph* presents a longitudinal study designed to specify the status, development, and interrelations of cognitive functions and processes that have been the focus of these three traditions. Specifically, these are speed of processing, controlled attention and inhibitory processes, short-term and working memory, and thinking and problem solving in different domains. The study to be presented in this *Monograph* was designed to answer the following questions:

1. How does each of these functions develop from middle childhood to middle adolescence?

2. How do changes in each of these functions become associated with changes in all of the other functions?

3. How is the condition of each of these functions associated with individual differences in the condition and functioning of the other functions at the successive phases of development?

The ultimate aim of the research was to advance an overarching model of the mental architecture and development that would contribute to the integration of the three traditions. To this end, first we describe and contrast the postulates and assumptions of each tradition in regard to the various constructs mentioned above. This exposition is presented in the context of an integrative model proposed by Demetriou and colleagues. The aim of this exposition is to highlight the common assumptions that an overarching model would need to integrate, the unresolved issues it would have to resolve, and the gaps it would have to fill in, if a satisfactory understanding of real-time intellectual functioning, development, and individual differences is to be achieved. Finally, we present the design and the predictions of the study that guide the chapters that follow.

AN INTEGRATIVE MODEL

The model developed by Demetriou and colleagues (Demetriou, 1998a, 1998b, 2000; Demetriou & Efklides, 1985, 1987, 1988, 1989; Demetriou, Efklides, & Platsidou, 1993; Demetriou & Kazi, 2001; Demetriou & Valanides, 1998) draws on all three traditions to describe and explain the architecture and development of the human mind and individual differences. According to this model, the mind is organized in three levels or layers, which must be distinguished from developmental levels. The most basic of these levels involves general processes and functions that define the processing potentials available at a given time. Thus, the condition of this level constrains the functioning of the systems included in the two *knowing levels*, so named because they involve systems and functions underlying understanding and problem solving. One of these two knowing levels involves systems of cognitive functions and abilities specializing in the representation and processing of the different aspects of the environment. The other knowing level involves systems underlying self-monitoring, self-representation, and self-regulation. Figure 1 illustrates this model. In the section below we will first outline this architecture and compare research and theorizing produced in the three traditions concerning each of the several constructs. Then the discussion will focus on research and theorizing concerned with the development and the dynamic interrelations between the constructs.

The levels in the present context are not identical with the levels or strata as defined by differential models. In differential models levels are

Core capacities (speed, span, control)

Specialized capacity spheres
(spatial, verbal/social, numerical, etc.)

Development Levels

Level 4

Level 3

Level 2

Level 1

Hypercognitive system
(builds model of all
other aspects of the
mind; maps lower order
structures onto each
other)

Semantic and
operational structures
within SCS

Stage transitions zones

(Note: For any individual,
these may occur at different
points, on different tasks,
and in different capacity
spheres.)

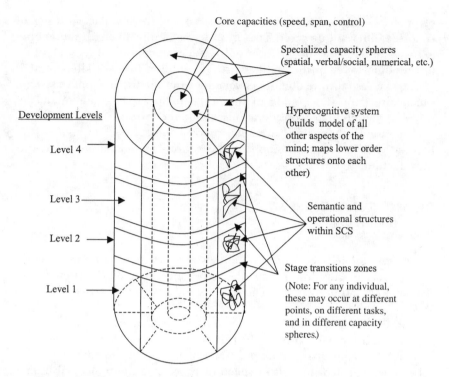

FIGURE 1.—The general model for the architecture of the developing mind

defined by the generality of the processes or abilities concerned. That is, the abilities residing at each next level or stratum involve abilities or processes of higher generality, so that the mind has a pyramid-like form. In the present context, the levels are defined in terms of their function and epistemic orientation. That is, both processing potentials and the hypercognitive system involve general-purpose processes and abilities (although both content and context may affect their functioning in particular situations or occasions). Their difference is that the processes and abilities involved in processing potentials *underlie* or *structurally participate in* all other processes and abilities. The processes and abilities involved in the hypercognitive system neither underlie nor participate in the other processes and functions. They *may just be applied on* all other functions and abilities, if this is considered necessary or useful. Only the processes and abilities involved in the systems related to the environment are specialized by construction. It may be noted that the two models are not technically incompatible. That is, the model shown in Figure 1 as an illustration of psychometric models may be used as a guide for the static architecture

5

of processes and abilities in the context of any theory. The meaning of factors is different, however. That is, in terms of our theory, psychometric *g*, for example, does not involve only what is common between all abilities residing lower in the architecture. In addition to these kinds of abilities, *g* may also involve abilities emanating from the hypercognitive system, which direct the functioning of the other abilities. Thus, our model involves, in addition to considerations about the construction of systems, considerations about their dynamic interrelations. These differences will become clear as the exposition of the various models advances in this introduction.

THE ARCHITECTURE OF THE MIND

Processing Potentials

In this model, processing potentials are specified in terms of three dimensions, mostly drawn from the experimental tradition (Demetriou, Efklides, & Platsidou, 1993). The dimensions are *speed of processing*, *control of processing*, and *working memory*.

All three dimensions have been studied systematically in the context of the experimental tradition. In this context, speed of processing basically refers to the maximum speed at which a given mental act may be efficiently executed. In tests of speed of processing the individual usually is asked to recognize a simple stimulus as quickly as possible, such as naming a letter, reading single words in one's native language, or identifying a geometrical figure. Under these conditions, speed of processing indicates the time needed by the system to record and give meaning to information. Traditionally, the faster an individual can recognize a stimulus, the more efficient his processing is considered to be (MacLeod, 1991; Posner & Raicle, 1997; Sternberg, 1975).

Controlled attention refers to processes that enable the thinker to stay focused on the information of interest while filtering out interfering and goal-irrelevant information (MacLeod, 1991; Navon, 1977; Neill, Valdes, & Terry, 1995). In laboratory situations, the Stroop phenomenon is the paradigmatic example of the conditions requiring efficient handling of conflicting information. In the classic version of the task, participants are presented with cards involving color words printed either in black ink or in an ink color that is different from the color denoted by the word itself (e.g., the word "red" is printed in blue ink). The participants may be examined under several conditions. For our present purposes, of primary interest is the classical condition used by Stroop (1935) of having to *read* the color words that are printed in black ink and the condition of having to *name* the ink color of words where meaning and ink color differ. Stroop

6

found that the mean time of reading the (100) words in the first condition was 43.30 s. The mean time of recognizing the ink color of the (100) words in the second condition was 110.3 s. According to Stroop, the longer time of the second condition results from the interference of the dominant aspect of the stimuli (the tendency to read a word) with the processing of their weaker but goal-relevant aspect (the recognition of ink color). Thus, the difference between the two kinds of measures is taken as an index of inhibition, which is the basic component of controlled attention (MacLeod, 1991; Stroop, 1935).

Working memory refers to the processes enabling a person to hold information in an active state while integrating it with other information until the current problem is solved. A common measure of working memory is the maximum amount of information and mental acts that the mind can efficiently activate simultaneously. The common assumption is that understanding, learning, and problem solving are positively related to working memory capacity because enhanced working memory increases the connections and associations that can be built either between the units of the newly encountered information or between this information and information already stored in long-term memory (Baddeley, 1990, 1993; Caplan & Waters, 1999; Swanson & Sachse-Lee, 2001).

Baddeley's (1990, 1993) model, which has received extensive empirical and theoretical scrutiny in the past 10 years, is widely regarded as a good approximation of the architecture of working memory (Engle, 2002; Caplan & Waters, 1999; Kemps, De Rammelaere, & Desmet, 2000; Morra, 2000; Ribaupierre & Bailleux, 2000; Schneider, in press; Swanson & Sachse-Lee, 2001). According to this model, which is graphically illustrated in Figure 2a, working memory consists of a central executive and two slave systems, a phonological loop and a visuo-spatial sketchpad. The *central executive* is an attentional control system that is responsible for (a) monitoring and coordinating the operations of the two slave systems, (b) strategy selection, and (c) coordinating the information in working memory with the information in long-term memory. The *phonological loop* involves a short-term phonological buffer and a subvocal rehearsal loop. The phonological buffer stores verbal information as encountered; the information in this buffer decays rapidly. The rehearsal loop counteracts this decay by refreshing memory traces through rehearsal—the faster the rehearsal, the more information that can be held in the phonological loop. The *visuo-spatial sketchpad* is responsible for the retention and manipulation of visual or spatial information. The two slave systems draw on partially different resources. As a result, each is amenable to interference from system-specific information that does not affect the other system. That is, the phonological loop is affected by interference from verbal but not visuo-spatial information; the visuo-spatial sketchpad is affected by visuo-spatial

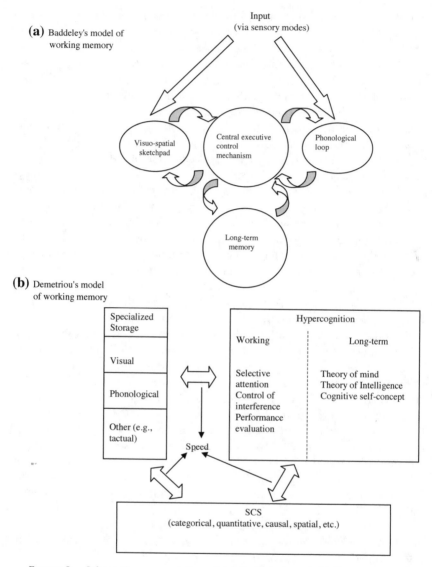

FIGURE 2.—Schematic representation of (a) Baddeley's and (b) Demetriou's model of the working memory

but not verbal information (Baddely, 1993; Shah & Miyake, 1996). However, these systems are interrelated and information from one can be translated into the code of the other through rehearsal guided by the central executive.

8

It must be noted that Baddeley and Hitch have recently added a fourth component to their model, namely an *episodic buffer*.

> This is assumed to act as a temporary storage system capable of holding information from the slave systems of working memory and long-term memory in some form of multimodal code. It is assumed to be controlled by the central executive, and to allow access through conscious awareness. As such, the mechanism is assumed to represent an approach to the binding problem, that is, the problem of how information from different sources is combined to create the perception of a single coherent episode. (Baddeley & Hitch, 2000, p. 135)

Thus, Baddeley's model allows for both specificity and generality in cognitive functioning. Specificity is defined in terms of the modality in which information is received (i.e., acoustic vs. visual) and the ensuing symbol systems, which are developed to handle information, presented in these modalities (i.e., language vs. mental imagery, respectively). Generality is defined in terms of the central executive and the episodic buffer. Their very existence ensures the communication and production of integrated mental products and their operating capacity sets the general constraints under which the two slave systems can function.

In the differential tradition many scholars believe that all of these three dimensions of processing potentials are important components of general intelligence or *g* (Cowan, 1999; Deary, 2000; Engle, 2002; Kyllonen, 2002). Technically, *g* in psychometric theories of intelligence is an index of performance on many different domain-specific tasks (such as speeded performance tasks; memory tasks; spatial, verbal, and mathematical reasoning tasks; and tasks addressed to general knowledge about the world) and it is taken to indicate what is common between them. Thus, in psychometric models of intelligence, individual differences in *g* are considered related to individual differences in one or more of these three basic dimensions of processing potentials (Deary, 2000; Jensen, 1998). It must be noted, however, that findings are inconclusive as to how each of these three constructs or possible combinations between them are actually related to general intelligence.

Many studies have investigated the relations between psychometric *g* and various measures of speed of processing (for reviews of these studies see Deary, 2000, and Mackintosh, 2000). It was found that these relations vary enormously (between −.2 and −.8) because the degree of correlation depends on the complexity of the speed of processing task. That is, the more complex and/or semantically laden the task is in terms of decisions required before responding, the higher the correlation (see Bors, MacLeod, & Forrin, 1993). Thus, it was suggested that general control processes rather than sheer speed are responsible for this relation (Embretson, 1995). Others have argued that the crucial variable in this relation is controlled attention capacity or selective or executive attention (Engle, 2002; Stankov & Roberts, 1997; Stankov, 2002). However, selective or executive attention is part of working memory as defined above in the context of Baddeley's model. Thus Kyllonen went so far as to argue that g *is* working memory (Kyllonen, 2002). Concurring with this claim, Conway, Cowan, Burting, Therriault, and Minkoff (in press) recently presented evidence suggesting that working memory but not speed of processing was related to g. And in agreement with these findings, L. T. Miller and Vernon (1992) showed that working memory predicts g better than speed of processing. However, these authors also noted that working memory mediates the relation between speed of processing and g because it is itself based on processing efficiency.

This research suggests that each of the three dimensions of processing potentials is directly or indirectly related to the problem solving and thinking processes involved in general intelligence. However, this research does not show clearly how and to what extent each of these three dimensions is actually related to general intelligence. For instance, one might assume that the contribution of working memory found by Kyllonen (2002) and Conway et al. (in press) may be overestimated, compared to measures of speed of processing or control of processing, because working memory depends on these dimensions. Thus, working memory and these two other measures of processing efficiency must be clearly dissociated if their relative contribution to thought is to be specified. This is one of the aims of the present study.

The Environment-Oriented Level

A large number of empirical studies have identified and delineated seven systems of thought that specialize in the representation and processing of different domains of relations in the environment (Case, Demetriou, Platsidou, & Kazi, 2001; Demetriou & Efklides, 1985, 1987, 1989; Demetriou, Efklides, Papadaki, Papantoniou, & Economou, 1993; Demetriou, Efklides, & Platsidou, 1993; Demetriou, Pachaury, Metallidou, & Kazi, 1996; Demetriou, Platsidou, Efklides, Metallidou, & Shayer, 1991; Shayer et al., 1988; Demetriou & Raftopoulos, 1999; Demetriou, Raftopoulos, & Kargopoulos, 1999). These systems are called *specialized capacity systems* or spheres (SCSs), because each of them includes a characteristic set of operations and processes which are appropriate for thinking and problem solving within its domain of application (Kargopoulos & Demetriou, 1998). Moreover, each of the seven systems is biased to a different symbol system, the one most appropriate for that specialized capacity system's representational and computational needs, such as language for the propositional system, mental images for the spatial system, and mathematical symbolisms for the quantitative system (Demetriou, Efklides, & Platsidou, 1993). Finally, because of these differences, the development of each system may proceed through partially different types of developmental sequences and at different rates of progression (Demetriou & Efklides, 1987; Demetriou & Raftopoulos, 1999; Demetrious, Raftopoulos, & Kargopoulos, 1999; Demetriou & Valanides, 1998). The domain and composition of each of these seven systems is presented below.

1. *The system of categorical thought.* This system has two important functions: (a) to identify and abstract from all the information in the environment those properties and characteristics that are important to the organism relative to its current goal; and (b) to reduce unnecessary complexity. This system is thus the basic mechanism underlying the construction, representation, and use of categorical structures. Browsing, scanning, and comparison, which enable an individual to identify the properties related to a categorization task, are examples of the operations involved in this system. Classification and rule-induction strategies, which primarily involve organization and reduction of information into more general mental schemes, are examples of processes aimed at the simplification of complexity for the sake of mental economy.

2. *The system of quantitative thought.* All elements of reality can potentially undergo quantitative transformations. Things aggregate or separate so that they increase, decrease, split, or multiply in space or time for many different reasons. Many of these aspects of reality are of adaptational value to living organisms. Thus, this system involves abilities and skills of quantitative specification—for example, counting, pointing, bringing in and removing, and sharing. Internalization of these skills into coordinated mental actions results in the four basic arithmetic operations, which provide understanding of the basic quantitative functions of increase, decrease, redistribution, and so forth. This system also involves rules and operations for identification of various types of quantitative relations, such as fractions. These processes constitute the basis of complex mathematical thinking, such as proportional or algebraic reasoning.

3. *The system of causal thought.* Objects and people are very often dynamically related, sometimes functioning as the cause of changes and other times as the recipients of causal effects. Cause-effect relations are rarely clear or directly available to the senses; often they are hidden due to the presence of unrelated elements, and frequently may be so concealed that they never strike onto the senses. In the physical world, all kinds of counter-intuitive phenomena, such as electromagnetic, nuclear, or astronomical phenomena, are examples of causal interactions. The immaterial effects exerted on human behavior by desires, ambitions, and feelings are examples

of masked causal relations in the psychological and the social world. That is, this system specializes in the representation and processing of all kinds of interactive reality structures. Thus, this system involves processes that enable the thinker to manipulate and represent causal relations. Specifically, it involves hypothesis formation, experimentation, and model construction.

4. *The system of spatial thought.* This system is directed to the representation and processing of two aspects of reality, orientation and movement in space and situations or scenes, which can be visualized mentally as integral wholes and processed as such. Therefore, anything that can be perceived and then somehow preserved as a mental image can become the object of the activity of this system. Formation of mental images and processes, such as perception of size, depth, and orientation of objects, constitutes the foundations of this system. Based on these foundations, the system involves processes and operations that enable the individual to apply onto mental images the actions that can be applied physically on the aspect of reality represented by these images. Thus, this system involves processes whereby the individual can transform an image through various mental actions such as removal, addition, rotation, and transposition of the elements involved in the image.

5. *The system of propositional thought.* This system serves two main functions: It enables the thinker to understand the relations between various actions mentioned in conversations and, thus, to abstract information from verbal interaction in a meaningful way. Thus, it facilitates interaction between persons, and it is used as a guide to action. In this sense, the system involves processes enabling the individual to check whether a series of statements are connected in a valid way, often independently of their content. Specifically, there are two types of processes: (a) processes that enable the individual to interpret and interrelate the components in verbal statements so that information may be abstracted in goal-relevant, meaningful, and coherent ways (interpretation of words or strings of words are examples of these skills); (b) skills that enable the individual to differentiate the contextual from the formal elements in a series of statements and to operate on the latter. For example, focusing on such verbs as *is* or *belongs to* or connectives such as *and, if,* and *or* directs thinking to the relations between the statements, rather than simply the statements themselves. These processes—the second in particular—enable one to grasp the basic logical relations of conjunction (. . . and . . .), disjunction (either . . . or), implication (if . . . then), and so forth (Efklides, Demetriou, & Metallidou, 1994).

6. *The system of social-interpersonal thought.* This system deals with the understanding of social relationships and interactions. This system involves operations and processes that enable understanding and manipu-

lation of the forces underlying verbal and nonverbal social interactions, such as motives and intentions (Demetriou & Kazi, 2001; Demetriou, Kazi, & Georgiou, 1999).

7. *The drawing-pictographic system.* This system involves multiple skills and operations that integrate many of the systems above into an idiosyncratic whole that is particular to humans. This system makes use of imaginal and kinetic processes and abilities for the sake of the pictorial representation of the relations associated with any of the systems summarized above. Through this system humans can represent their environment or their thoughts themselves by the production of drawings or any other kinds of signs (Demetriou & Kazi, 2001).

These systems of thought were induced on the basis of evidence generated by a large number of studies. That is, in factorial studies looking for underlying dimensions or factors standing for different abilities, SCSs always come out as independent factors, as illustrated in the model shown in Figure 1 (Demetriou et al., 1991; Demetriou, Efklides, Papadaki et al., 1993; Demetriou, Efklides, & Platsidou, 1993; Demetriou et al., 1996; Efklides et al., 1994). One of these studies was specifically designed to test what is common between Case's central conceptual structures (i.e., Case's, 1992a, definition of *domain-specific structures of thought*), Demetriou's SCS, and psychometric abilities (Case et al., 2001). This study shows that most of the SCSs coincide, to a large extent, with the broad abilities identified by psychometric research. That is, the quantitative, the spatial, and the propositional systems coincide with numerical, spatial, and verbal reasoning, which are frequently identified by psychometric research. The systems that do not exist as such in psychometric models of intelligence, such as the causal and the social SCSs, seem to underlie the operation of other powerful abilities that are known under different names in psychometric literature. That is, causal thought seems to be related to practical abilities (measured by picture arrangement) and social thought seems to be related to crystallized intelligence underlying knowledge about the world.

The Hypercognitive System

It was argued above that the SCSs are domain-specific, computationally specific, and symbolically biased. Obviously, problem-solving entities other than humans, such as animals and computers, may possess SCS-like systems governed by these three principles. However, possession of SCS-like systems is not sufficient to credit these entities with mind. For this to be possible, a cognitive system must be capable of *self-mapping*. That is, it must be able to record its own cognitive experiences and represent them as different if they differ from one another with regard to domain specificity, procedural specificity, and symbolic bias. This is the minimum requirement for the construction of a "theory of mind" and a self-system that can be used for understanding and regulating one's own and others' behavior, thinking, and problem solving (Demetriou, 2000; Demetriou & Efklides, 1989; Demetriou, Efklides, & Platsidou, 1993; Demetriou & Kazi, 2001; Demetriou, Kazi, & Georgiou, 1999).

Positing this principle implies that creatures capable of self-mapping involve a second-order level of knowing. In our terms, this is the *hypercognitive system* (the adverb *hyper* in Greek means *higher than* or *on top of* or *going beyond*; when added to the word cognitive it indicates the supervising and coordinating functions of the hypercognitive system). The input to this system is information coming from the first level (sensations, feelings, and conceptions caused by mental activity). This information is organized into the maps or models of mental functions, to be described below, which are used to guide the control of the functioning of the SCSs and the processing potentials available. Thus, the hypercognitive system involves self-awareness and self-regulation knowledge and strategies. It is conceived as the interface between (a) mind and reality, (b) any of the SCSs or any other cognitive functions, and (c) the processing potentials described above and the SCSs. The hypercognitive system is considered to involve *working hypercognition* and *long-term hypercognition*.

Working hypercognition comprises self-monitoring and self-regulation processes used during on-line problem solving or decision making. These include processes related to the control of attention, allocation of mental resources, selection of problem-specific processes and skills, and evaluation of problem-solving or decision-making outcomes. Thus, working hypercognition involves the control and executive functions ascribed by Baddeley's model to the central executive and the episodic buffer of working memory, or by experimental researchers to functions underlying control of processing and inhibition. The ascription of these functions to the hypercognitive system rather than to working memory or control of processing simply conveys the assumption of our theory that self-awareness and control emanate from a higher order system that specializes in the surveillance and regulation of cognitive functions and processes directly responsible for the representation and processes of environment-relevant information. In fact, the recent addition of an episodic buffer into the model of working memory by Baddeley himself and the ascription of conscious awareness to it is a move in the direction of our theory, which has long recognized that self-awareness must somehow be part of cognitive control. Figure 2b illustrates our conception of processing capacity as a system that involves executive processes associated with working hypercognition and storage.

This conception is consistent with current findings about the organization of the brain. According to these findings, the brain involves circuits specializing in the representation of environment-relevant information (such as spatial, quantitative, and categorical information) and circuits (such as the frontal lobe) specializing in the surveillance, coordination, and regulation of these environment-relevant circuits (Case, 1992b; Thatcher, 1994). Our assumption that working hypercognition operates as a higher order control system directing the functioning of various more-specialized control systems (such as control of processing operating at the level of perceptual recognition or the control of information to be stored in temporary storage buffers) suggests that all of these specialized control systems must be reducible to a common construct or factor. This study is designed to provide evidence related to this question.

Long-term hypercognition involves models and representations about past cognitive experiences that result from the functioning of on-line self-monitoring and self-regulation involved in working hypercognition. These models involve descriptions about the general structural and dynamic characteristics of the mind—for example, that there are different cognitive functions, such as perception, attention, and memory, and different cognitive structures, such as the SCSs described above. Moreover, these models involve prescriptions and rules about the efficient use of the functions—for instance, that excessive information requires organization if it is to be retained in memory or that rehearsal is needed if one is to learn quickly and permanently. Research on theory of mind (e.g., Flavell, Green, & Flavell, 1995; Fabricius & Schwanenflugel, 1994; Wellman, 1990) and on implicit theories of intelligence (Sternberg, Conway, Ketron, & Bernstein, 1981) sheds light on this aspect of long-term hypercognition. Moreover, research on self-evaluation and self-representation with regard to intellectual functioning is related to the evaluative and regulatory aspects of hypercognition (Demetriou & Kazi, 2001; Harter, 1990). Of the theories of intelligence, R. J. Sternberg's (1985) theory has explicitly integrated constructs similar to our hypercognitive system as integral parts of the architecture of intelligence. Sternberg termed these constructs *metacomponents* and they are assumed to be self-monitoring and self-awareness components which are applied on the components specializing in the solution of problems related to the environment.

The assumptions about hypercognition were tested and verified in a series of studies investigating the various "hypercognitive maps" that persons hold about their own minds. In these studies, participants were first asked to solve tasks addressing the different environment-oriented systems. They were then given descriptions of various processes that according to the theory are employed in processing each type of task, and they were asked to specify which processes were used and to what degree in solving each task. Overall, participants associated the processes in accordance with the theory (Demetriou & Efklides, 1989; Demetriou, Efklides,

15

& Platsidou, 1993; Demetriou & Kazi, 2001). In fact, a recent study has shown that even 4- and 5-year-olds are able to differentiate between different tasks, such as mathematical and classification tasks, on the basis of the thought activity required for each task (Kazi, 2002). Demetriou and Kazi (2001) also showed that persons fast in processing and good in syllogistic reasoning have a more positive image of themselves with regard to reasoning and learning ability compared to persons who are slow in processing and not so good in syllogistic reasoning. This finding suggests that the hypercognitive system directly registers and represents the condition of the processing system and the environment-oriented reasoning processes.

Therefore, the SCSs, the hypercognitive system, and the processing system are at one and the same time distinct and dynamically intertwined. That is, the SCSs are formulated in response to the structure of the environment, become operative via the processing system, and become known via the hypercognitive system. The processing system is void if not fed by the SCSs and undirected if not controlled by the hypercognitive system. One might argue that working hypercognition carries over to the processing system, so to speak, both the person's personhood and the person's more general views about the mind, thereby shaping one's personal processing style. At the same time, however, the hypercognitive system draws on and is nourished by the SCSs and is constrained by the processing system in the kinds and the scope of controls it can exercise (Demetriou & Raftopoulos, 1999, p. 325).

Developmental Dynamics

Research over recent decades has generated detailed evidence about developmental changes in each of the three functions of processing potentials (i.e., speed of processing, control of processing, and working memory), each of the SCSs, and the hypercognitive system. Overall, it is accurate to say that, with development, processing becomes faster and more efficient and storage increases until each stabilizes in early adulthood (Case, 1985, 1992a; Demetriou, Efklides, & Platsidou, 1993; Kail, 1991; Pascual-Leone, 1970). Similarly, with development, each of the SCSs becomes increasingly able to deal with more complex, abstract, unfamiliar, and counterintuitive problems (Case, 1992a; Demetriou, Efklides, & Platsidou, 1993; Inhelder & Piaget, 1958; Shayer et al., 1988). Finally, self-awareness and self-regulation become more accurate, detailed, focused, differentiated, and skillful (Demetriou, 2000; Demetriou & Kazi, 2001; Harter, 1999). All functions and processes remain relatively stable from early adulthood to late middle age, when they enter a period of negative changes that limit their efficiency to varying degrees. That is, processing becomes slower and vulnerable to interference, working memory capacity decreases, facility to deal with new and abstract problems weakens, and self-monitoring and self-regulation become less accurate and flexible (Salthouse, 1991).

How are the changes in the various levels of the systems of the mind interrelated? No generally accepted answer exists, as different researchers have provided different answers to this question. In general, the models that have been proposed may be classified into three categories. (a) One set of models emphasizes the role of processing efficiency as a driver of development. According to these models, changes in some dimension of processing efficiency, such as speed or inhibition, open the way for changes in cognitive functions residing higher in the cognitive architecture. (b) A second set of models emphasizes the role of working memory as the main driver of cognitive change in the SCSs or self-awareness and self-regulation. (c) The third set of models espouses a synergic conception of developmental dynamics. These models assume that developmental causality may be both bottom-up and top-down such that changes in lower level processes may open the way for changes in higher level processes, and changes in these latter processes may, in turn, open the way for changes in lower level processes. These three sets of models are summarized below.

Processing Efficiency as the Driver of Cognitive Change

There is abundant evidence that the speed of processing increases systematically with age until early adulthood. Kail (1991, 2000) has shown that reaction times for a wide range of tasks, including motor, perceptual, and cognitive tasks (such as mental addition, mental rotation, and memory search) decrease exponentially with age, leveling off at about the age of 17–18 years. According to Kail, the similarity in the patterns of change in the speed of processing so many different types of information suggests the operation of a common underlying mechanism, which may be associated with age-related changes in the rate of neural communication or other parameters related to the representation and processing of information in the brain.

Kail and Salthouse (1994) extended this model to account for cognitive changes that occur in the later years of life. Specifically, they argued that impairment in cognitive performance, which occurs after middle age (Baltes, 1991; Schaie, Willis, Jay, & Chipuer, 1989), is caused by a slowing in speed of processing that begins at about the age of 40 years and continues systematically until death. Salthouse (1996) ascribes this effect of cognitive slowing to two mechanisms, the limited-time mechanism and the simultaneity mechanism. According to the first mechanism, when processing speed is slower than the demand of a given task, performance is degraded because there is competition between the currently executed operations and the operations of the immediate past. That is, "the time to perform later operations is greatly restricted when large proportions of the available time is occupied by the execution of early operations" (Salthouse, 1996, p. 404), with the result that processing always lags behind current needs. According to the second mechanism, "products of early processing may be lost by the time that later processing is completed. To the extent this is the case, relevant information may no longer be available when it is needed" (Salthouse, 1996, p. 405). Thus, the operation of higher level mental functions, such as working memory or reasoning, may be impaired due to lack of critical information.

Inhibition may be conceived as the gatekeeper of information processing. It refers to active suppression processes that protect processing from the interference of irrelevant information, remove task-irrelevant information from the field or space of processing, and block mental or overt actions that may divert processing from the current goal (Bjorklund & Harnishfeger, 1995; Dempster, 1991, 1992, 1993; Harnishfeger, 1995). Recent empirical research has shown that inhibition changes systematically with age, following a pattern similar to that observed in the development of speed of processing. That is, it improves from early childhood to late adolescence, remains stable until middle age, and declines thereafter. This pattern was observed in the context of various task conditions, including the Stroop phenomenon (Comalli, Wapner, & Werner 1962; Demetriou, Efklides, & Platsidou, 1993; Harnishfeger, 1995; see also MacLeod, 1991) and working memory. In the case of working memory, children become more able, with development, to retain relevant information in storage and ignore distracting information (Gathercole, 1998). In the later years of life, the tendency to distribute attention over both relevant information and distractors surges again, thereby impairing working memory performance (Baltes, 1991; Baltes, Lindenberger, & Staudinger, 1998; Salthouse, 1991).

Working Memory as the Driver of Cognitive Change

In the developmental tradition, there is a class of models, known as the *neo-Piagetian models* of cognitive development (see Demetriou, 1988), which have attempted to explain stages in the development of thinking and problem solving by invoking changes in storage capacity or working memory as the causal factor of stage transitions. These are the models proposed by Pascual-Leone (1970, 1988; Pascual-Leone & Goodman, 1979), Case (1985, 1992a), and Halford (1993). Despite their common assumption that working memory development is the main driver of cognitive change at the level of thinking and problem solving, these models differ considerably in how they define working memory. In this section we summarize the main postulates of these three models in order to highlight their similarities and differences as related to the nature and role of working memory. The aim of this exposition is to enable the reader to grasp the implications of the study to be presented here with respect to the validity of these three models.

The model of Pascual-Leone. In the early 1960s several researchers discussed the possibility that storage capacity may be a crucial factor in the development of thinking along the Piagetian stages (e.g., McLaughlin, 1963). Pascual-Leone (1970) was the first to advance a complete model of cognitive development in which the fundamental assumptions of information processing theory were systematically integrated with the fundamental assumptions of Piagetian theory. Specifically, he argued that human thought is organized as a two-level system. The first and more basic level involves a number of constructs and functions which define the volume of information an individual can represent and process at a given time, and also the style and preferred ways of processing. The second level involves both the mental operations the thinker can execute and the concepts or knowledge that she has about the world. Pascual-Leone accepted that this level involves the structures of thought described by Piaget. Therefore, in Pascual-Leone's theory, the first of the two levels of mental architecture is derived from information processing theory and the second originated from Piaget's theory. Pascual-Leone invoked the first level to explain the functioning and the development of the second level.

Mental attention is the fundamental construct of the causal level. It involves three constituents: The *M-operator*, which reflects the mental energy available at a given moment; the *I-operator*, which reflects central inhibition processes that enable the person to stay focused on a goal; and the currently dominant set of *executive schemes*, which specify the current goal. Working memory involves, in addition to all of these operators, the various content schemes that need to be held in memory when working on tasks. Mental power, or *Mp*, is the measured manifestation of working memory as defined above (Pascual-Leone & Baillargeon, 1994). Thus, in Pascual-Leone's theory, *Mp* is an inclusive construct that involves the hidden representational and inhibitory resources available at a given age, executive processes, and also domain-specific information, which may be phonological or visual. Therefore, Pascual-Leone's *Mp* is very similar but not identical to Baddeley's working memory. Technically speaking, *Mp* refers to the maximum number of independent information units or mental schemes that the person can hold simultaneously in mind at a given moment and it is quantitatively defined by Equation (1):

$$Mp = e + k, \tag{1}$$

where e = the mental energy required to hold the current goal (or executive) active and k = the number of independent schemes (both operative and content schemes) that can be represented and operated on. According to Pascual-Leone, e grows during the period of sensorimotor development until it stabilizes at age 2 to 3 years; k is equal to one scheme or unit of information at the age of 3 years and it increases by one unit every second year until reaching its maximum of 7 units—which coincides with G. A. Miller's (1956) magical number 7—at age 15 years.

Pascual-Leone attempted very systematically to show that the increase in Mp is the *cause* of the transition from one Piagetian stage or substage to the next. Thus, he maintained that the classical Piagetian tasks that can be solved at the stage of preoperational, intuitive, early concrete, late concrete, transitional from concrete to formal, early formal, and late formal thought require an Mp of 1, 2, 3, 4, 5, 6, and 7 mental schemes, respectively. Having mental power that is lower than required by a task makes solving the task impossible. Thus, each increase in the capacity of Mp opens the way for the construction of concepts and skills up to the new level of capacity. Pascual-Leone and colleagues presented a number of empirical studies confirming the expected relation between Mp development and stage attainment by children and adolescents (Johnson, Pascual-Leone, & Agostino, 2001; Pascual-Leone & Baillargeon, 1994; Pascual-Leone & Goodman, 1979; Pascual-Leone & Morra, 1991; Ribaupierre & Pascual-Leone, 1984; Stewart & Pascual-Leone, 1992).

The model of Case. Case (1985, 1992a) advanced a model that is similar to Pascual-Leone's model in some respects and different in others. Specifically, the mental architecture in Case's theory is the same as in Pascual-Leone's theory—that is, it involves two levels, one defined in terms of processing capacity and the other defined in terms of mental structures. Moreover, causality in the relations between the two levels runs in the same direction as in Pascual-Leone's theory: The development of processing capacity drives the development of mental structures.

However, there are some crucial differences between the two models. First, Case rejected the idea that changes in processing capacity can be described as a progression along a single line of development as suggested by Pascual-Leone. Instead, Case maintained that processing capacity development recycles over a succession of four main stages, each characterized by its own executive control structures. Executive control structures are systems of goal-directed representations and strategies rather than operational systems organized according to the laws of some kind of logic. In Case's words,

An executive control structure is an internal mental blueprint, which represents a subject's habitual way of construing a particular problem situation, together with his or her habitual procedure for dealing with it. All executive control structures are supposed to contain (1) a representation of the *problem situation*, (2) a representation of their most common *objectives* in such a situation, and (3) a representation of the *strategy* needed to go from the problem situation to the objectives in as efficient manner as possible. (1985, pp. 68–69)

Case maintained that there are four types of executive control structures: sensorimotor (e.g., seeing or grasping; 1 to 18 months), interrelational (e.g., words or mental images; 18 months to 5 years), dimensional (e.g., numbers; 5 to 11 years), and vectorial (ratios or numbers; 11 to 19 years).

Second, Case maintained that development within each of these four main stages evolves along the same sequence of four levels: (a) operational consolidation, (b) unifocal coordination, (c) bifocal coordination, and (d) elaborated coordination. As implied by their names, structures of increasing complexity can be understood or assembled at each of the four levels. The successive stages are not unrelated, however. According to Case, the final level of a given stage is at the same time the first level of the following stage. Thus, when the structures of a given stage reach a given level of complexity (which corresponds to the level of elaborated coordination) a new mental unit is created and the cycle starts up from the beginning.

Case used the term *total processing space* (TPS) to refer to processing capacity. In a way similar to Pascual-Leone, he defined TPS as the sum of operating space (OS) and short-term storage space (STSS). Equation (2) is a formal expression of Case's model:

$$TPS = OS + STSS. \tag{2}$$

The operating space refers to the operations that need to be performed by the thinker in order to attain the goal. The STSS refers to the maximum number of mental schemes that the thinker can focus on at a single centration of attention. An example is when one has to count how many elements are involved in several groups of objects and at the end recall all values found. In this example the operation of counting occupies the operating space component of total processing space and the values found as a result of counting occupy the STSS. Thus, at each of the four major stages of development the operating space is occupied by sensorimotor, relational, dimensional, and vectorial operations, respectively.

This architecture of TPS is similar in some respects to Baddeley's and Pascual-Leone's architectures. That is, Case's operating space is similar to Baddeley's central executive, and STSS is very similar to Baddeley's storage buffers although Case does not differentiate between different buffers. Moreover, Case's operating space overlaps but does not coincide with Pascual-Leone's e. In Pascual-Leone's model, the operations to be performed are counted as part of the k schemes; see Equation (1), which defines Pascual-Leone's Mp. The executive schemes (e in Equation (1)) are only concerned with the representation of the problem goal. In the example above, counting is what must be performed on the numbers; however, the counting as such is part of the k rather than the e scheme.

Moreover, Case, unlike Pascual-Leone, maintained that TPS does not change with development. Only the relations between the OS and the STSS change. That is, Case asserted that, with development, the quantity of mental resources required by the OS decreases due to increasing processing efficiency. The space left free because of these changes is used by the STSS. Thus, the STSS increases as processing efficiency increases. Case maintained that the capacity of the STSS is 1, 2, 3, and 4 schemes, at the levels of operational consolidation, unifocal coordination, bifocal coordination, respectively.

Case (1985, 1992a; Case, Kurland, & Goldberg, 1982; Case & Okamoto, 1996) presented extensive evidence to support his position. To show that the development of the STSS recycles through the same levels across the four main stages of development, he devised STSS tasks appropriate for each of those stages (described above). The tasks addressed to each of the four stages require that the child keep in mind sensorimotor actions, relational representations, dimensional representations, and vectorial representations.

In another series of experiments Case tried to show that increases in the STSS are indeed related to increases in operational efficiency. In these experiments, operational efficiency was defined as the speed of execution of the required operation. For instance, to measure operational efficiency in the dimensional stage, children were asked to count the elements of different sets of objects as fast as possible. In this experiment, the children were also tested for their STSS of the sets involved. It was found that the faster the children executed the counting operation, the more items they were able to store in the STSS.

The model of Halford. Halford (1993; Halford, Wilson, & Phillips, 1998) raised a number of objections regarding Case's definition of processing capacity and its role in cognitive growth. First, Halford rejected Case's position that total processing space does not increase with age, because there is evidence to suggest that total capacity does increase with age (Halford, 1993).

Second, he also objected to Case's fundamental assumption that development in problem solving is due to the increase in STSS, because evidence gathered in the context of Baddeley's model (Baddeley, 1990; see also Halford, Maybery, O'Hare, & Grant, 1994) suggests that STSS *is not* the workspace of thinking. According to this evidence, a person can keep one type of information in storage and still be able to work on a problem of a different type. This is taken to imply that it is the central executive that is involved in current problem solving and not either of the two storage systems (the phonological loop or the visuo-spatial sketch-pad). Halford believed that the two storage systems are only used to store information that will be used at steps subsequent to the current one in a given problem-solving attempt.

The third main objection refers to Case's analysis of the complexity of problems. The reader is reminded that, according to Case, the complexity of a problem is a function of the number of goals or subgoals that must be represented as subservient to the attainment of the main goal. The more numerous they are, the larger the STSS needs to be in order to represent them. Halford (1993) argued that Case's definition of complexity and ensuing processing load in terms of processing steps or subroutine hierarchies is flawed for two reasons. First, subroutine hierarchies are not intrinsically constrained—that is, nothing inherent in them ensures that everybody will always analyze the goal stack of the problem in the same way. Thus, there is no way to standardize problem difficulty, making it impossible to ascribe problems unequivocally to a specific developmental level. Second, Case's assumption that more steps or subgoals make a problem more difficult is contradicted by a rather common assumption in cognitive psychology that breaking a problem into more steps makes it simpler or easier to solve (Halford, 1993).

Halford (1993; Halford et al., 1998) proposed an alternative way to analyze the processing demands of problems to explain the most crucial component of problem solving: understanding what the problem is about, as the construction of a representation of the problem which is meaningful to the person and which fully captures all the crucial relations involved. According to Halford, this understanding is built through *structure mapping*. Structure mapping is analogical reasoning that thinkers use to give meaning to problems by translating the givens of a problem into a representation or mental model that they already have and that allows them to understand the problem. The structure mappings that can be constructed depend on the relational complexity of structures they involve. The relational complexity of structures depends on the number of entities or the number of dimensions that are involved in the structure. The processing load of a task corresponds to the number of dimensions, which must be simultaneously represented if their relations are to be understood. For example, to understand any comparison between two entities (e.g., "larger than," "better than,"), one must be able to represent two

23

entities and one relation between them. To understand a transititive relation (e.g., that A > C because A > B and B > C) one must be able to
represent at least three entities (A, B, and, C) and two relations (A > B;
C < B); otherwise it would not be possible to mentally arrange the entities in the right order to reveal the relations between all entities involved
(Andrews & Halford, in press).

Halford (1993; Halford et al., 1998) identified four levels of dimensionality. The first is the level of unary relations or element mappings.
Mappings at this level are effected on the basis of a single attribute. For
instance, the mental image of a cat is a valid representation of the animal
cat because it is similar to it—they have many characteristics in common,
such as a particular shape of head, ears, etc. The second is the level of
binary relations or relational mappings. At this level two-dimensional concepts of the type "larger than" can be constructed. Thus, two elements
connected by a given relation can be considered at this level. The next is
the level of system mappings, which requires that three elements or two
relations be considered simultaneously. At this level ternary relations or
binary operations can be represented. The example of transitivity, which
can be understood at this level, has already been explained above. The
ability to solve simple arithmetic problems where one term is missing,
such as $3 + ? = 8$ or $4 ? 2 = 8$, also depends on system mappings because
all three known factors given must be considered simultaneously if the
missing element or operation is to be specified. At the final level, multiple-
system mappings can be constructed. At this level quaternary relations or
relations between binary operations can be constructed. For example, problems with two unknowns (e.g., $2 ? 2 ? 4 = 4$) or problems of proportionality can be solved. That is, at this level four dimensions can be considered
at once.

The four levels correspond to Piaget's sensorimotor, intuitive, concrete, and formal stages, or Case's sensorimotor, interrelational, dimensional, and vectorial stages, respectively, and are thought to be attainable
at the ages of 1, 3, 5, and 10 years. It is noted that higher levels provide
more flexibility to thinking and problem solving because they emanci-
pate structure mapping from its dependence on physical similarity between mental models and problems. However, this flexibility is attained
at the cost of a higher processing load because more dimensions need to
be considered at the same time.

To conclude, in Pascual-Leone's and Case's theories the crucial developmental factor for both across-stages and within-stage transitions is the
increase in short-term storage as such. In Halford's theory, the crucial
developmental factor for transitions across the main stages of thought is
the development of the central executive, whereas the crucial developmental factor for within-stage transitions may be the development of

short-term storage. Halford (1993) maintained that the first kind of developmental progression depends more on maturation than on experience because it draws on the capacity of the brain to represent information. The second kind of progression depends more on experience because it depends on conceptual chunking and segmentation, which can be learned.

Models of Synergic Developmental Relations

We now consider the third category of models of the mind. In this set of models developmental causality is conceived as synergic. That is, change can initiate from any of the three fundamental levels of mind and can radiate to all other levels.

> This is so because the systems are functionally tuned to each other. Therefore, a change in any of them is a disturbance factor which puts the dynamic tuning of the whole system in jeopardy. The direction of change is dictated by the system that has changed first, which will tend to pull the other systems in the direction toward which it has already moved. (Demetriou, Efklides, & Platsidou, 1993, p. 130)

Thus, this theory allows for multiple paths in the direction of causality during development. At a general level, three main types of developmental change are described: bottom-up changes, horizontal changes, and top-down changes (Demetriou & Raftopoulos, 1999; Demetriou, Raftopoulos, & Kargopoulos, 1999; Demetriou & Valanides, 1998).

Bottom-up changes. These changes begin at the more basic levels of the mental architecture and spread to the hierarchically more advanced levels. The most characteristic example of this type of change can be seen when a change in speed of processing, which is the most fundamental function in the cognitive architecture, spreads upward until it affects the SCSs and the hypercognitive system. Obviously, all of the models discussed above, which ascribe the development of thinking to changes either in processing efficiency or working memory, conceptualize change as a bottom-up process. The difference between these models and the synergic model discussed here is that they consider bottom-up changes to be the dominant, if not the only really important type of change. Moreover, these models do not specify in detail how the change spreads from the one function or process to the other.

Our studies have attempted to specify in detail how changes in processing speed are followed in time by changes in inhibition efficiency, and how these in turn are followed by changes in working memory, which are then followed by changes in the SCSs (Demetriou, Efklides, & Platsidou,

25

1993). This pattern of change was interpreted to imply that changes in higher levels become necessary in order to cope with the consequences of the changes occurring at the lower levels. That is, changes in the flow of information, which result from increases in speed of processing, necessitate improvements in the control of incoming information because an increase in encoding speed increases the likelihood that irrelevant information may pass into the system. As a result, the mind must work to improve its control of processing. Improvements in handling the flow of information in the system contribute to more efficient utilization of the available storage space or capabilities. One reason is that the storage space is protected from the intrusion of irrelevant information, and thus more space is left free for the storage of relevant information. These changes enhance the likelihood of constructing new specific skills that would improve the functioning of processes involved in working hypercognition, such as information search, selection, and evaluation. Naturally, these changes affect the functioning the SCSs.

Horizontal changes. These changes affect systems within the same hierarchical level. For instance, a change in a particular component within an SCS, such as the acquisition of a new, more efficient counting strategy in the preschool years, eventually affects positively the general concept of numbers, because it enables the child to realize that spatial arrangements of objects is not related to their numerocity. Many learning and cognitive acceleration studies (Adey & Shayer, 1994; Demetriou, Efklides, & Platsidou, 1993, Study 2), which have examined the transfer of learning effects from one domain or subdomain of thinking, provide examples of this type of change. Demetriou and Raftopoulos (1999; Demetriou, Raftopoulos, & Kargopoulos, 1999) have described extensively several cases of this type of cognitive changes that occur both within and across the SCSs and proposed connectionist models that describe how they are activated and effected.

Top-down changes. Changes of this type initiate at a given level in the mental architecture and then spread downward, thereby affecting the functioning of more fundamental systems in the mind. Changes initiating in the hypercognitive system and then affecting the functioning of the SCSs and the processing potentials constitute the classical example of top-down changes. That is, changes in awareness about the limitations of a given strategy for handling information result first in improvements in the functioning of the strategy itself and then in the performance in particular domains where the strategy is applied. Research on the training of metacognitive strategies is related to this type of change transfer across the levels of mental architecture. This research indicates that giving the thinker a particular self-management strategy, such as knowing how, when, and why the strategy should be used, eventually influences the functioning of the SCSs and aspects of processing potentials, such as working memory (Kuhn, Garcia-Mila, Zohar, & Anderson, 1995; Adey & Shayer, 1994).

It may be noted here that Piaget's (2001) reflective abstraction and Karmiloff-Smith's (1992) representational redescription are examples of top-down changes. Both models ascribe cognitive change to the reorganization of lower level mental operations into more abstract and inclusive operations, which comes as a result of gaining awareness about and reflecting on these mental operations and their relations. That is, awareness and reflection open the way for looking into the similarities and differences between the lower level operations and their eventual reduction into a new mental construct that would be better able to represent, mentally manipulate, and express the reality concerned.

The analysis above suggests that, in synergic models of development, bottom-up changes may be seen as the developmental process that transforms changes in the operating possibilities of the mind into actual cognitive and hypercognitive skills, concepts, and abilities. Horizontal and top-down changes may be seen as the developmental processes that contribute to the broadening and expansion of possibilities that are made available to the developing mind by bottom-up changes. Thus, one is justified in asking if bottom-up changes are related more to transitions across the main phases of development and horizontal and top-down changes are related more to within-phase transitions. The theories reviewed here do not provide the basis for assumptions in this regard. Results generated by the present study will provide evidence relevant to this important issue.

COMMON ASSUMPTIONS AND UNRESOLVED ISSUES

The above review suggests that the three traditions and the models converge on a number of important issues regarding the architecture of the human mind. At the same time, however, the review also suggests that many issues are still unresolved or unclear regarding the relative standing of the various functions and processes in both the architecture and the development of the mind. This study was designed to contribute to the resolution and clarification of these issues.

The three traditions agree that there are both central and specialized processes in intellectual functioning and development. With regard to the central processes, there is considerable agreement between the three traditions as to their nature. More specifically, the three traditions accept that these central processes involve a strong executive function which is

27

responsible for monitoring, planning, coordinating, and assembling mental acts and information vis-à-vis the current mental goal and for deactivating or canceling out irrelevant mental acts or information. Baddeley's central executive, psychometric *g*, Pascual-Leone's mental attention, Case's total processing space, and Demetriou's working hypercognition are all different names for the same mental function.

There is less agreement as to what is actually involved in this function and, thus, how this function is to be specified. In the experimental tradition, selective attention and executive control are considered to be its best manifestation. Thus, priming and operation under conflicting information are considered representative of this function. In the differential and the developmental traditions, the emphasis is on efficiency of operation and the capacity of this function to represent and operate on information. Thus, in the differential tradition, speed of processing is considered as its best manifestation. In the developmental tradition, working memory is considered its best manifestation. It is noted, however, that control is a part of both processes in both of these traditions. In the differential tradition, the tasks used to address speed of processing frequently require selection of the stimulus to be responded to from among others or selection of the response (Jensen, 1998). In the developmental tradition, executive control is always part of the conditions under which memory capacity is examined. Also, some theories in the developmental tradition (Demetriou, 2000; Demetriou & Kazi, 2001; Demetriou, Efklides, & Platsidou, 1993; Perner, Lang, & Kloo, 2002) have emphasized the role of self-awareness and reflection as part of executive control.

There is also broad agreement that the central executive operates in liaison with more specialized processes. It is generally accepted that, in addition to whatever storage capacity is embedded in or occupied by the central executive, there is modality-specific storage that specializes in the representation of different types of information. The experimental and the differential tradition have explicitly recognized at least two types of specialized short-term storage, phonological and visual storage. The central executive is activated, together with modality-specific storage, in all acts of understanding and information processing. This coactivation may cause differentiation in performance according to type of information (i.e., phonological vs. visual) due to possible differences in the capacity or the efficiency of the different storage systems. In fact, in the differential tradition, this specialization in the construction of processing capacity is considered to explain the operation of at least two modes of thinking and problem solving, namely verbal and spatial reasoning. In an effort to test this association between the construction of underlying processes and the structure of thinking and problem-solving processes, research in the psychometric tradition has shown that phonological memory is related more closely to verbal than to spatial IQ, whereas spatial working memory is related more closely to spatial than to verbal IQ (Mackintosh, 2000). Moreover, psychometric studies have found that speed of processing measures involving figural stimuli are more highly related to visuo-spatial than to acoustic tasks (Neubauer & Busik, 1996). However, this research is scanty and has not yet fully disentangled what is truly general and what is specific in each domain of thought.

Similar comments may be made about the state of our understanding with respect to the roles of and interrelations among the various processes in the context of the processing system or in the context of problem solving. On the one hand, there is general agreement that both processing efficiency and working memory are associated with individual or developmental differences in thinking and problem solving. The reader is reminded that the differential tradition ascribes individual differences in understanding and problem solving to differences in processing efficiency (Jensen, 1998) or working memory (Cowan, 2001; Kyllonen, 2002) and the developmental tradition ascribes changes in understanding and problem solving to changes in processing efficiency (Kail, 1991) or working memory (Case, 1992a; Halford, 1993; Pascual-Leone, 1970).

On the other hand, there is no general agreement on the exact status and role of each of the various processes and their dynamic relations. We have noted above that different scholars emphasize different processes as important in cognitive functioning and development. Some models emphasize the role of processing efficiency. These models do have a strong advantage over other models of intellectual development. Specifically, they explain the development of higher level intellectual processes in reference to changes in very simple content-free processes. This provides parsimony to the theory of intellectual development. Parsimony, however, is bought at the expense of interpretive power. That is, these models underestimate both the role of working memory in cognitive development and functioning and the role of domain-specific processes in the functioning and development of thinking. As a result, these models do not generally take into account the variability that exists across different types of thinking and problem solving. In fact, these models substitute one type of general characterization of intellectual development (such as Spearman's g or Piaget's general stages) for another (speed of processing or power of inhibition). As a result, a large part of individual differences or developmental changes in thinking and problem-solving processes and abilities remains unaccountable in these models. Moreover, the models do not specify how changes in these supposedly pivotal functions are transformed into actual new cognitive processes and abilities. Thus, these models, even if correct, would highlight only a small part of the puzzle of the operation and development of the human mind.

29

The models emphasizing the role of working memory, such as the models proposed by Cowan (2001) in the experimental tradition, Kyllonen (2002) in the differential tradition, and the neo-Piagetian models in the developmental tradition, seem also to be parsimonious in that they explain differences or development in complex thought processes by means of reference to a simpler and rather easily measured type of processes. However, there is no agreement as to what component of working memory is actually the crucial factor in the development of thinking. Each of the three neo-Piagetian models summarized here emphasizes the role that a different aspect of working may have in the development of thought (Pascual-Leone and Case emphasize storage, although each defines it differently, and Halford emphasizes the central executive). It may be that the basic premises of each of these three models are complementary to each other. If so, a complete model of cognitive development would have to integrate these premises into an overarching system capable of describing explicitly how the various aspects of processing capacity are related to each other and to the various functions and processes residing in the other levels of the mind. However, the neo-Piagetian theorists themselves have not moved in the direction of their integration.

With respect to theoretical integration, in recent years several studies have compared Pascual-Leone's model to Baddeley's (Ribaupierre & Bailleux, 1994, 1995; Kemps et al., 2000; Morra, 2000) and have concluded that the two models are complementary. These studies found, on the one hand, that Pascual-Leone's theory can accommodate the evidence related to the development of the central aspects of working memory because the pattern of age differences found approximates the developmental pattern proposed by this theory. On the other hand, they concluded that Baddeley's model is better able to accommodate the evidence referring to the architecture of working memory and the phenomena related to this architecture. That is, Baddeley's model can accommodate the differentiation between phonological and visual memory and also the effect of processes used to facilitate the retention of information, such as rehearsal.

It is important to note, however, that the two theorists themselves are unwilling to accept the complementarity of their models. Pascual-Leone (2000) believes that Baddeley's architecture can be fully accounted for by the tenets of the theory of constructive operators. Specifically, Pascual-Leone suggests that Baddeley's central executive lies at the intersection of four of his constructs: (a) control executive schemes (the e schemes in Equation (1)), (b) the "mental energy" capacity, (c) the interrupt or inhibition mechanism, and (d) a gestalt or field mechanism that is responsible for the synthesis or integration of the currently active schemes. The two slave systems are considered to represent the operation of learning and experiential factors that result in the differentiation of information that is related to different modalities and, by implication, to different types of problems. Thus, Pascual-Leone believes that Baddeley's model is actually a subcase of his theory rather than being complementary to it. Baddeley and Hitch (2000) believe that integrating the two models may still be premature because of important differences in their empirical and epistemological backgrounds. However, they note that the *episodic buffer*, which they have recently introduced into the model to account for the active and self-conscious combination of information from different sources, brings their model closer to that of Pascual-Leone.

It does appear that there are critical differences between these two models. One difference is concerned with the nature of the two slave systems. According to Pascual-Leone, their differentiation is only due to experiential and learning differences between visual and phonological information. According to Baddeley, their differentiation is structural rather than experiential—that is, it results from the association of each of these two slave systems with different circuits in the brain. Research on the neural bases of memory seems to support Baddeley's rather than Pascual-Leone's position (Fischbach, 1993).

The several models discussed here are also open to criticisms that need to be addressed and satisfactorily answered. First, the theories do not agree on the upper limit of capacity, the exact nature of capacity, and, by implication, the exact nature of intellectual development itself. In Pascual-Leone's theory, intellectual development is linear and its sequence of stages is patterned along the 1–7 sequence in the development of Mp. In Case's theory, development is recycling over four major cycles (i.e., sensorimotor, relational, dimensional, and vectorial) and each cycle develops along four levels of complexity, each patterned along its own type of short-term storage. Finally, Halford's theory includes a sequence of four major levels patterned along the development of the capacity of the central executive, which evolves from holding one relation to holding four relations.

With respect to the upper limit of capacity, recent research (summarized by Cowan, 2001) suggests, in line with Case and Halford and contrary to Pascual-Leone, that the upper capacity limit for the adult human is 4 rather than 7 chunks of information. However, Pascual-Leone (2000) argues that the difference is apparent rather than real because his measures of Mp are purified from the need for executive control; on the contrary, according to Pascual-Leone, the measures of working memory obtained by Case and other researchers of working memory confound storage as such with executive control. Thus, they obtain lower values of working memory because a part of the capacity available is spent for the support of executive control. Obviously, the role of working memory

31

in intellectual development will be accurately specified only if this dispute is resolved. To resolve the dispute, we need to systematically vary the executive demand of the tasks addressed to working memory so that the developmental state and role of each of these two fundamental components of working memory may be specified. This is one of the aims of this study.

How does development proceed in a system where developmental causality runs in multiple directions because this system is a multilevel and multistructural organization? Normally, a system of this kind cannot have neat developmental sequences as in the models of linear growth proposed by Pascual-Leone (1970, 1988) or Halford (1993) or the model of recycling growth proposed by Case (1985, 1992a). In fact, it has proven very difficult to confirm either the neat horizontal relations between levels of working memory development and the supposedly corresponding levels of thought development or the vertical relations between levels of equivalent complexity which reside in different major stages or tiers of development, such as Case's recycling levels of STSS (Demetriou, Efklides, & Platsidou, 1993). This is understandable from the viewpoint of dynamic models of development (Demetriou, Efklides, & Platsidou, 1993; Fischer & Bidell, 1998; van Geert, 1994). That is, the relative autonomy of the systems and functions (which vary depending on the structural distance between any two systems or functions) suggests that a given change in a particular system or function may not always affect the functioning of another system of function (Demetriou & Raftopoulos, 1999). For instance, all of the models discussed above accept that a change in speed of processing will eventually beneficially affect working memory capacity and this, in turn, will beneficially affect the functioning of the SCSs. We have found that this is not always the case (see Demetriou, Efklides, & Platsidou, 1993, Study 4).

Our studies of working memory (Demetriou, Efklides, & Platsidou, 1993) failed to confirm the relations expected between successive stages, according to the models of Pascual-Leone and Case. These studies showed, contrary to Pascual-Leone and in line with Case's model, that development recycles over successive cycles of memory development that include levels of increasing complexity. That is, it is indeed the case that the retention of the more complex units of the latter level is lower than that of the units of the earlier level and both appear to have a common ceiling close to 4 or 5 units. However, the expected relation between the various levels of successive cycles was not observed

Thus, the *functional shift* model was proposed to account for this pattern of working memory development (Demetriou, Efklides, & Platsidou, 1993). This model does not presume an exact formal equivalence between the corresponding levels of successive developmental cycles. Recycling is thus considered more as a gross correspondence between two or more hierarchies of ascending complexity than as a self-repetition of a single hierarchy of different contents or representation systems. Transition to a new cycle occurs when the structures of a given cycle reach a maximum degree of complexity that makes them not easily manageable. Thus, the new cycle is needed for the sake of functional efficiency. When a new mental unit is created, the system prefers to work with this rather than with those used before because of its functional advantages. However, the development of the earlier units may continue concomitantly with development in the new cycle and, sometimes, returning to them may be preferable or more functional.

Functionality may vary between individuals, depending on their particular social and cultural niche. That is, differences in the environmental contexts of development between individuals may interact with the intra-individual dynamics of change and result in alternative developmental pathways. For example, the same type of change in processing efficiency in two groups of the population who have the same age but different learning needs may affect differently the functioning of working memory or the various SCSs. One is justified in assuming that in cases such as this a number of alternative developmental pathways may spring from the same initial change in the state of a given fundamental system. Thus, it is important for developmental theories of change to be able to systematically describe and explain alternative patterns of change. The interest in dynamic systems theory, which is increasing rapidly in developmental psychology, aims to capture this complexity and multiplicity of development. Van Geert (1994) and Fischer and Bidell (1998) have been very instrumental in developing models and methods for studying the dynamic characteristics and the variability of development. One of the main aims of the study presented in this *Monograph* is to use these models and methods to specify both the dynamic bottom-up and top-down interactions between the various processes this study focuses on and the possible alternative developmental pathways that may result from differences in the relations between the various processes.

The question of transitions across and within major phases of development is also an important issue that remains unresolved. This is so because none of the theories explains convincingly how both transitions *across* and transitions *within* the major stages of thought development take place. Pascual-Leone posits a linear increase in Mp as responsible for both types of transitions. That is, a change of one unit along the sequence of k units (i.e., 1–7 units from 3 to 15 years of age) causes a transition within a stage and a change of two units cause a transition across major stages. However, it is not explained why this must be so. Halford criticized Case for failing to explain transitions across the main stages and

33

this criticism may be valid. However, the criticism may be inverted and leveled against Halford's theory itself, for that theory, although supposedly able to explain transitions across the main stages, does not explain transitions within them. Specifically, it does not explain why and how changes in the storage buffers take the lead as causal factors of change within a stage after a major stage transition has occurred as a result of changes in the central executive.

Also, none of the three theories presented above elaborates systematically on how changes in speed or control of processing are related to changes in working memory capacity. Halford never studied the development of processing efficiency, and the evidence presented by Pascual-Leone (1988) and Case (1985) in this regard is very weak. Thus, their assumptions about these relations are subject to criticism. For example, Baddely and Hitch (2000) suggested that Case's findings concerning the connection between changes in processing efficiency and storage (the reader is reminded that, according to Case, improvements in processing efficiency free resources that result in increases in storage space, which is then used for the construction of more complex concepts or executive structures) do not seem justified. This is so because, in his experiment concerning the efficiency-storage relation, Case did not directly observe the resource demands of processing, but rather inferred them from changes in processing speed. Thus, an alternative to the assumption that increased processing efficiency frees resources that can then be used to retain more information in storage might be that faster processing enables one to process more items per time unit, thereby increasing span. If this is the case, changes in storage are not actually the cause of changes in thinking. Rather, changes in speed of processing cause changes in both storage and thinking.

Finally, these three theories, like the processing efficiency models discussed above, underestimate the role of domain specificities in the development and functioning of thinking. That is, these theories assume that concepts and operations in different domains, such as the domain of spatial relations and the domain of mathematical relations, are equivalent in their demand in processing capacity. However, this may not be the case, as is suggested by the fact that performance in different domains is rarely the same even if problem complexity appears to be comparable (Demetriou, Efklides, & Platsidou, 1993). It is admitted that all of these theories accept that differences in experience across domains may cause considerable variations in performance or rate of development between domains both within and across individuals. However, domains in these theories are not clearly delimited and the principles of their differentiation are not explicitly defined. Even in Case's theory, which assumes the operation central conceptual structures as the equivalent of our SCSs (Case,

1992a; Case et al., 2001), there are no clearly specified criteria for delimiting domains. Thus, a comprehensive theory of intellectual development would have to be able to account for both general patterns of development and performance variations across domains.

DESIGN OF THE STUDY AND PREDICTIONS

The present study was designed to decipher the status, development, and interrelation among the several processes discussed above and to examine their relative contributions to the development of problem solving. Specifically, the study was designed to examine if speed and control of processing are indeed discrete aspects of processing efficiency, if memory actually involves the functions described by Baddeley's model, and if problem solving is indeed organized in domain-specific systems as assumed by psychometric theory and Demetriou's model. Moreover, the study was designed to uncover how each of these functions and abilities develops during a crucial phase of cognitive development, namely the phase between middle childhood and middle adolescence. It is well known that this phase is associated with major changes in the quality of thought and problem solving. Finally, the study aimed to specify the structural and dynamic relations among these processes during development. Specifically, the study sought to clarify how the various parameters of processing efficiency are related to working memory and how all these parameters are associated with problem solving.

To answer these questions, a complex design was implemented. Specifically, we obtained measures of all the cognitive functions or dimensions of interest; that is, we obtained measures of speed and control (inhibition) of processing under three symbol systems, numerical, verbal, and visual. Likewise, we obtained measures of all three components supposedly included in working memory—measures addressed to processes supposedly involved in the central executive of working memory, phonological storage, and visual storage under the same symbol systems. Finally, we tested three SCSs, the quantitative-relational, the verbal-propositional, and the spatial-imaginal. Moreover, each process and ability was measured three times in the framework of a cross-lagged sequential design, such that four age cohorts, originally sampled among 8-, 10-, 12-, and 14-year-olds, were retested two more times spaced one year apart.

Thus, the very design of the study is rooted in all three traditions discussed here. That is, the tasks addressed to processing efficiency and working memory come directly from the experimental tradition. The tasks addressed to the problem solving come primarily from the developmental tradition and tests similar to some of them are found in psychometric tests of intelligence. Finally, the use of multiple tasks to address each of the various processes and abilities is clearly psychometric in origin. The same blending of methods is used for the analysis of results. That is, confirmatory factor analysis and structural equation modeling, primarily associated with the psychometric tradition, are used to test the structural predictions of the study. Multivariate analysis of variance, coming from the experimental tradition, is used to uncover differences in performance across tasks and groups of persons. Finally, dynamic systems modeling by the use of logistic equations, which comes from the developmental tradition, is used to uncover the exact form of development of the various processes as well as their reciprocal interactions during development.

This design provides a very powerful database and the analyses offer a very detailed and exact picture of the phenomena of interest that enabled us to pinpoint and cross-check in detail the development and interrelations of the various processes and abilities. Specifically, the study is able to test the following predictions.

Prediction 1

From a structural point of view, a three-stratum hierarchy must be able to model performance on the tasks addressed to the various processes and abilities. The first stratum should involve the various constructs representing the dimensions or processes involved in each of the main systems addressed by the study—that is, speed and control of processing in the Stroop-like tasks addressed to processing efficiency; phonological, visual, and executive memory in tasks addressed to working memory; and quantitative, verbal, and spatial reasoning in the tasks addressed to problem solving. The second stratum should involve constructs representing the three systems (i.e., the two processing efficiency dimensions should be subsumed under one second-order construct representing processing efficiency); the three first-stratum memory constructs should be related to another second-order construct representing working memory; and the three SCS-specific constructs should be related to another second-order construct representing thinking and problem solving. In psychometric terms, the nature of the tasks used in the study suggests that this second-order factor is a close approximation of fluid intelligence. Finally, all three second-order constructs should be subsumed under a third-order construct, which in psychometric terms may be taken to be equivalent to g.

Prediction 2

With respect to the various relations among these dimensions and abilities, it is expected that, in agreement with the model of synergic growth proposed by Demetriou, Efklides, and Platsidou (1993), developmental interrelations will run both bottom-up and top-down in the hierarchy of the mental architecture. Regarding bottom-up relations, a cascade-like model is expected to accommodate the data. According to this model, the more fundamental constructs in the mental hierarchy are embedded in or are part of the constructs residing higher in the hierarchy. In other words, at a general level, it is expected that processing efficiency will be an integral component of working memory and working memory will be an integral component of problem solving. More precise hypotheses are difficult to formulate; however, it can be expected that, if there is a general mechanism underlying controlled processing, then speed of processing must be the most fundamental factor because it is the clearer approximation to processes requiring the focusing of attention on a particular stimulus (see Ribaupierre & Bailleux, 2000; Stankov & Roberts, 1997). Moreover, processing efficiency may be related to the executive component of working memory more closely than to its storage components, because the executive processes needed to efficiently store and recall information from working memory require, by definition, selection and control. In terms of the relative contribution of the various components of working memory to the development of thinking, the models presented above lead to different predictions. On the one hand, the models of Baddeley and Halford would predict that the executive component of working memory must be more closely related to the development of thinking because this is the workspace of thinking. On the other hand, the models of Pascual-Leone and Case would predict that storage is more crucial in the development of thinking, because in these models the space occupied by executive processes either remains stable (Pascual-Leone) or decreases, thereby leaving space for storage, which is the critical factor in the operation and development of thinking (Case). Moreover, it is to be expected that visual memory will be more closely related to the spatial SCS, whereas phonological memory will be more related to the verbal and the quantitative SCSs.

Prediction 3

Regarding top-down relations, we may expect that changes in thinking may be associated with improvements in processing efficiency and/or working memory performance, mainly because they provide more efficient storing strategies. Several researchers (Chi, 1976; Schneider, in press; Schneider & Bjorklund, 1998) have shown that the acquisition of strategies enabling one to focus processing on goal-relevant information and to organize information in problem appropriate ways beneficially affects processing capacity. At the very least, these strategies enable the individual to make use of the processing capacity potential available closer to its upper limits. However, more precise predictions cannot be made in this regard due to lack of relevant evidence.

Prediction 4

All of the processes and abilities must undergo systematic changes within the age span covered by this study. Normally, change at some age phases must be faster than at some other phases. Given the tasks used in the present study, change in the period of 10–12 years of age must be faster than change in the period of 14–16 years of age. This pattern agrees with both the classical developmental assumption (Piaget, 2001) and its modern expression in terms of dynamic systems theory (Fischer & Bidell, 1998; van Geert, 1994) that change in periods of major developmental transitions is faster than in periods of consolidation of cognitive acquisitions. According to dynamic systems theory, the dominant form of development is logistic. That is, change is rather slow at the beginning of a given period, it then accelerates once a minimum degree of momentum is gained, and it decelerates again when it approaches ceiling.

Prediction 5

Theorists of the dynamic nature of development (Fischer & Bidell, 1998; van Geert, 1994) argue that there are multiple paths in the development of the same sets of processes and abilities. Each of these paths may represent a different combination or interpatterning of the state of the various abilities at different ages. Differences of this kind reflect differences in the environmental opportunities or disadvantages of different individuals or differences in the interests and preferences of different individuals, which shape dynamic contexts for self-development. Therefore, it is predicted that there will be more than one systematic pattern of development of the bundle of processes and abilities investigated here. However, more specific predictions about the exact nature of different patterns cannot be formulated due to the absence of relevant evidence and theorizing.

II. THE STUDY METHODS

PARTICIPANTS

This study included 113 participants; these were about equally distributed at the first testing among 8-year-olds (28 total; 13 female, 15 male), 10-year-olds (30 total; 14 female, 16 male), 12-year-olds (29 total; 14 female, 15 male) and 14-year-olds (26 total; 13 female, 13 male). Participants were tested two more times, with the tests separated by one-year intervals. The mean age in months of the four groups at the first testing wave was 97.2 (SD = 4.6), 121.5 (SD = 4.6), 145.2 (SD = 3.4), and 168.8 (SD = 4.2), respectively. At each subsequent testing, participants of each age group were 12 months older than at the previous testing.

All participants were Greek and came from middle-class families, with at least one of the parents having university education. The participants were students at the Experimental School of the Aristotle University of Thessaloniki. Thessaloniki is the second largest city in Greece with a population of about one million inhabitants.

ASSESSMENT BATTERIES

The general principles that guided the experimental design of this study were presented in Chapter I. A wide array of tasks were used to measure the various processes and abilities involved in processing efficiency, working memory, and domain-specific problem solving. Table 1 presents an overview of these tasks

Processing Efficiency Tasks

A series of Stroop-like tasks were devised to measure speed of processing and control of processing under different symbol systems. Specifically, three stimuli were used for each of the two dimensions of the

39

TABLE 1

Tasks Used in the Study

Processing System	Working Memory	Problem Solving and Thinking
Speed of processing	Storage buffers	Specialized capacity systems
Verbal	Verbal	Verbal
Recognition of words written in the same ink color.	Serial recall of unrelated words.	Inductive and deductive reasoning.
Numerical	Numerical	Quantitative
Recognition of large number digit composed of many of the same small digit.	Serial recall of unrelated number digits.	Arithmetical operations and proportional reasoning.
Imaginal	Visual	Spatial
Recognition of large geometrical figure composed of many of the same small figure.	Reproduction of patterns of geometrical figures.	Mental rotation and integration of perspectives.
Control of processing	Central executive	
Verbal	Numerical/Verbal	
Ink-color recognition of words demoting a different color.	Serial recall, upon instructions, of number digits or words abstracted from complete sentences.	
Numerical	Visual/Verbal	
Recognition of the small number digit the large number digit is composed of.	Serial recall, upon instructions, of words or the ink color of words present.	
Imaginal		
Recognition of the small geometrical the large figure is composed of.		

processing system (i.e., speed of processing and control of processing) for each of the three symbol systems, giving a total of 18 reaction times. Each stimulus was written on a 21 × 15 cm card.

To measure *verbal* speed of processing, participants were asked to read a number of words denoting a color written in the same ink color (e.g., the word *red* written in red ink) as described below. For verbal control of processing, participants were asked to recognize the ink color of words denoting a color different than the ink (e.g., the word *red* written in blue ink). Both tasks employed the following three Greek words, which have the same number of letters: κόκκινο (red), πράσινο (green), κίτρινο (yellow). Examples are shown in Figure 3a.

To measure the two dimensions of *numerical* processing, several "large" digits, which were composed of "small" digits, were prepared. This task involved the numbers 4, 7, and 9. In the compatible condition, the large digit (e.g., 7) was composed of the same small digit (i.e., 7). In the incompatible condition, the large digit (e.g., 7) was composed of one of the other digits (e.g., 4). To measure speed of processing, the participants were asked to recognize the large number digit of the compatible stimuli. To measure control of processing the participants were asked to recognize the small digit of the incompatible stimuli. Examples of these tasks are shown in Figure 3b.

The tasks addressed to the *imaginal* system were similar to those used for the numerical system, and comprised three geometrical figures: circle, triangle, and square (see Figure 3c for some examples). In the tasks addressed to speed of processing the large geometrical figure was composed of the same small figure. For the control of processing tasks, the large figure was composed of one of the other figures.

Reaction times to all three types of the compatible conditions described above were taken to indicate speed of processing for the following three reasons: (a) participants were asked to provide a familiar and well-practiced response to a perceptually dominant and familiar stimulus; (b) ideally, nothing interfered in the encoding of this stimulus or the production of the response; and (c) the encoding of this dominant and familiar stimulus was facilitated by the fact that the secondary stimulus is the same. Reaction times to the incompatible conditions can be considered indicative of the individual's efficient control of processing because he must inhibit the tendency to react to the perceptually dominant but irrelevant stimuli in order to encode and respond to the secondary but relevant stimuli. That is, the difference between reaction time to the incompatible and the corresponding compatible condition is a measure of the individual's efficiency in suppressing the processing of the irrelevant stimulus in order to process and respond to the relevant one (see Demetriou, Efklides, & Platsidou, 1993; Jensen & Rohwer, 1966).

A. VERBAL SYSTEM

a. **KÓKKINO** (red)
b. **KÍTPINO** (yellow)
c. **πράσινο** (green)

B. NUMERICAL SYSTEM

Compatible

a.

b.

Incompatible

c.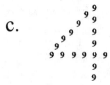

d.

C. FIGURAL SYSTEM

Compatible

a.

b.

Incompatible

c.

d.

FIGURE 3.—Examples of Stroop-like tasks addressed to speed of processing and control of processing

Reliability of Processing Efficiency Tasks

The reliability of the processing efficiency tasks was extremely high. Specifically, the Cronbach's alphas for the whole battery were .95, .94, and .92, at first, second, and third testing waves respectively.

Working Memory Tasks

Short-Term Memory Tasks

Three tasks addressed storage in short-term memory, one for each of the three symbol systems. The *verbal task* included six levels of difficulty, each of which was tested by two different trials. Difficulty here was defined in terms of the number of words; thus, from easy to difficult, the number of words ranged from two to seven concrete nouns. All were two-syllable words. A one-item level was not included as it was judged too easy for all participants. The two trials within a level were differentiated in terms of the grammatical complexity of the words. That is, in the easy trial the nouns were presented in the singular nominative case and in the difficult trial both singular and plural Greek nouns in various cases were used (Table 2).

The *numerical task* was structurally identical to the verbal task, including six levels of difficulty defined by the number of the numbers to be stored (i.e., 2 to 7 for the six successive difficulty levels). Each level was tested in two different trials, each of which involved two-digit numbers of variable complexity (Table 3). Specifically, in the easy trial only decade numbers were used (60, 40, etc.); in the difficult trial the two digits of the numbers were different (32, 57, etc.).

It may be noted here that this manipulation can generate results directly related to the word length effect. Specifically, attention is drawn to the fact that each stimulus in the difficult number task includes two number names attached to each other, whereas each stimulus in the easy condition includes only one number name. This is not the case in the verbal task. Stating the nouns in cases other than the singular nominative case makes them only one or two letters longer than when they are stated in the singular nominative case. Therefore, based on Baddeley's (1990) postulates about the word length effect, one can expect an interaction between symbol system and difficulty. That is, we may expect that the differences in performance between the easy and the difficult number levels in the numerical task must be considerably larger than the corresponding differences in the levels of the verbal task, reflecting the respective differences in the length of the words involved.

In the *imaginal task* the stimuli were presented visually and had to be reproduced visuospatially. Specifically, for each item participants were shown

TABLE 2

WORD LIST USED IN THE VERBAL TASK ADDRESSED TO PHONOLOGICAL MEMORY

Difficulty Level	Stimuli
2	χτένα, βροχή (comb, rain) λάμπας, ρυζιού (lamp's, rice's)
3	λόφους, πουλιών, τρύπας (hills, birds', hole's) μύγα, δάσος, τοίχος (fly, forest, wall)
4	λάδι, πόρτα, χέρι, κουτί (oil, door, hand, box) γλάρο, ψωμιού, πέτρας, κήπου (seagull, bread's, stone's, garden's)
5	γάτας, πόλης, ναών, καπνού, νησιού (cat's, town's, temple's, smoke's, island's) μύτη, πάρκο, ψάρι, γάλα, φωτιά (nose, park, fish, milk, fire)
6	τροχών, στυλούς, αυλών, λύρας, φυτού, τρένων (wheels', pencils, courts', lyre's, plant's, trains') στόμα, άμμος, σκάλα, δίχτυ, σκύλος, χαρτί (mouth, sand, ladder, net, dog, paper)
7	βιολί, αγρός, πανί, γλάστρα, νερό, στολή, βυθός (violin, field, douse, flower-pot, water, uniform, bed) χτένας, μωρών, γραμμών, βάρκας, τυριών, κύκλων, αυτιού (comb's, babies', lines', boat's, cheeses', circles', ear's)

Note.—One row in each difficulty level was presented in singular and nominative case; the other row in plural or singular and in possessive and/or accusative cases. It is noted that the various cases are stated as simple words in Greek.

a card (21 × 15 cm) on which a number of geometrical figures were drawn (e.g., a rectangle and a triangle; see Figure 4 for examples). Participants were shown the target card for 2 seconds per figure (e.g., two-figure cards were shown for 4 seconds) and were given twice as many ready-made cardboard figures from which to choose as the number of figures on the target card. Participants were asked to fully reproduce the target card by choosing the appropriate figures from among the several cardboard geometrical figures (which were identical in size and shape to the figures drawn on the target card) and then placing them on a white card, also identical in size and shape to the target card. Thus, instructions were to place on the blank card the figures seen on the target card in exactly the same position and orientation.

The imaginal task was designed to be as structurally similar to the visual and numerical tasks as possible. Thus, this task also included six levels of difficulty, each defined with reference to the number of items to be recalled (i.e., from the lowest to the highest difficulty level the target cards involved 2 to 7 geometrical figures), and each difficulty level also involved two trials. In the easy trial, all figures were presented in their

44

TABLE 3

Numbers List Used in the
Numerical Task Addressed to
Phonological Memory

Difficulty Level	Stimuli
2	32 57 60 40
3	30 70 90 73 48 64
4	50 80 20 60 58 23 52 79
5	49 67 34 72 93 80 20 50 40 70
6	90 20 60 80 50 30 75 29 43 85 63 46
7	50 80 30 70 40 20 90 28 36 59 83 45 94 68

standard orientation relative to the three dimensions of space (e.g., triangles were presented vertically: Δ). In the difficult trial the figures on the target card were presented in orientations diverging from the standard (e.g., they were inclined by 45° relative to their vertical axis).

Executive Memory

Two tasks addressed the operation of executive processes in working memory. To activate executive processes in the storage and recall of information, two types of information were integrated in each of the items included in these tasks. The children's task was to recall one of these two types of information, according to the instruction associated with each of the items. Specifically, one of the tasks integrated numerical and verbal information and the other integrated visual and verbal information. That is, it was known from the beginning that two types of information were to be presented and that only one of them would have to be recalled at each trial, according to instructions. However, it was not known which of the two types was to be recalled until the presentation of the instruction for each trial, which was always given after the presentation of all of the information to be stored. Thus, children had to systematically organize storage of each of these two types of information in discriminable storage

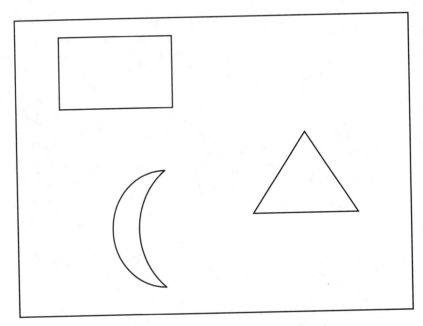

FIGURE 4.—Example of items addressed to visual storage

clusters and then access only the cluster specified in the instructions. Obviously, executive processes were required in order to both organize storage and select information for recall. It is noted that tasks like the present ones, which require storing different types of information and recalling part of it upon instruction, were used in earlier research as indicators of executive processes in working memory (Just & Carpenter, 1992).

The *numerical-verbal task* included 12 sets of verbal propositions. Each proposition was comprised of a subject, a verb, a numerical specification, and an object (e.g., "The man ate three apples." "The father bought two breads." "The boy has seven balls."). The subject and the object were always concrete nouns and the numerical specification was a number varying from one to nine. In pairs, the sets 1 to 12 included 2 to 7 propositions, respectively. Once all of the propositions in a set were presented, the participant was trained to recall either the subject or the numerical specification of all of the propositions in the set, as a response to the instruction "Who?" or "How many?" In the examples presented above, the response to the Who? question would be "man, father, boy" and the response to the How many? question would be "three, two, seven." The participants were asked to recall the subject (Who?) of the propositions in one set of each pair and the numerical specification (How many?) of the propositions in the other set. The items included in each set and the recall instruction associated with each set are shown in Table 4.

The *visual-verbal task* was structurally equivalent to the numerical-verbal task described above. That is, it included 12 sets of stimuli integrating visual and verbal information, and the participant's task was to store both but recall one of the two kinds according to the instructions. In a sense, this task was an adaptation of the Stroop task, designed to test working memory rather than perceptual recognition. In pairs, the sets 2 through 12 involved 2 to 7 items, respectively. Specifically, each set of stimuli included a series of 21 × 15 cm cards, each involving one of the following color words: red, green, yellow, blue. Each word was written either in the same or a different ink color. All items included in this task are shown in Table 5. The cards in each set were presented at a rate of 2 seconds per card. The end of a set was indicated with the presentation of a blank card and the instruction specifying the information to be recalled. The instruction "Word" indicated that the participant would have to recall, in their order of presentation, the words written on the cards of a set. The instruction "Color" indicated that the ink color of the words would have to be recalled. The participants were asked to recall the words in one set of each pair and the ink color in the other.

Scoring of Memory Tasks

Participants obtained two scores on each of the three short-term memory tasks and the two executive memory tasks, one for each of the two trials. All scores equaled the number of items at the highest level which were errorlessly recalled, so that all six short-term memory scores varied from 2 to 7. For instance, a participant who obtained a score of 4 on a trial was able to recall correctly all four items involved in the given trial of the corresponding level as well as the items involved in all lower levels of this trial.

Three scores were given to the performance attained on the imaginal task. That is, a score was given for (a) the choice of figures (one point for each figure seen on the target card), (b) the specification of positions (one point for each position occupied on the card), and (c) the specification of the orientation of the figures (one point for each correct orientation of the figure seen on the target card). The three scores were independent of each other. It may be noted here that this task is very similar to the Cucui task originally developed by Case (1985) and used in subsequent research (Ribaupierre & Bailleux, 1994; Kemps et al., 2000) as a measure of working memory.

TABLE 4

THE VERBAL/NUMERICAL TASK ADDRESSED TO EXECUTIVE PROCESSES IN WORKING MEMORY

Difficulty Level	Sentences	Instruction
1	Ο άνδρας έφαγε τρία μήλα (The man eats three apples).	Ποιος (Who)
1	Στο λιβάδι βόσκουν δύο ζώα (Two animals browse in grassland).	Πόσα (How many)
2	Το τετράδιο έχει εννιά φύλλα (The workbook has nine sheets). Πέντε κάδρα έχει ο τοίχος (The wall has five frames).	Πόσα (How many)
3	Ο μηχανικός χάραξε επτά γραμμές (The engineer notches seven lines). Δύο ψωμιά αγόρασε ο πατέρας (The father buys two breads). Η φωτιά έκαψε έξι δένδρα (The fire burns six trees).	Ποιος (Who)
2	Τρία αβγά γέννησε η κότα (The chicken whelps three eggs). Ο ναύτης διέκρινε εννιά βάρκες (The seaman perceives nine boats).	Ποιος (Who)
3	Ο εργάτης έχει να βάψει οκτώ πόρτες (The worker has to color eight doors). Πέντε σκύλους έχει ο αγρότης (The farmer has five dogs). Ο δρόμος περνά μέσα από τρία δάση (The road passes through three forests).	Πόσα (How many)
4	Ο ψαράς απλώνει τέσσερα δίχτυα (The fisherman spread four nets). Έφτιαξε δύο φαγητά η μητέρα (The mother cooks two foods). Ο τοίχος έχει μήκος επτά μέτρα (The length of the wall is seven meters). Έξι δώρα πήρε το αγόρι (The boy gets six gifts).	Ποιος (Who)
5	Οκτώ κορυφές έχει το βουνό (The mountain has eight crowns). Η γάτα έφαγε τέσσερα ψάρια (The cat eats four fishes). Τρία πάρκα έχει η γειτονιά (The neighborhood has three parks). Το δένδρο έχει εννιά κλαδιά (The tree has nine boughs). Η νοσοκόμα προσέχει επτά μωρά (The nurse cares for seven babies).	Πόσα (How many)
4	Έξι γάτες έχει η αυλή μας (Our court has six cats). Το σχολείο έχει οκτώ τάξεις (The school has eight classes). Ο δάσκαλος κρατάει πέντε χαρτιά (The teacher holds five papers). Δύο φυτά έχει στη γλάστρα (The flowerpot has two plants).	Πόσα (How many)
5	Τέσσερα πουλιά έπιασε ο κυνηγός (The hunter catches four birds). Ο πατέρας λείπει έξι ημέρες (The father is absent six days). Η καρέκλα έχει τρία πόδια (The chair has three legs). Τέσσερις μάσκες αγόρασε το κορίτσι (The girl purchases four masks). Ο βοσκός έχει εννιά αρνιά (The shepherd has nine lambs).	Ποιος (Who)
6	Δύο τσάντες κρατάει ο καθηγητής (The professor holds two bags). Ο εργάτης κουβάλησε πέντε τούβλα (The worker carries five bricks). Ο ναύτης είδε επτά γλάρους (The seaman sees seven seagulls). Η μαργαρίτα έχει τρία φύλλα (The daisy has three petals). Ο κηπουρός φροντίζει οκτώ κήπους (The gardener takes care of eight gardens). Τέσσερα μέτρα πήδηξε ο αθλητής (The long jumper jumps four meters).	Ποιος (Who)

continued

TABLE 4 *continued*

Difficulty Level	Sentences	Instruction
7	Επτά μπάλες έχει το αγόρι (The boy has seven balls). Ο μανάβης έβαλε τρία κιλά μήλα (The greengrocer put three kilos of apples). Ο αστυνόμος έπιασε έξι κλέφτες (The policeman catches six burglars). Πέντε μπλούζες έχει η μητέρα (The mother has four blouses). Τέσσερα κιλά έχασε η γυναίκα (The woman shrinks four kilos). Η θάλασσα έχει επτά καράβια (The sea has seven ships). Πέντε μαξιλάρια έχει ο καναπές (The sofa has five cushions).	Πόσα (How many)
6	Τρία αυτοκίνητα έχει ο πρόεδρος (The president has three cars). Ο μάγειρας έφταιξε δύο φαγητά (The chef cooks two foods). Η τάξη έχει εννιά μαθητές (The class has nine students). Το σπίτι έχει τέσσερα δωμάτια (The house has four rooms). Πέντε βιβλία έχει η βιβλιοθήκη (The bookcase has five books). Το πακέτο έχει έξι καραμέλες (The packet has six candies).	Πόσα (How many)
7	Το χέρι έχει πέντε δάχτυλα (The hand has five fingers). Τέσσερα κοστούμια έχει η ντουλάπα (The wardrobe has four costumes). Το τρένο σφύριξε δύο φορές (The train whistles two times). Οκτώ στροφές έχει ο δρόμος (The road has eight turns). Το ποδήλατο έχει τρεις ρόδες (The bicycle has three wheels). Ο άνδρας έφαγε επτά φρούτα (The man eats seven fruits). Πέντε παιχνίδια έχει το μωρό (The baby has five toys).	Ποιος (Who)

Reliability of Working Memory Tasks

The reliability of the cognitive battery was good. Specifically, the Cronbach's alphas for the whole battery were .81, .73, and .76, at first, second, and third testing waves respectively.

Cognitive Tasks

The cognitive tasks were designed to assess *verbal, quantitative, and spatial reasoning*. The aim was to map the three symbolic systems (i.e., verbal, numerical, and imaginal systems) that were represented in the tasks addressed to the three dimensions of the processing system. Thus, verbal reasoning was addressed by a verbal analogies task and a syllogistic reasoning task. Quantitative reasoning was addressed by a task requiring execution of arithmetic operations and a proportional reasoning task. Finally, a mental rotation task and the tilted bottle task were used to address spatial reasoning.

The tasks addressed to each domain included a series of items systematically varying in developmental affiliation and difficulty. That is, the

49

TABLE 5

The Visual/Verbal Task Addressed to Executive Processes in Working Memory

Difficulty Level	Meaning of Printed Word (Color of the Printed Words)	Instruction
1	Κόκκινο Red	Λέξη
	(κόκκινο) (Red)	(Word)
	Πράσινο Green	Χρώμα
	(γαλάζιο) (Green)	(Color)
2	Κίτρινο γαλάζιο Yellow blue	Χρώμα
	(κίτρινο πράσινο) (Yellow green)	(Color)
	Πράσινο κίτρινο Green yellow	Λέξη
	(κόκκινο πράσινο) (Red green)	(Word)
3	Γαλάζιο πράσινο κόκκινο Blue green red	Χρώμα
	(γαλάζιο κίτρινο πράσινο) (Blue yellow green)	(Color)
	Κόκκινο κίτρινο γαλάζιο Red yellow blue	Λέξη
	(γαλάζιο κόκκινο κίτρινο) (Blue red yellow)	(Word)
4	Κίτρινο πράσινο γαλάζιο κόκκινο Yellow green blue red	Λέξη
	(γαλάζιο πράσινο κόκκινο κίτρινο) (Blue green red yellow)	(Word)
	Κίτρινο πράσινο γαλάζιο κόκκινο Yellow green blue red	Χρώμα
	(κόκκινο κίτρινο πράσινο γαλάζιο) (Red yellow green blue)	(Color)
5	Κόκκινο πράσινο κόκκινο γαλάζιο κίτρινο Red green red blue yellow	Χρώμα
	(γαλάζιο κίτρινο κόκκινο γαλάζιο πράσινο) (Blue yellow red blue green)	(Color)
	Πράσινο κόκκινο γαλάζιο κίτρινο πράσινο	Λέξη
	Green red blue yellow green	(Word)
	(κόκκινο κίτρινο πράσινο κίτρινο πράσινο)	
	(Red yellow green yellow green)	
6	Κόκκινο κίτρινο πράσινο κόκκινο γαλάζιο πράσινο	Λέξη
	Red yellow green red blue green	(Word)
	(κόκκινο πράσινο κόκκινο γαλάζιο κίτρινο πράσινο)	
	(Red green red blue yellow green)	
	Κίτρινο γαλάζιο πράσινο κόκκινο γαλάζιο κίτρινο	Κρώμα
	Yellow blue green red blue yellow	(Color)
	(κίτρινο γαλάζιο κίτρινο πράσινο κόκκινο γαλάζιο)	
	(Yellow blue yellow green red blue)	
7	Πράσινο κίτρινο κόκκινο πράσινο γαλάζιο κόκκινο κίτρινο	Λέξη
	Green yellow red green blue red yellow	
	(κόκκινο κίτρινο γαλάζιο γαλάζιο κίτρινο κόκκινο πράσινο)	
	(Red yellow blue blue yellow red green)	
	Γαλάζιο πράσινο κίτρινο πράσινο κόκκινο γαλάζιο κίτρινο	Κρώμα
	Blue green yellow green red blue yellow	(Color)
	(κόκκινο πράσινο κόκκινο κίτρινο πράσινο γαλάζιο πράσινο)	
	(Red green red yellow green blue green)	

Note.—The first row in each difficulty level refers to the meaning of the words shown on each card; the second refers to the ink color of the word.

tasks were constructed to address abilities acquired throughout the age span covered by the study, across all three SCSs. Moreover, it was attempted, based on extant literature (see below), to have tasks tapping equivalent developmental levels across the three SCSs. The developmental affiliation of the tasks below is analyzed in reference to Fischer's (1980) theory of skill levels. This analysis aims to show similarities and differences between tasks vis-à-vis a standard developmental hierarchy and also their modal association with age. It is admitted that the tasks were not constructed from the beginning to systematically represent Fischer's levels. It may be noted, however, that Fischer himself (personal communication, June 2002) and Dawson (personal communication, June 2002) have also ascribed our tasks to Fischer's system of levels with almost perfect agreement with the analysis presented below. Finally, we point out that these tasks were individually addressed and an example was given to the child at the beginning of each set to ensure that the tasks were treated similarly by the participants and in the way intended by the researchers.

One might argue that more and better tasks may be used to uncover the cognitive abilities targeted by the study. We would argue that using more tasks would make the study practically impossible to realize because the examination of processing efficiency and working memory, in addition to problem solving, posed very heavy demands on our testing conditions. Better tasks may, of course, always be used or invented and thus one must approach our findings and conditions under this ever-present limitation. However, as is shown below, despite this possible limitation the cognitive battery was satisfactorily reliable, allowing the specification of the relations of problem solving with the rest of the processes and abilities investigated. The structure and affiliation of the tasks is explained below.

Verbal reasoning. The four verbal analogies were as follows:

1. ink : pen :: paint : - [color, *brush*, paper].

2. bed : sleep :: - [paper, *table*, water] : --- [*eating*, rain, book].

3. (children : parents :: family) ::: (students : teachers :: - [school, *education*, lesson])

4. {(tail : fish :: feet : mammals) ::: - [*movement*, animals, vertebrates]} :::: {(propeller : ship :: wheels : car) ::: - [vehicles, *transportation*, carriers]}

The participant's task was to choose the correct word (italicized here) among the three alternatives provided for each missing element.

It can be seen that difficulty in this task is primarily related to the abstractness of the relationships involved. Second-, third-, and fourth-order relationships have to be abstracted for the solution of analogies 1 and 2, 3, and 4, respectively. The number of the missing elements was also manipulated in the case of the first two analogies, both of which were of the same order. The first analogy required completion of the target pair, whereas the second required analogy to fully construct the target pair. This manipulation aimed to differentiate between children at the lower end of the developmental continuum.

In terms of Fischer's (1980) model of skill levels, we propose that these four verbal analogies tap two major levels: The first analogy taps the level of single abstractions because it requires the participant to abstract the semantic relation underlying two concretely based relations. The second analogy also taps the level of single abstractions and is structurally and semantically similar to the first; however, it is more difficult because it requires the participant to fully construct the target pair. The third analogy taps the level of abstract relations or mappings because it requires the participant to abstract the relation between two semantic relations of the type tapped by the first analogy. The fourth analogy also taps the level of abstract relations or mappings in that it requires the participant to abstract the relations between semantic relations of the type tapped by the third analogy; however, it is more complex than the third analogy because it involves more relations. According to Fischer, the level of single abstractions and abstract mappings are acquired at the ages of 10–11 and 14–15 years, respectively. Normally, the second and the fourth analogies, being more difficult than the first and the third analogies, ought to be solved later, at the ages of 12–13 and 16–17 years, respectively.

The second task assessing verbal reasoning used the following four syllogisms:

1. If peacocks have more beautiful feathers than cocks and sparrows have uglier feathers than cocks ⇒ [sparrows have more beautiful feathers than peacocks, *sparrows have uglier feathers than peacocks*, none of the two].

2. If elephants are heavier than horses and if elephants are heavier than dogs ⇒ [horses are heavier than dogs, elephants are heavier than dogs, *none of the two*].

3. If animals live in a cage then they are not happy. The bird is happy ⇒ [the bird lives in the cage, *the bird does not live in the cage*, none of the two].

4. If the bird is in the nest then it sings; the bird sings ⇒ [the bird is not in the nest, the bird is in the nest, *none of the two*].

In pairs, the first two syllogisms addressed transitivity, the third and fourth addressed implication. In each pair the first syllogism was decidable and the second was undecidable. Many studies have suggested that transitivity is generally easier than implication and that decidable tasks are more difficult than undecidable ones (Moshman, 1990, 1994, 1995; Efklides et al., 1994). In terms of Fischer's levels, we would propose that items 1 and 3 tap single abstractions and items 2 and 4 tap abstract mappings.

Quantitative reasoning. Four problems addressed the ability to decipher arithmetic operations:

1. $9 * 3 = 6$

2. $(2 \# 4) @ 2 = 6$

3. $(3 * 2 @ 4) \# 3 = 7$

4. $(3 \# 3) * 1 = (12 @ 3) \$ 2.$

The participants were told that the symbols in each of these equations stand for different operations and they were asked to specify all of them in each of the equations. Thus, difficulty here was manipulated with reference to the number of operations missing from each equation, as one, two, three, and four operations were missing from items 1–4, respectively. In terms of Fischer's levels, problem 1 may be considered as addressing systems of representations, which is attainable at the age of 6–7 years. Problems 2 and 3 tap the level of single abstractions, with problem 3 more complex due to an extra missing operation. Problem 4 taps abstract mappings because the two parts of the equation involve missing elements that must be mapped onto each other.

The proportional reasoning task included the following six items:

1. $6 : 12 :: 8 : ?$

2. $6 : 3 :: 8 : ?$

3. $3 : 9 :: 6 : ?$

4. $3 : 1 :: 6 : ?$

5. $6 : 8 :: 9 : ?$

6. $6 : 4 :: 9 : ?$

Formally, all of these tasks appear to tap single abstractions, because they require the participant to abstract the relation between two relations. However, it can be seen that difficulty here was manipulated with reference to the type of mathematical relation involved. Specifically, in three of the items the numbers increased and in the other three they decreased; numbers in both sets increased or decreased by a factor of 2 (items 1 and 2, respectively), 3 (items 3 and 4, respectively), or 1/3 (items 5 and 6, respectively). Evidence suggests that increase can be estimated more easily than decrease and that changes by a factor of 2 are more easily specifiable than changes by a factor of 3, and these in turn are more easily specifiable than fractional changes (Demetriou, Efklides, & Platsidou, 1993; Lamon, 1994; Lesh, Post, & Behr, 1988). In fact, the two most difficult items (5 and 6) may require abstract mappings because the difficulty in specifying the relation between the numbers of the first pair might require producing a set of alternative tentative estimations, which would then be mapped onto the second pair until a consistent solution was found and verified.

Spatial reasoning. The spatial-imaginal SCS was also addressed by two tasks. The first was a mental rotation task comprising six items (see Figure 5). In this task, each item depicted a clock face with one hand pointing to the 12:00 position and the other pointing to 12:15, 12:30, or 12:45. The hand pointing to the 12:00 position included figures of varying complexity. The participant was directed to imagine that the 12:00 hand was going to move until it sat on top of the other hand, then draw the figure on the rotating hand as it would look after the rotation. Difficulty in this task was controlled in reference to two dimensions, the complexity of the shapes involved and the degree of rotation. Clocks 3 and 5 each had a simple geometrical figure, clocks 2 and 4 a figure with diagonal lines, and clocks 1 and 6 two figures with one embedded in the other. The degrees of rotation were 45°, 90°, and 145°. Research has established that rotations of different degrees exhibit differential difficulty and that the more information one needs to integrate into an image the more difficult the task is (Shepard & Cooper, 1982); that is, imagining the rotation of a complex figure is more difficult than imagining the rotation of a simple figure.

In terms of Fischer's levels, we would argue that clocks 3 and 5, each involving a single figure, tap systems of representations because they require the thinker to transform a simple representation into another one by changing its orientation. Clocks 2 and 4, each having one figure with diagonal lines, require single abstractions because they require the participant to disentangle mentally the effects of rotation on each of the two main components of the target figure (i.e., the main figure and the lines

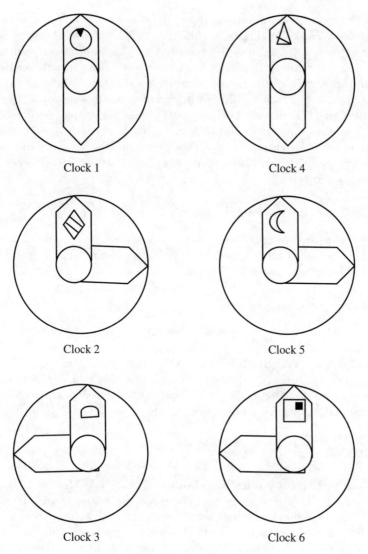

Clock 1   Clock 4

Clock 2   Clock 5

Clock 3   Clock 6

FIGURE 5.—The mental rotation task

embedded in it) and project them (i.e., map them) onto the integrated representation to come from the rotation. Finally, clocks 1 and 6 require abstract mappings because they require the participant to conceive of the effects of rotation on two aspects of each of the two figures involved: the orientation and the position of the two figures relative to each other.

The second task addressing the spatial-imaginal SCS was a version of the classical Piagetian (Piaget & Inhelder, 1967) water-level task in which a picture of a half-full bottle is presented and the subject is instructed to draw a line indicating the water level when the bottle is inclined first by 45° and then 90°. There is vast literature on this task indicating that it is a good test of a person's ability to integrate multiple systems of reference in space (see Thomas & Lohaus, 1993). This task seems to tap single abstractions, because it requires the participant to conceive of the orientation of one dimension of the configuration (the level of the water) relative to both the container and an external system of reference (the surface of the earth).

Scoring of Cognitive Tasks

All items in the cognitive battery were scored on a pass-fail basis (0 and 1). The mean scores used in the analyses below were computed by averaging over the items involved in each task.

Reliability of Cognitive Tasks

The reliability of the cognitive battery was very satisfactory. Specifically, the Cronbach's alphas for the whole battery were .87, .82, and .80, at first, second, and third testing waves respectively. The slight decrease of this index across testing waves is due to the fact that performance on some tasks approached ceiling with time, an expected phenomenon in a longitudinal study such as the present one.

PROCEDURE

Each participant was tested individually on all tasks. Testing took place in a quiet room provided by the school for the purposes of this experiment. Experimenter and participant sat facing each other across a table. The testing was conducted in three sessions: Session 1: the Stroop-like tasks and, for practical reasons, of the memory tasks the visual-verbal task addressed to executive memory; Session 2: all the memory tasks but the task mentioned before; and Session 3: the cognitive tasks were given at separate sessions, each lasting for approximately one hour. The presentation order of the three sessions was counterbalanced across participants.

The Stroop-Like Tasks

The experimenter introduced the three tasks to the child, one by one, using first the demonstration cards and then the practice cards to familiarize the child with the tasks. The aim was to make clear to the subjects that the cards in the main task were going to be presented in succession and that their task was to name the attribute specified by the instruction word quickly and correctly. The instruction word was stated by the experimenter simultaneously with the presentation of each card. In the verbal task the instruction words were *Word* for reading the word and and *Color* for naming the ink-color. In the numerical and the figural tasks, the instruction words were *Large* and *Small* for naming the large and the small number or figure, respectively. Once it was clear that the child was able to follow the instructions, testing proceeded to the main tasks described above. For practical reasons, the presentation order of items within the symbol systems was the same across subjects. However, the presentation order of the three symbol systems was counterbalanced across subjects.

Testing on the main tasks was tape-recorded. The records of each subject were then loaded into a computer with special hardware and software that enabled response reaction time to be specified. In this process, reaction time was defined as the time between the first phoneme of the instruction word and the first phoneme of the participant's response. The reaction time to a stimulus was not used for incorrect responses; however, incorrect responses were very rare, varying from .07% to 1.04% in the compatible conditions and from 1.9% to 3.2% in the incompatible conditions.

We recognize that an automated system of stimulus presentation might have some advantages over the human-dependent system that was used here, such as the complete standardization of the flow of stimuli and instructions. However, in this study an automated system might also have had several disadvantages, given that the participants were school-aged children. An automated system may be less appropriate than a human-driven system to monitor and keep a child's attention constantly focused on what is relevant in the experiment. Moreover, a human-driven system may be more tuned to the child's pace of responding than an automated system. Thus, we opted for the human-driven method and attempted to minimize variations in the flow of card presentation and instructions as much as possible through extensive relevant training of the experimenter. This, together with the complete automation of the specification of response times, ensures the validity of the measures taken.

The Memory Tasks

For verbal and numerical tasks the subjects were instructed to recall the words or the numbers in the order of presentation as soon as the experimenter finished stating a series, as indicated by a nonverbal sign. The instructions were as follows: "I am going to present a series of words (numbers) to you. Your task is to recall them and tell them back to me as soon I tell you to do so by raising my right hand."

In the imaginal task the participant was instructed to carefully reproduce the figures on a target card in exactly the same position and orientation. The instructions were as follows: "I am going to show to you a series of cards which have various geometrical figures drawn on them. I will give you some time to study each of the cards and then I will remove it. As soon as I remove the card, I want you to choose from the geometrical figures here (the experimenter pointed to the cardboard figures which were placed below the blank card) all of the figures you saw on the target card and put them on the blank card. Be careful to put them at exactly the right position and right orientation."

In the verbal-numerical executive memory task the instructions were as follows: "I am going to present sets of verbal statements to you. Each of these statements describes an episode, which is associated with a number. You will have to keep in memory both the actor and the number mentioned in each statement and, when all of the statements in a set are presented to you, recall only the actors or the numbers of each statement, according to my question. If the question is Who?, you will have to recall the actors; if the question is How many? you will have to recall the numbers."

In the visual-verbal tasks the instructions were as follows: "I am going to present sets of cards to you. Each card has a color word written on it. Your will have to keep in memory both the word itself and the ink color in which it is written. When a set is presented you will have to recall either the words or the ink colors, according to my instruction. If the instruction is Word, you will have to recall the words; if the instruction is Color, you will have to recall the colors."

Items within a series were presented at a rate of one item per second. The presentation order of the two trials within each of the six difficulty levels was randomized across levels; the presentation order of difficulty levels was the same across subjects, going from easy to difficult. Administration of a task stopped if the subject failed to recall errorlessly the two trials involved in a level.

The Cognitive Tasks

The cognitive tasks were presented in a paper-and-pencil form and were individually administered. The presentation order of tasks was counterbalanced across participants, and the items within tasks were always presented according to difficulty, with simpler tasks presented before complex tasks. The experimenter explained each task and was available to answer questions as needed.

III. RESULTS: THE ARCHITECTURE OF THE MIND

Confirmatory factor analysis and structural equation modeling were used to examine our hypotheses on the organization of the various processes and abilities tested by this study, and to specify the relations among them both within and across the three testing waves. Two sets of models were tested. The first set aimed to test the organization of processes within each type of measure (speed of performance, memory, and problem solving measures), their hierarchical structure, and the stability of this organization across the three testing waves. The second set of models aimed to specify the structural relations among the processes underlying the three types of measures. That is, this set of models aimed to specify how each of the various processes was associated with each of the other processes both within and across the three testing waves.

THE ORGANIZATION OF PROCESSES AND ABILITIES

To test for the organization of processes and abilities, the model shown in Figure 6 was tested. This model is a test of the three-stratum model of intelligence, and thus it includes the following factors. At a first stratum there was a factor for each of the various dimensions or components represented in the battery; specifically, there was a factor for speed of processing and a factor for control of processing. Each of these factors was specified with reference to three mean scores computed by averaging across the three items addressed to each symbol system. These two factors were related to a second-order factor representing processing efficiency. Moreover, there was one factor specified by the central executive with reference to the four respective items, one factor for phonological memory specified with reference to the two verbal and the two numerical items, and one factor for visual memory specified with reference to the three visual memory items. These three factors were regressed on a second-order factor which therefore stands for working memory. Finally, there was one factor for each of the three SCSs, specified with reference to the

59

respective pair of measures. These three factors were regressed on a second-order factor, which therefore represents the common thought processes involved in problem solving. Finally, the three second-order factors were regressed on a third-order factor, which may be taken to stand for g. This model was tested separately on the performance attained at each testing wave. The parameter estimates of the model are shown in Figure 6. The fit of this model for the three testing waves was as follows:

1. first testing:
χ^2 (218) = 235.369, p = .19, χ^2/df = 1.078, CFI = .984, RMSEA = .028
(χ^2 (218) = 239.828, p = .14, χ^2/df = 1.090, CFI = .982, RMSEA = .031).

2. second testing:
χ^2 (219) = 242.158, p = .14, χ^2/df = 1.106, CFI = .975, RMSEA = .032
(χ^2 (219) = 244.460, p = .11, χ^2/df = 1.116, CFI = .975, RMSEA = .033).

3. third testing:
χ^2 (218) = 264.202, p = .02, χ^2/df = 1.212, CFI = .944, RMSEA = .044
(χ^2 (218) = 268.692, p = .01, χ^2/df = 1.233, CFI = .945, RMSEA = .046).

The fit was excellent and the values of the estimates were very high in all cases. (It is noted that to have a good fit to the data a model must have a fit index, such as the comparative fit index (CFI), higher than .9. Also, ideally, the p value for the χ^2 must be higher than .05, indicating that the model does not differ significantly from the data. When this is not possible, because the sample size is large, a χ^2/df ratio of less than 2 is considered satisfactory). It is clear, therefore, that the three-stratum architecture accurately captures the data. The correlations between the variables included in this model are shown in Appendix A.

TESTING THE STABILITY OF THE ARCHITECTURE OF MIND

We might hypothesize that the organization of cognitive processes suggested by the various models presented earlier is more a function of differential effects of growth rather than stable, functional-organizational differences between the processes involved. To test for this possibility, all the models presented earlier were tested after removing the effects of age. To remove the effects of age, each of the manifest variables included in each model was regressed on the participants' age at the first testing wave. The parameter estimates of these models are shown in Figure 6 (in italics). The fit statistics of each of the models is shown in parentheses following the fit statistics of each model before partialing out the effect

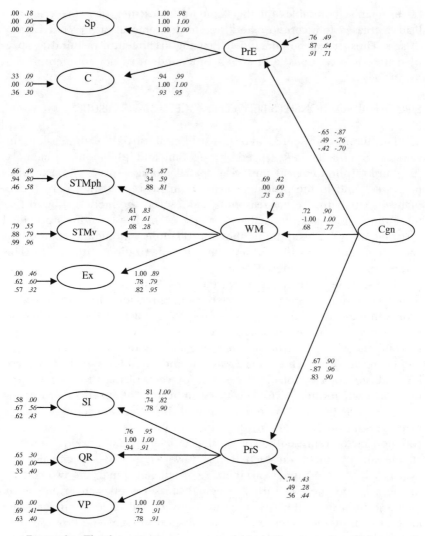

FIGURE 6.—The three-stratum common model including processing efficiency, working memory, and problem solving. (Sp = speed of processing, C = control of processing, PrE = processing efficiency, STMph = short-term memory—phonological, STMv = short-term memory—verbal, Ex = executive, WM = working memory, Ggn = general cognitive ability (or factor?), SI = spatial imaginal system, QR = qualitative-relational system, VP = verbal-propositional system, PrS = problem solving.)

of age. It can be seen that removing the effect of age did not result in any significant change in the fit of the models. Moreover, there was only a slight effect on the various estimates, where, understandably, the loadings of the manifest variables on the latent variables they were prescribed to load decreased to a certain extent due to the removal of the contribution of age. Thus, it can be concluded that the architecture of mind as specified here is very robust and largely independent of development.

STRUCTURAL RELATIONSHIPS BETWEEN PROCESSES AND ABILITIES

The models presented above clearly established the dimensions involved in Stroop-like tasks (speed of processing and inhibition), in memory-span tasks (phonological and visuospatial storage space and executive processes), and in the problem-solving domains represented here (quantitative, spatial, and verbal reasoning). Moreover, the models showed that these dimensions are very stable during growth. These findings provided a strong basis for examining the interrelations among the dimensions above that represent different levels in the organization of the mind. This is the issue to be considered next.

To examine these relations we included indicators of all dimensions in the same model. Specifically, there were three indicators for speed of processing and three for control of processing. Each of the six indicators was the average of performance attained on the three speed of processing and the three control of processing tasks addressed to each symbol system, respectively. Thus, there was one indicator for speed of processing and one for control of processing, for each of the three symbol systems, in each testing wave. The three indicators of speed of processing were prescribed to load on one factor and the three indicators of control of processing on another. In turn, these two factors were regressed on a common factor representing processing efficiency. For working memory, all measures available at each testing wave were used—specifically, the two verbal, the two numerical, the three spatial-imaginal, the two verbal/numerical, and the two verbal/imaginal measures of each testing wave. Of these indicators, the first four were prescribed to load on the same factor, which therefore represents phonological storage. The three spatial/imaginal indicators were prescribed to load on another factor to represent visuospatial memory and the last four indicators were prescribed to load on another factor representing the executive processes of memory. These three factors were regressed on a common working memory factor. Finally, the same two mean scores per cognitive domain were used to indicate the domains of quantitative, spatial, and verbal reasoning, and were therefore prescribed to load on their respective factors in pairs. These three SCS-specific factors were regressed on a general problem-solving factor. The correlations between the variables included in these models are shown in Appendix A.

To specify the relations among the three aspects of the mind, two approaches were adopted and compared. First, we tested the approach followed by Conway et al. (in press) and Kyllonen (2002), according to which the processing efficiency and working memory factors are specified as independent factors that are allowed to correlate, and the problem-solving factor is regressed on both of these factors. Second, we tested the cascade model proposed by Demetriou, Efklides, and Platsidou (1993). The reader is reminded that this model assumes that dimensions are hierarchically organized so that the processes at each subsequent higher level in the hierarchy include the processes of all previous levels together with processes specific to this level. To implement this assumption in the present case, the working memory factor was regressed on the processing efficiency factor and the problem-solving factor was regressed on both the processing efficiency factor and the *residual* of the working memory factor.

These two types of models were tested separately on the performance attained by the whole sample at each testing wave. Moreover, the models were tested on the performance attained on processing efficiency at the first testing wave, on memory tasks at the second testing wave, and on the cognitive tasks at the third testing wave. This latter model is obviously a very robust test of the relations of interest because it involves measures of the different structures and levels of the mind examined at different points in time.

The two types of models are illustrated in Figure 7. The fit of both types of models was very good and statistically indiscriminate in all four cases. It is noted, however, that the Conway–Kyllonen approach (Figure 7a) faced technical problems, which are clearly reflected in the fact that the parameter estimates of the regression of the problem-solving factor on the working memory factor exceeded unity in two cases, indicating colinearity between processing efficiency and working memory. To remedy these problems, these two models were rerun with the problem-solving–processing efficiency relations left out. Obviously, both tests of this model suggested a very strong dependence of problem solving on working memory. Thus, taken at face value, these results are in line with the Conway–Kyllonen conclusion that "*g* is working memory." However, the technical problems noted above suggest that this is due to the fact that working memory is confounded with processing efficiency in this approach. That is, the strong relations of working memory with problem solving come from both the processing efficiency engrafted in the functioning of working memory and the storage and executive components that are particular to it (see Figure 7a). This confounding does not exist in the cascade model (see Figure 7b) because the regression of working memory on processing efficiency and the regression of problem solving on both processing efficiency and the *residual* of working memory separate the effects

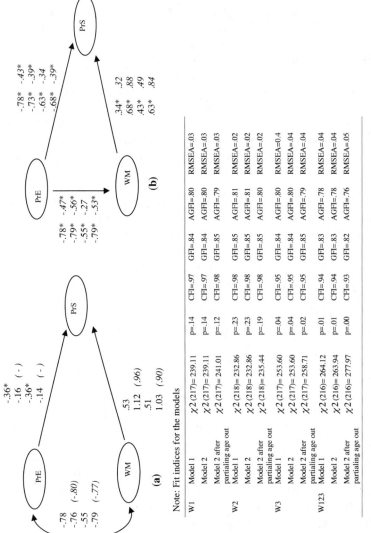

FIGURE 7.—Structural equation models for relations between processing efficiency, working memory, and problem solving. Model 1 assumes that processing efficiency and working memory are correlated and independently affect problem solving. Model 2 takes processing efficiency as the independent factor on which both others can be regressed. Problem solving is also regressed on the residuals of working memory. (PrE = processing efficiency, WM = working memory, PrS = problem solving.)

of each of these two aspects of the mind on problem solving. As a result, the cascade problem is free of any colinearity problems. In fact, removing the processing efficiency–problem-solving relation in the Conway–Kyllonen model in order to solve the colinearity problems resulted in slightly lower fit indexes of this model as compared to the corresponding cascade model. Therefore, the cascade model is both conceptually and technically superior. Inspection of this model (see Figure 7b) suggests clearly that processing efficiency is strongly and almost equally related to problem solving (all parameter estimates were in the .6–.7 range). Moreover, working memory is also significantly related, although this relation is weaker.

The model above is rather global in that the component processes involved in each of the three main constellations of functions of the mind (speed and control of processing, the three aspects of working memory, and the three domains of problem solving) were masked under their respective general factors. However, it is interesting to disentangle the interrelations among these components both within and across levels. To specify these interrelations, the three general factors were removed from the model and the following structural relations among the component-specific factors were built into the model: (1) The control of processing factor was regressed on the speed of processing factor. (2) The executive memory factor was regressed on (a) the speed of processing factor and (b) the residual of the control of processing factor. (3) Each of the two short-term storage factors (i.e., phonological and visual memory) was regressed on the constructs noted in (1) and (2) and also on the residual of the executive memory factor. (4) Each of the three SCS-specific factors was regressed on the constructs noted in (1)–(3) and also on the residual of one of the storage-specific factors of working memory. That is, the spatial reasoning factor was regressed on the residual of the visual memory factor and the quantitative and verbal reasoning factors were regressed on the residual of the phonological memory factor. This model is shown in Figure 8.

Obviously, this model implements the cascade model (the model claiming that more fundamental processes are embedded in more complex processes) at the analytical level of the component processes involved in the three levels of the mind investigated here. Thus, in the present realization of the model, it is assumed that control of processing includes the processes needed to perform on the sheer speed of processing tasks together with the encoding and inhibition processes required by control of processing tasks. In turn, the executive aspects of working memory (the strategies used to organize the storage and the retrieval of information) require both aspects of processing efficiency together with the executive strategies required to efficiently store and recall information. In a similar fashion, the short-term memory (STM) tasks need all of these processes

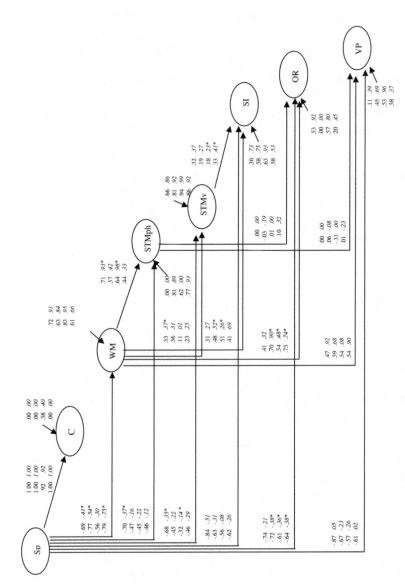

FIGURE 8.—Model of the structural relations between factors across the three testing waves. (Sp = speed of processing, C = control of processing, WM = working memory, STMph = short-term memory—phonological, STMv = short-term memory—verbal, SI = spatial imaginal system, QR = qualitative-relational system, VP = verbal-propositional system.)

as well as the buffer-specific storage and retrieval processes (such as phonological rehearsal) needed by the respective tasks. Finally, tasks addressed to the various SCSs require all of these processes together with specific processes and operations that are characteristic of each of the SCSs concerned.

This model was again tested separately on the performance attained by the whole sample at each testing wave. Moreover, the model was also tested on the performance attained on speed and control of processing tasks at the first testing wave, the memory tasks at the second testing wave, and the cognitive tasks at the third testing wave. The fit of this model at and across the testing waves was always very good:

    1. first testing:

χ^2 (212) = 236.601, p = .12, χ^2/df = 1.116, CFI = .977, RMSEA = .034
(χ^2 (215) = 301.112, p = .00, χ^2/df = 1.401, CFI = .929, RMSEA = .061).

    2. second testing:

χ^2 (214) = 238.357, p = .12, χ^2/df = 1.114, CFI = .974, RMSEA = .033
(χ^2 (219) = 238.170, p = .12, χ^2/df = 1.113, CFI = .976, RMSEA = .033).

    3. third testing:

χ^2 (209) = 241.873, p = .06, χ^2/df = 1.573, CFI = .960, RMSEA = .039
(χ^2 (213) = 269.737, p = .01, χ^2/df = 1.266, CFI = .938, RMSEA = .050).

    4. across the three testing waves:

χ^2 (212) = 260.522, p = .01, χ^2/df = 1.229, CFI = .945, RMSEA = .046
(χ^2 (213) = 265.811, p = .01, χ^2/df = 1.248, CFI = .949, RMSEA = .048).

The parameters of interest are those reflecting the structural relations among factors as specified above. It can be seen that speed of processing is strongly associated with all the other factors (parameter estimates generally ranging from .6 to .7). In fact, this factor accounted for all of the variance of the control of processing factor so that the regression of the residual of control of processing on the other factors was constrained to 0. The association of executive memory with visual memory was stronger than its association with phonological memory. Interestingly, the relation of the central executive processes of working memory with all of the SCS-specific factors was much stronger than the corresponding relation to the storage buffers. Therefore, these results suggest strongly that speed of processing is an important component of all other systems. Control of processing is fully absorbed by speed of processing so that it disappears as a factor of performance on memory or problem-solving tasks. Memory is important and it accounts for a considerable additional amount of variance of the cognitive tasks. Of the two basic components of working memory, the executive and the storage components, the executive is more important than the storage component in cognitive performance. In conclusion, speed of processing and the executive processes of working memory are the crucial factors that define problem solving.

How are these relations impacted by age? A first answer to this question is suggested by a closer inspection of the three wave-specific models. Comparing the parameter estimates of these three models suggests that the relation of speed of processing with all other factors decreases systematically from one wave to the next, whereas the relation of the executive component of working memory with problem solving remains generally stable. This trend suggests that, with development, factors other than efficiency (such as general hypercognitive strategies or factors related to the operation within particular domains) become more important in the use of problem-solving skills, operations, and concepts. In other words, changes in processing efficiency appear to open the way for the construction of problem-solving skills, operations, and concepts. To be constructed, however, skills, operations, and concepts need the involvement of general management processes and domain-specific experiences. Moreover, after they are constructed, domain-specific skills or operations tend to mask the initial involvement of processing efficiency.

A stricter test of the role of age in the relations among dimensions would be to fit the models above after partialing out the effect of age. Thus, each of the models was rerun with one additional set of relations built into it. Specifically, each of the manifest variables included in the models was regressed on the age at the first testing wave, in addition to its regression on the latent variable to which it is supposedly related. Partialing out age differences in starting age purifies the models of the presence of cohort and individual differences, which at the beginning are confounded with age differences. Thus, one can see how this manipulation affects both the pattern of interfactor relations within each age group (which reveals the effects of individual differences between the factors) and the pattern of relations among the estimates of each factor across testing waves (which reveals the effect of sheer growth, so to speak, on the relative status of each factor).

The parameter estimates and statistics of these models are shown in Figure 8 in italics. It can be seen that partialing out initial age differences results in a drastic decrease of the association of processing efficiency with all other factors. Obviously this finding implies strongly that speed of processing covaries closely with age. It is also noticeable that the decrease in the strength of the association of speed of processing was not uniform across dimensions. At one extreme, its association with executive memory remained significant and noticeable, implying that executive processes in working memory are tightly linked with processing efficiency. At the other extreme, this association decreased extensively in the case of the three problem-solving domains and vanished completely in the case of the verbal reasoning. This change implies that many other factors are required to transform a given level of processing efficiency into actual reasoning in the various domains. In fact, the more a domain depends on domain-specific meaning and knowledge, such as verbal reasoning, the more important these other factors turn out to be. Finally, it is to be noted that the association of executive memory with all other factors remained very stable after partialing out age, implying the direct involvement of this aspect of working memory in all aspects of problem solving.

The differential effect of the age partialing-out manipulation on the relations between processing speed and working memory on the one hand and problem solving on the other suggests that these two aspects are related differently with problem solving. Speed of processing appears to set the limits for the operation of the executive processes of working memory and opens possibilities for the operation of problem solving in various domains. However, the executive processes that are required to organize and choose between information are part of both working memory and problem solving. Thus, these two aspects of the mind are partly inseparable. Of course, the implementation of these executive processes together with domain-specific processes poses efficiency requirements, which vary from domain to domain. These requirements are responsible for the relations between speed of processing and problem solving after partialing out the relations with age.

CONCLUSIONS

The findings of the structural analyses presented above suggest the following conclusions. First, all dimensions addressed by the study (speed and control of processing in processing efficiency; phonological memory, visual memory, and central executive processes in working memory; and verbal, quantitative, and spatial reasoning in problem solving) were identified in the performance of the participants. This is the meaning of the fact that all of these dimensions stood up as first-order factors in the models found to fit our data.

Second, these dimensions are hierarchically organized, as expected (see prediction 1 in the final section of Chapter I). This is clearly suggested by both the hierarchical model shown in Figure 6 and the structural models shown in Figures 7 and 8, which indicate that more fundamental processes are embedded in more complex processes. It must be noted, however, that the number of strata or levels in the architecture of the mind is not a fixed number, as is implied by the three-stratum model of intelligence proposed by Carroll (1993). Rather, this number is a function of the resolution of the experimental manipulations used to uncover cognitive processes or of the analyses used to specify them. The reader is reminded that there were many more levels of inclusion of processes within each other in the analytic cascade model shown in Figure 8 as compared to the global model shown in Figure 7. Therefore, on the one hand, the three strata suggested by general theories of intelligence, such as those proposed by Carroll (1993) or Gustafsson and Undheim (1996), represent a relatively refined and appropriate architecture that reflects both particular processes and functions as well as their intertwining into broader systems that have conceptual and functional unity. On the other hand, we need to remember that more dimensions and more strata may be found if the analysis focuses on the composition of each of the particular dimensions or functions involved, or on the effects exerted on these dimensions by particular aspects of the environment. In any case, the architecture described here is not affected by growth, as suggested by the fact that it was the same across both age cohorts and testing waves.

Third, the more fundamental functions are embedded in more complex functions, as suggested by the model of functional and developmental synergy advanced in the Introduction (see prediction 2 in Chapter I). It may be noted, however, that the role of some dimensions is more powerful than that of others in this synergy. Specifically, of the two dimensions of processing efficiency, speed of processing is a more powerful predictor of both working memory and problem solving. Most probably this is due to the fact that both dimensions represent the same underlying mechanism of selective attention, and speed of processing, as measured here, is a purer measure of this mechanism. Moreover, of the three components of working memory, the executive processes are implicated more strongly in problem solving than are the storage buffers. This is most probably due to the fact that the fundamental executive processes addressed by working memory tasks (organization of incoming information and selection of information according to the requirements of the current goal) are part of any problem-solving endeavor. In effect, both of the strong predictors of problem solving—speed of processing and the executive processes permeating working memory—are complementary manifestations of the same underlying construct: guided processing under time constraints. Passolunghi and Sigel (2001) have recently presented evidence fully in line with our findings; they show that inhibitory control of information in working memory is related more to problem solving than to passive storage of information.

These findings do have clear implications for the neo-Piagetian models summarized in the introduction. The reader is reminded that there is no general agreement between neo-Piagetian models with regard to the organization of working memory and the role of its various components. On the one hand, according to both Pascual-Leone and Case, storage as such is the causal component in the development and functioning of thinking. According to Pascual-Leone the crucial parameter insofar as thought development is concerned is the k parameter in Equation (1), and according to Case the crucial parameter is the STSS in Equation (2)— that is, the number of schemes that can be simultaneously held active in the processing space. The parameter that stands for executive processes in these theories either remains constant (the e parameter for Pascual-Leone) or decreases (the OS parameter for Case) with age. On the other hand, Halford, following Baddeley, maintained that the central executive and not storage as such is the workspace of thinking. We have demonstrated above (see the models shown in Figure 8) that storage is much less closely associated with any of the SCSs than are executive processes. In fact, only visual storage was found to be significantly associated with the spatial SCS. Therefore, it is to be concluded that our results are largely in line with Halford and Baddeley in indicating that the central executive is more important than storage as such in the relations between working memory and thinking. However, storage does play a role in one domain of thinking, namely spatial thinking.

Contrary to the architecture, which does not change with growth, the strength of relations between dimensions does change with growth. The reader is reminded that the role of speed of processing diminishes with age, whereas the role of working memory remains stable. Thus, the function of these aspects of processing in the development of thought is not the same. Speed of processing opens possibilities for thought but other factors need to be activated if these possibilities are to be transformed into actual thought abilities. Working memory does not just open possibilities for thought. It is part of it. Thus, its enlargement alters thought by definition.

In the three following chapters we focus on development in order to study in detail the conditions of each dimension and their dynamic interactions during the age span covered by this study. Three different methods are adopted. First, we try to capture and depict the exact condition of each of these processes through a series of multivariate analyses of variance. Then we use growth modeling to decipher developmental changes from possible changes in individual differences and mixture growth modeling to specify different types or styles of development. Finally, we use dynamic modeling by logistic equations to specify both the exact developmental function of each of these processes and their dynamic interactions during growth.

71

IV. RESULTS: THE DEVELOPMENT OF
COGNITIVE FUNCTIONS

THE DEVELOPMENT OF PROCESSING EFFICIENCY

To specify the changes in processing efficiency with time, and the possible effects exerted on these changes by the factors involved in the study (the dimension of processing and symbol system), a $4 \times 3 \times 2 \times 3$ (Age cohorts × Testing waves × Speed vs. control of processing × Symbol systems) MANOVA with repeated measures on the last three factors was run. The main findings of this analysis are summarized in Figure 9, which shows that the effect of age cohort was highly significant and very strong, $F_{(3,109)} = 49.718$, $p < .0001$, $\eta^2 = .58$ (η^2 shows the percentage of variance in the dependent variable accounted for by the independent variable; i.e., in the present case, 58% of the variance in processing efficiency is explained by variation in the variable standing for age cohort), indicating that older subjects performed faster on all tasks used here. Moreover, the effect of testing wave was also highly significant and very strong, $F_{(2,108)} = 49.895$, $p < .0001$, $\eta^2 = .48$, indicating that reaction times decreased systematically across the three testing waves. The dimension effect was very strong, $F_{(1,109)} = 356.963$, $p < .0001$, $\eta^2 = .77$, indicating that reaction times for speed of processing tasks were much lower than for the control of processing tasks. Thus, it appears that the control of interference of the stronger but irrelevant aspect of the stimuli takes time in addition to the encoding time required by speed of processing tasks. The symbol system effect was also highly significant and very strong, $F_{(2,108)} = 144.130$, $p < .0001$, $\eta^2 = .73$, indicating that performance on the figural tasks was considerably lower than performance on the numerical and verbal tasks, which were very similar. Finally, the dimension × symbol system effect was significant and strong, $F_{(2,108)} = 18.099$, $p < .0001$, $\eta^2 = .25$, indicating that the difference between the figural system and the two other systems, in terms of control of processing, was considerably higher than their corresponding difference in terms of speed of processing. This

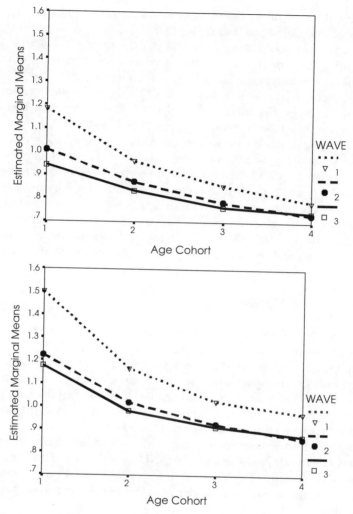

FIGURE 9.—Mean performance on speed and control of processing tasks across age cohorts and testing waves

suggests that interference of the dominant dimension was stronger in the figural system.

The interaction of age cohort with testing wave was significant, $F_{(6,216)} = 7.104$, $p < .0001$, $\eta^2 = .15$, indicating that improvement in performance from the one testing wave to the next diminished extensively and systematically from the younger to the older age cohorts. This finding is consistent with the assumption that growth decelerates as it approaches ceiling.

Moreover, the age cohort × dimension interaction was significant, $F_{(3,109)} = 7.905$, $p < .0001$, $\eta^2 = .18$, indicating that the difference between the two dimensions was larger among the younger than among the older cohorts. This finding suggests that the ability to control interference grows faster than sheer speed of processing. The age cohort also interacted with the symbol system, $F_{(6,218)} = 6.307$, $p < .0001$, $\eta^2 = .14$, indicating that the difference between the three symbol systems diminished with increasing age. The wave × symbol system, $F_{(4,106)} = 19.958$, $p < .0001$, $\eta^2 = .43$, and the wave × symbol system × dimension interactions were significant, $F_{(4,106)} = 9.903$, $p < .0001$, $\eta^2 = .27$, indicating that the pattern of improvement across testing waves and dimensions was not the same for the three symbol systems. Specifically, in the verbal system little improvement was observed from the first to the second testing, whereas there was considerable improvement from the second to the third testing. In contrast, in the numerical and the figural systems there was considerable improvement from first to second testing and very little from second to third testing.

DEVELOPMENT OF MEMORY

To specify the changes in memory with time and the factors examined by the study (symbol system and complexity of information), a series of multivariate analyses of variance were run. The first of these analyses focused only on the short-term memory tasks and it involved all the verbal and numerical short-term memory tasks; of the figural tasks we included the figure naming and position specification tasks in order to have a fully balanced factorial design. Thus, technically speaking, this was a 4 × 3 × 3 × 2 (Age cohorts × Testing waves × Symbol systems × Levels of complexity in each symbol system) MANOVA with repeated measures on the last three factors. The main findings of the analysis are summarized in Figure 10; the means and standard deviations resulting from this analysis are shown in Table 6.

The effect of age cohort was highly significant and strong, $F_{(3,109)} = 24.129$, $p < .0001$, $\eta^2 = .40$ ($F_{(3,106)} = 7.216$, $p < .0001$, $\eta^2 = .17$), indicating that older participants performed better than younger participants. Similarly, the effect of testing wave was also highly significant and very strong, $F_{(2,108)} = 153.071$, $p < .0001$, $\eta^2 = .74$ ($F_{(2,105)} = .798$, $p > .05$, $\eta^2 = .02$), indicating that performance improved from one testing wave to the next. The symbol system effect was also highly significant and very strong, $F_{(2,108)} = 79.014$, $p < .0001$, $\eta^2 = .59$ ($F_{(2,105)} = .228$, $p > .14$, $\eta^2 = .00$), indicating that performance on the verbal tasks was better than performance on the numerical tasks by an average of .3 of a unit and that performance on these latter tasks was better than performance on the imaginal tasks by

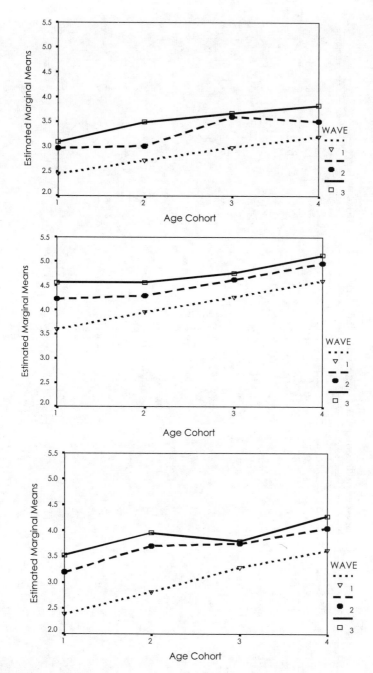

FIGURE 10.—Performance on the three components of working memory across age cohorts and testing waves

TABLE 6

Mean Performance and Standard Deviations (in parentheses) on the Memory Tasks

Tasks	Testing Waves	Age (in years)								
		8	9	10	11	12	13	14	15	16
Numerical Easy	1	4.25 (.75)		4.63 (.81)		4.86 (.74)		5.15 (.61)		
	2		4.71 (.94)		4.97 (.93)		5.45 (.87)		5.77 (.95)	
	3			5.29 (.76)		5.20 (.81)		5.66 (.77)		5.92 (.98)
Difficult	1	2.64 (.73)		3.17 (.65)		3.48 (.78)		3.77 (.82)		
	2		3.32 (.77)		3.43 (.63)		3.62 (.62)		3.96 (.77)	
	3			3.71 (.46)		3.50 (.63)		3.62 (.68)		4.08 (.80)
Verbal Easy	1	4.04 (.64)		4.30 (.65)		4.62 (.78)		4.96 (.77)		
	2		4.57 (.88)		4.63 (.81)		5.03 (.82)		5.27 (.67)	
	3			4.89 (.74)		5.13 (.73)		5.34 (.81)		5.69 (.68)
Difficult	1	3.43 (.69)		3.70 (.75)		4.10 (.67)		4.50 (.86)		
	2		4.29 (.71)		4.13 (.78)		4.38 (.68)		4.85 (.61)	
	3			4.36 (.62)		4.43 (.86)		4.41 (.73)		4.81 (.75)

Spatial-object	1	2.86 (.97)		3.40 (.89)		3.93 (1.00)		4.19 (.94)	
	2		4.07 (.81)		4.47 (1.14)		4.52 (1.06)		4.96 (1.04)
	3			3.93 (.81)		4.43 (.94)		4.45 (.74)		5.00 (1.17)
Spatial-positions	1	2.14 (.93)		2.43 (.82)		2.90 (.86)		3.27 (1.08)	
	2		2.68 (.98)		3.50 (1.04)		3.55 (1.15)		3.62 (.98)
	3			3.64 (.68)		3.97 (.76)		3.62 (.90)		4.31 (1.16)
Spatial-orientation	1	2.14 (.71)		2.60 (.81)		3.03 (1.05)		3.38 (1.06)	
	2		2.82 (.82)		3.13 (.90)		3.17 (.80)		3.58 (.99)
	3			3.00 (.77)		3.47 (1.01)		3.31 (.85)		3.54 (.86)
Numerical-verbal Who	1	2.29 (.94)		2.67 (.80)		2.69 (1.07)		3.19 (.69)	
	2		2.71 (.66)		2.83 (.70)		3.28 (.80)		3.31 (.62)
	3			3.07 (.66)		3.33 (.66)		3.34 (.72)		3.65 (.63)

continued

TABLE 6—*Continued*

Tasks	Testing Waves	Age (in years)								
		8	9	10	11	12	13	14	15	16
Numerical-verbal How many	1	1.96 (.84)		2.33 (.99)		2.69 (1.23)		2.92 (1.16)		
	2		2.68 (1.33)		2.67 (.96)		3.55 (1.06)		3.12 (1.18)	
	3			2.96 (1.07)		3.43 (.63)		3.38 (1.12)		3.92 (1.02)
Imaginal-verbal Object	1	2.82 (.98)		3.20 (1.13)		3.45 (.99)		3.50 (.91)		
	2		3.32 (.90)		3.27 (.91)		3.79 (.98)		3.96 (.92)	
	3							4.03 (.94)		4.04 (.87)
Imaginal-verbal Color	1	2.71 (1.01)		2.67 (.96)		3.10 (.98)		3.15 (1.16)		
	2		3.14 (.80)		3.27 (.83)		3.76 (.87)		3.62 (.75)	
	3			3.11 (.79)		3.57 (.82)		3.93 (.59)		3.69 (.62)
Pascual-Leone's K		3	4	4	5	5	6	6	7	7
Case's STSS Dimensional-vectorial		3	4	4	2	2	3	3	4	4
			1	1						

about .5 per item (see Table 6). The effect of complexity was extremely high and strong, $F_{(1,109)} = 1021.248$, $p < .0001$, $\eta^2 = .90$ ($F_{(1,106)} = 19.630$, $p < .0001$, $\eta^2 = .16$), indicating that performance on the simpler tasks was higher than performance on the complex tasks by about one memory item. Some of the interactions among these factors were significant. Specifically, the interaction between age cohort and testing wave was significant, $F_{(6,218)} = 3.321$, $p < .003$, $\eta^2 = .09$ ($F_{(6,212)} = 1.151$, $p > .05$, $\eta^2 = .03$), indicating that, overall, the improvement from the first to the second testing wave was greater than the improvement from the second to the third wave, especially for the two older age cohorts. This effect is perfectly understandable because it reflects the fact that performance among older subjects approached ceiling so that there was little room for improvement from the second to the third testing. Moreover, the wave × symbol system interaction was significant, $F_{(4,106)} = 4.657$, $p < .002$, $\eta^2 = .15$ ($F_{(4,103)} = 1.011$, $p > .05$, $\eta^2 = .04$). This interaction simply reflected the fact that the difference between performance on the imaginal tasks on the one hand and the two other symbol systems on the other hand was greater in the first testing wave as compared to the other two. Both effects are consistent with the trend observed in the two dimensions of processing efficiency, where the growth of processing potentials tends to decelerate with increasing age. The symbol system × complexity interaction was significant and very strong, $F_{(2,108)} = 146.199$, $p < .0001$, $\eta^2 = .73$ ($F_{(2,105)} = 4.467$, $p < .02$, $\eta^2 = .08$), indicating that the difference between the simple and the complex items in the numerical system was much greater (close to two memory items) than the corresponding items in the verbal system (about one memory item). Finally, the testing wave × symbol system × complexity interaction was significant, $F_{(4,106)} = 10.801$, $p < .0001$, $\eta^2 = .29$ ($F_{(4,103)} = 2.643$, $p < .04$, $\eta^2 = .09$). This interaction reflected some interesting trends. First, in the case of the three simpler tasks, performance on the numerical tasks was higher than performance on the verbal tasks and performance on these latter tasks was higher than performance on the imaginal tasks. However, in the case of the complex tasks, performance on the verbal tasks was higher than performance on the numerical tasks. Performance on the figural tasks was again the lowest, although its difference from the other two symbol systems tended to diminish across testing waves more than in the case of the simple tasks (see Table 7). These effects concur with Baddeley's (1990) claim that word length exerts an effect on the number of units that can be retained in the phonological buffer. Attention is drawn to the fact that, in this regard, the difficult number items are about twice as long as the easy items, which is not true for the corresponding verbal items.

The reader is reminded that the structural models presented in Chapter III suggested that memory is closely associated with speed of processing. One is then justified to ask if, and to what extent, the significant effects noted above derive from differences in this fundamental variable of speed of processing rather than from the various factors involved in the analysis above. To answer this question, we reran the MANOVA above using three indicators of speed of processing as covariates. Specifically, we used one index of speed of processing for each of the three symbol systems in the first testing wave; this was the mean performance attained on all three trials addressed to speed of processing within each symbol system. The values obtained from this analysis are shown above in parentheses, next to the corresponding values of the analysis, which did not include any covariate. Comparing these values suggests that partialing out the effect of speed of processing resulted in a dramatic decrease of all significant effects discussed above. In fact, of the various effects, only three remained significant after the effect of speed of processing was partialed out: the effect of age cohort, complexity, and the testing wave × symbol system × complexity interaction. These findings suggest that a major part of age changes in memory performance derives from changes in speed of processing. A lesser but still significant part of memory development is particular to memory itself. In a similar vein, it is also suggested that dealing with complex information that needs to be stored and recalled in working memory is, to a very large extent, a function of speed of processing. At the same time, however, dealing with complexity requires processes particular to memory itself.

To contrast the modality-specific storage buffers (SB) (i.e., the phonological buffer and the visual buffer) with the central executive (CE) of working memory, two MANOVAs were run. The first included the verbal and the number symbol systems and the second the verbal and the imaginal symbol system. Specifically, the first was a $4 \times 3 \times 2 \times 2$ (Age cohorts × Testing waves × SB vs. CE × Verbal vs. number symbol systems) MANOVA with repeated measures on the last three factors. Specifically, this analysis involved the simple verbal and number tasks for short-term memory and the two complex tasks that required their coordination. The second was a $4 \times 3 \times 2 \times 2$ (Age cohorts × Testing waves × SB vs. CE × Verbal vs. imaginal symbol systems) MANOVA with repeated measures on the last three factors. This analysis involved the simple verbal and figural tasks for the storage buffers and the two complex tasks that required their coordination.

The results of the two analyses showed only the following to be significant:

1. First analysis
   age cohort: $F_{(3,109)} = 15.930$, $p < .0001$, $\eta^2 = .31$
   $(F_{(3,109)} = 5.560$, $p < .001$, $\eta^2 = .14)$
   testing wave: $F_{(2,108)} = 111.819$, $p < .0001$, $\eta^2 = .67$
   $(F_{(2,105)} = .303$, $p > .05$, $\eta^2 = .01)$

memory type: $F_{(1,109)} = 1246.799$, $p < .0001$, $\eta^2 = .92$
$(F_{(1,106)} = 14.356$, $p < .0001$, $\eta^2 = .12)$
memory type × symbol system interaction effects:
$F_{(1,109)} = 17.703$, $p < .0001$, $\eta^2 = .14$
$(F_{(3,106)} = 3.813$, $p > .05$, $\eta^2 = .03)$.

2. Second analysis
age cohort: $F_{(3,109)} = 23.227$, $p < .0001$, $\eta^2 = .39$
$(F_{(3,109)} = 7.693$, $p < .0001$, $\eta^2 = .18)$
testing wave: $F_{(2,108)} = 78.861$, $p < .0001$, $\eta^2 = .59$
$(F_{(2,105)} = 2.919$, $p > .05$, $\eta^2 = .05)$
memory type: $F_{(1,109)} = 467.279$, $p < .0001$, $\eta^2 = .81$
$(F_{(1,106)} = 18.004$, $p < .0001$, $\eta^2 = .14)$
symbol system: $F_{(1,109)} = 93.497$, $p < .0001$, $\eta^2 = .46$
$(F_{(1,106)} = 1.236$, $p > .05$, $\eta^2 = .01)$
wave × symbol system: $F_{(2,108)} = 5.961$, $p < .004$, $\eta^2 = .10$
$(F_{(2,105)} = 3.330$, $p < .05$, $\eta^2 = .06$
memory type × symbol system interaction effects:
$F_{(1,109)} = 30.071$, $p < .0001$, $\eta^2 = .22$
$(F_{(1,106)} = 1.561$, $p > .05$, $\eta^2 = .01)$.

In both analyses only the effects of age cohort and memory type remained significant after partialing out the effect of speed of processing, which suggests that executive processes in memory are, to a certain extent, independent of processing efficiency. It is to be stressed, however, that even in these cases, partialing out the effect of speed of processing resulted in a dramatic decrease (by 80% in the first analysis and by 67% in the second analysis) of the effect of memory type. This indicates that the executive processes that differentiate the tasks addressed to executive processes and storage can be reduced, to a large extent, to processing efficiency as such.

Which model of memory development is supported by our findings? Strictly speaking, none of the models discussed in the Introduction is fully supported by these findings. The data agree with Pascual-Leone's model in that they show a systematic increase in memory capacity throughout the age span studied here. However, inspection of Table 6 makes it clear that the values obtained do not fully support this model because the memory capacity of the various age groups deviates, to one degree or another, from the capacity expected for each age according to Pascual-Leone's model. In fact, the rate of change is variable and depends on the age phase concerned. In Pascual-Leone's model the rate is stable from 3 to 15 years of age and it is one unit for every two years of age. In a similar way, the findings only partially agree with Case's model. Thus, in agreement with Case's model, we found that increasing the executive load of tasks is related to a systematic decrease in the amount of information that can be held in short-term storage. However, there was no sign that the space required for executive control of the task decreases with age. In fact, the difference between the short-term memory tasks, which required executive control at the minimum, and the complex tasks where much more extensive control was indeed required, remained stable across age cohorts and testing waves (i.e., it was the equivalent of 1 unit of information, plus or minus .5). These values are shown in Table 6. Applying a 4 × 3 × 3 (Age cohorts × Symbol systems × Testing waves) MANOVA on these differences indicated that effects of both age (i.e., cohort, $F_{(3,109)} = 1.663$, $p > .05$, $n^2 = .04$) and wave ($F_{(2,108)} = 1.227$, $p > .05$, $n^2 = .02$) were nonsignificant. Obviously, these findings suggest, in agreement with Pascual-Leone and Halford, and contrary to Case, that capacity increases with development.

Therefore, these findings suggest that the space occupied by executive processes does not vary systematically with age, at the least for the age span covered by this study. At first, this might be taken to support Pascual-Leone's position that the space required by the executive remains stable after the age of 2 years. However, this interpretation is not tenable because the executive processes activated by our tasks do not fully coincide with Pascual-Leone's executive (i.e., e in Equation (1), which stands for the capacity required for the representation of the task goal). That is, the tasks addressed to the central executive in this study involve, in addition to the representation of the task goal, actual operations applied on information (e.g., the organization of information in different sets according to symbol system). These are counted as k schemes (see Equation (1)) in Pascual-Leone's model.

Our findings also have implications with respect to the upper limit of working memory capacity. The reader may remember that the maximum capacity of Pascual-Leone's Mp is 7 schemes; the maximum capacity for Case's STSS for each cycle of development is 4 schemes; the maximum level of Halford's dimensionality is 4 dimensions. Our results (see Table 6) suggest that under appropriate conditions all models are, by and large, valid. Specifically, when familiar single units are to be stored and when the task demands for executive processes are limited as much as possible, as is the case with our tasks addressed to numerical and verbal storage, the upper limit does approach or reach Pascual-Leone's limit of 7 units. To do justice to Pascual-Leone, we note here that he insists (Pascual-Leone, 1970, personal communication, May 8, 2002) that the specification of Mp can only be effected under conditions of maximum facilitation so that executive processes do not consume any of the mental energy available beyond what is needed for the representation of the task's goal, (i.e., e in Equation (1)). When the tasks do require the activation of executive process, as is the case with our tasks addressed to working memory, the upper limit varies depending on the complexity of the executive processes required, and, in general, is close to 4 schemes.

Thus, it is clear that a functional conception of working memory is preferable over a fixed conception. We need a model that will specify, in the direction of the functional shift model (Demetriou, Efklides, & Platsidou, 1993) summarized in Chapter I, the relation between alternative metrics of working memory capacity. Different systems for measuring working memory capacity may be used, depending on the particular needs of the task at hand. Obviously, these needs are related to the specificities of the domain, the content, or context of the developmental or cognitive phenomenon to be described or explained. This would allow one to specify the role and functionality of the various aspects of working memory vis-à-vis the specificities of the task at hand.

Finally, it must be noted that none of these developmental models made any systematic provisions for possible differences in memory capacity as a function of the kind of information. Only Baddeley's model and our model allow prediction of possible differences among kinds of information, although possible differences are not precisely specified. The present findings show that these differences exist and they favor phonological memory, for we found that performance on the phonological memory tasks was superior to performance on the visual memory tasks. However, we recognize that these differences may have been caused by differences in the type of response required by the visual task; having to reconstruct the visual pattern may require executive memory that is not required by the verbal and numerical tasks.

SCS DEVELOPMENT

To study the development of the three domains of reasoning involved in this study, we constructed an index for each of them, which was the sum of the mean performance attained on each of the two tasks addressed to each specialized capacity sphere. These indexes were then used in a 4 × 3 × 3 (Age cohorts × Testing waves × SCSs) MANOVA with repeated measures on the last factor. The main findings of this analysis are summarized in Figure 11. It can be seen that the effect of age cohort was highly significant and very strong, $F_{(3,108)} = 45.320$, $p < .0001$, $\eta^2 = .56$ ($F_{(3,103)} = 15.570$, $p < .0001$, $\eta^2 = .31$), indicating that older participants performed better than younger participants. Moreover, the effect of testing wave was highly significant and very strong, $F_{(2,107)} = 158.620$, $p < .0001$, $\eta^2 = .75$, ($F_{(2,102)} = 4.967$, $p < .009$, $\eta^2 = .09$), indicating that performance

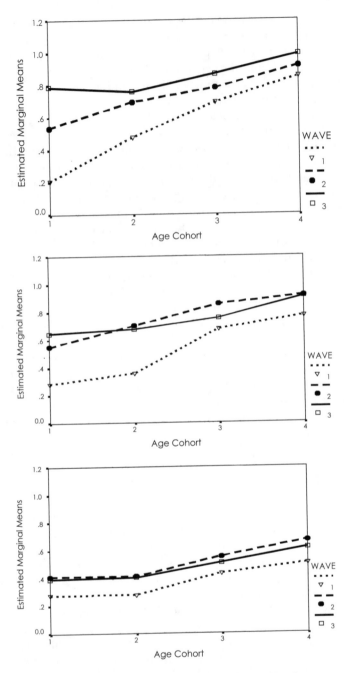

FIGURE 11.—Performances on the three specialized capacity spheres across age cohorts and testing waves

improved extensively from one testing to the next. The SCS effect was also highly significant and very strong, $F_{(2,107)} = 204.122$, $p < .0001$, $\eta^2 = .79$ ($F_{(2,102)} = 4.294$, $p < .02$, $\eta^2 = .08$), reflecting the fact that performance on the spatial-imaginal tasks was better than performance on the quantitative tasks and performance on these latter tasks was better than performance on the verbal reasoning tasks. Moreover, the interaction between age cohort and testing wave was significant, $F_{(6,216)} = 8.676$, $p < .0001$, $\eta^2 = .18$ ($F_{(6,204)} = 6.689$, $p < .0001$, $\eta^2 = .16$), indicating that improvement in performance from one wave to the next varied as a function of cohort. That is, performance improvement from the first to the second testing was much greater than the corresponding improvement from the second to the third testing; the same trend was revealed by the analyses applied on processing efficiency and memory. In fact, there was considerable improvement in performance from first to second testing in all cohorts, but from second to third testing only the younger age cohort improved noticeably. Moreover, the age cohort × SCS, $F_{(6,216)} = 3.711$, $p < .002$, $\eta^2 = .09$ ($F_{(6,204)} = .732$, $p > .05$, $\eta^2 = .02$), the testing wave × SCS, $F_{(4,105)} = 9.696$, $p < .002$, $\eta^2 = .09$ ($F_{(4,100)} = 1.281$, $p > .05$, $\eta^2 = .05$), and the age cohort × testing wave × SCS interactions were significant, $F_{(12,278)} = 3.707$, $p < .0001$, $\eta^2 = .12$ ($F_{(2,264)} = 2.435$, $p < .005$, $\eta^2 = .09$), indicating that the pattern of change was not the same across the three SCSs. In general, improvement in the verbal reasoning SCS was less marked and stable, especially from the second to the third testing wave. Moreover, this was the only SCS in which there was no difference between 8- and 10-year-olds, suggesting that reasoning problems require abilities acquired in adolescence.

It must be stressed that most of these effects remained significant even after controlling for the effect of speed of processing and short-term memory (an index of speed of processing for each symbol system at the first testing wave and an index of each of the two tasks addressed to the executive processes of working memory at the first testing wave). This finding indicates clearly that both the architecture of the three SCSs and their development are affected by processes other than those involved in these general processes.

The tasks that can be solved at each age are illustrated more clearly in Appendix B, which shows percentage success across age cohorts, testing waves, and items (and also class of participants as revealed by the analyses to be presented in the next chapter). Performance on the different tasks varied according to expectations; that is, in each set of tasks success was proportional to the constructional complexity of the tasks. In the set of quantitative tasks (the number operations items), success was a direct function of the number of missing operations. In general, if success by at least 50% of an age group is taken as a criterion for crediting this group with the ability represented by an item, the easiest item (having one operation missing) was attainable by the age of 8 years and all the rest were attainable by the age of 9 years. Of the items addressed to proportionality, the easiest one (involving increase by a factor of 2) proved to be within the reach of 8-year-olds, the most difficult one (involving decrease by a factor of $1/3$) was attainable only at the age of 15–16 years, and the others were solved by the age groups in between. In conclusion, development of quantitative thought, in the present context, proceeds from the ability to grasp the relations between a minimum of two numbers under facilitating conditions to the ability to operate on multiple sets of numbers and grasp their nonapparent relations.

Verbal reasoning appeared to evolve along the same pattern. The easy transitivity item and one of the two first-order analogies proved to be within the ability of the 8-year-olds, the easy implication item was solved at the age of 9 years, the first of the two first-order analogies was solved at the age of 12 years, and the difficult transitivity item and the fourth of the verbal analogies were solved at the age of 15–16 years. Two items, the difficult implication and the third-order verbal analogy, proved to be beyond the reach of our oldest adolescents. Thus it appears, in line with both classical Piagetian theory (Inhelder & Piaget, 1958) and more recent studies of the development of propositional reasoning (Moshman, 1990), that verbal reasoning proceeds from the ability to grasp relations between concrete aspects of reality to the ability to process their nonapparent relations under indeterminate conditions. In fact, even when present, this ability may fail when the semantics of the terms manipulated are unclear or ambivalent, as indicated by failure on the indeterminate implication item and the third-order analogy, which were apparently easy but elusive.

The development of spatial reasoning was similar, although it appeared to reach its final state faster. Children were able to solve the easiest of the mental rotation items by the age of 8 years, at age 9 years they were able to solve the tilted bottle task, and by the age of 10–11 years they were able to solve the most complex of the mental rotation items.

CONCLUSIONS

The analyses presented above suggest the following conclusions.

1. All dimensions of processing efficiency, working memory, and problem solving improve systematically with age. The rate of development decelerates as it approaches ceiling, at about middle adolescence.

2. The symbol system in which one operates is related to performance in all dimensions. Obviously, this indicates that differences in experience or the specificities of information mediate the implementation or functioning of central processing, storage, or problem-solving mechanisms.

3. Processing efficiency as indicated by speed of processing is an important feature of memory development. Development in processing efficiency seems to have a privileged relation with executive processes in memory in contrast to storage. However, it must also be noted that memory involves executive and storage processes that go beyond processing efficiency.

4. The operations to be performed on information require capacity. The more demanding they are, the less the capacity available for storing information. However, capacity seems to increase with age. In fact, the association of working memory with processing efficiency indicates that the development of processing efficiency is highly related to capacity increases.

5. Baddeley's model is supported by our findings regarding the architecture of working memory or the association of the type of information with it. However, none of the models available can fully accommodate the data concerning working memory development. In agreement with Pascual-Leone and Halford, and contrary to Case, executive processes in memory are more important than storage as factors of problem solving. However, the exact capacity available at successive phases of development cannot be specified in reference to any absolute number that can be attached to each of these phases. Both the nature of information and the operational or executive demands of the current problem are associated with what can be stored.

The development of problem solving depends on processing efficiency and capacity. The degree and the kind of dependence vary from domain to domain. Moreover, there is considerable autonomy in the development of the various domains. This of course provides full support to a theory of the human mind that accommodates both the domain-general and the domain-specific aspects of the human mind.

In the chapters that follow, we focus on the more dynamic aspects of development and try to specify both the nature of change within each of the dimensions and their interactions.

V. RESULTS: SPECIFYING PATTERNS OF CHANGE BY GROWTH MODELING

To specify the nature of change in the three main aspects of the mind investigated here (processing efficiency, working memory, and problem solving), and the possible interrelations in the patterns of change in these aspects, growth modeling was used. In particular, we focused on a structural equation modeling (SEM) approach using latent growth models. Latent growth models were estimated based on the observed mean vector and covariance matrix. The basic latent growth model was composed of two latent factors. The first latent factor represented the initial status (or intercept) and was defined by fixing all factor loadings of the repeated measures to 1.0. This factor captured the starting point of the growth trajectory at time 1. The second latent factor was the latent growth rate (or slope), and the factor loadings of the repeated measures were a mixture of fixed and freely estimated parameters that defined the shape of the growth trajectory over time. The mean of the initial status and growth rate factors represented the group parameter values of the intercept and slope of the growth trajectory. The variance of the initial status and growth rate factors represented the individual variability of each subject around the group parameters. Larger factor variances reflected greater individual differences in growth over time; smaller variances reflected more similar patterns of growth over time.

In the present chapter latent growth modeling is used to provide answers to the questions of the study as defined in Chapter I. In particular, we first analyze the development of memory, information processing, and problem solving of our sample over the three years of repeated testing; and, second, we investigate whether there are distinct subclasses of individuals who develop along different trajectories.

THE GROWTH PATTERN OF THE DEVELOPMENT OF PROCESSING EFFICIENCY, WORKING MEMORY, AND PROBLEM SOLVING

The general model tested here is illustrated in Figure 12. This model was estimated with the Mplus (Version 2) program (Muthen & Muthen, 2001) under the STREAMS 2.5 (Gustafsson & Stahl, 2000). The figure shows that nine manifest variables were used in this model: three for processing efficiency, three for working memory, and three for problem solving. Each variable was a composite measure of the performance attained

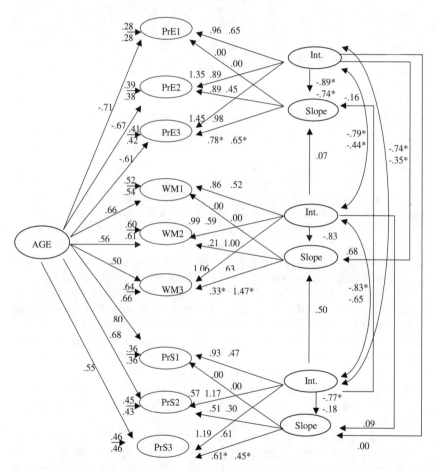

FIGURE 12.—The best-fitting growth model for processing efficiency, working memory, and problem solving across the three testing waves. (PrE = processing efficiency, WM = working memory, PrS = problem solving, Int. = intercept variable.)

TABLE 7

CORRELATIONS BETWEEN THE VARIABLES USED IN THE GROWTH MODELS
PRESENTED IN CHAPTER V

	AGE	PREFF1	PREFF2	PREFF3	WM1	WM2	WM3	PS1	PS2
PREFF1	−.707*	1.000							
PREFF2	−.658*	.823*	1.000						
PREFF3	−.628*	.768*	.839*	1.000					
WM1	.644*	−.645*	−.543*	−.507*	1.000				
WM2	.568*	−.582*	−.522*	−.523*	.661*	1.000			
WM3	.498*	−.480*	−.483*	−.476*	.667*	.609*	1.000		
PS1	.800*	−.655*	−.640*	−.580*	.652*	.657*	.604*	1.000	
PS2	.690*	−.624*	−.589*	−.449*	.605*	.616*	.501*	.785*	1.000
PS3	.546*	−.513*	−.538*	−.472*	.537*	.543*	.503*	.700*	.783*

*Correlation is significant at the .05 level (two-tailed).

Note.—The symbols PREFF, WM, and PS stand for processing efficiency, working memory, and problem solving, respectively. Numbers refer to testing waves.

on the respective tasks at each of the three testing waves. Thus, processing efficiency was the mean of performance attained on the processing speed and control of processing tasks; working memory was the mean of performance attained on the executive, phonological, and visual memory tasks; problem solving was the sum of the means of performance attained on the quantitative, verbal, and spatial reasoning tasks. The correlations between the variables included in this model are shown in Table 7.

The intercept variable for each of the three tasks in the study was fixed at a constant value of 1 as indicated in Figure 12 by the three lines from the intercept to their respective manifest variables. At an initial run of the model, the slope variable was fixed to have a relation of 0, 1, and 2 with all manifest variables at the first, second, and third testing waves, respectively. This constraint expresses the modeling assumption that change is a linear function of time. However, this model was found impossible to converge. Thus, the relation of the manifest variables in the third testing wave with the slope parameter was allowed to vary freely, which enabled the model to converge, indicating that change was not linear. Obviously, this finding is in full agreement with the results of our earlier multivariate analyses of variance which indicated that change tends to decelerate with age.

The overall model fit statistics were χ^2 ($df = 25$, $N = 112$) = 35.00, $p < .09$, RMSEA = .06, suggesting an excellent fit of the model to the data. Moreover, as can be seen in Figure 12, each of the slope variables was regressed on all three intercept variables and the three intercepts were allowed to correlate. The means and variances of the latent vari-

90

TABLE 8

Mean, Variances, and Correlations of Intercept and Slope Before and After Partialing Out the Effect of Age on Processing Efficiency, Working Memory, and Problem Solving

Variable	Mean		Variance	
	Age In	Age Out	Age In	Age Out
Processing efficiency intercept	1.06*	1.88*	.05*	.02*
Slope	.28*	.31*		
Working memory intercept	3.31*	1.48*	.24*	.09*
Slope	.66	.96*		−.01
Problem-solving intercept	2.95*	−2.23*	1.49*	.38*
Slope	1.77	2.45*		
Correlations				
Working memory and processing efficiency	−.79	−.44		
Problem solving and processing efficiency	−.74	−.35		
Problem solving and working memory	.83	.65		

ables are shown in Table 8; the parameter estimates of the model are shown in Figure 12.

Table 8 shows that the estimate of the mean of the intercept was 1.06 for processing efficiency, 3.31 for working memory, and 2.95 for problem solving. These means for all three aspects of the mind were significantly different from 0 ($t_{processing} = 47.89$, $t_{memory} = 61.42$, and $t_{problem\ solving} = 23.76$). The means of the slopes for working memory and problem solving were 0.66 and 1.77, respectively, indicating that these estimates were not significantly different from 0 ($t = 1.28$ for memory and $t = 1.48$ for problem solving). However, the mean of the slope for processing efficiency was 0.28, an estimate that was marginally significantly different from 0 ($t = 1.68$), indicating that there was an increase in processing efficiency over time.

The next question concerns the extent to which individuals in the sample vary around their group average (mean) trajectories in the three aspects of mind. This was evaluated by looking at the variances (or equivalently, the standard deviations). Table 8 depicts the variance estimates of the intercepts, reflecting the variation of individual intercepts and the variance of the slopes, explaining why, between the ages of 8 and 16 years, some individuals exhibit a more rapid development in the three aspects of mind than others. Their corresponding variance estimates for the intercepts ($V_{processing} = 0.05$, $V_{memory} = 0.24$, and $V_{problem\ solving} = 1.49$) were statistically significant, indicating significant individual variability in the initial states of processing, memory, and problem solving across the three waves of measurement ($t_{processing}$ = 6.87, t_{memory} = 5.57, and $t_{problem\ solving}$ = 6.45). The variance of slope estimates for processing and problem solving were significant ($t_{processing}$ = 3.48 and $t_{problem\ solving}$ = 3.05), showing a variable rate of change in these two aspects of mind. However, the variance estimated for the slope of working memory was not significant.

Moreover, of the various regressions of the slope variable on the intercept variable, only two were significant: the regression of the processing efficiency slope on the processing efficiency intercept and the regression of the problem-solving slope on the problem-solving intercept. The nonsignificant regression of the working memory slope on the working memory intercept was consistent with the nonsignificant variance of the memory intercept and slope.

The correlation between the intercept and the slope is important. In the present study, all correlations between the three intercept and slope factors were significant. The correlations between the intercept and slope in the processing and working memory tasks were negative (–.8, –.9, respectively), meaning that individuals who had higher initial scores had a weaker rate of increase (slope). The correlation between the intercept and slope in the problem-solving tasks was positive (.32), indicating that individuals who started out with a high initial level of problem solving became increasingly more capable in problem solving than others. The correlations among the intercepts in the three factors were also high and significant. In the processing efficiency and working memory aspects of mind the correlation among the intercepts was –.79, meaning that individuals with high initial levels of processing did not necessarily have high initial levels of working memory and vice versa. Negative correlations were also observed among the intercepts of processing efficiency and problem solving (–.74), while correlation among the intercepts of working memory and problem solving was positive (.83).

THE EFFECTS OF AGE AND COHORT

It might be thought that the pattern of relations and change suggested by the above model are no more than spurious manifestations of the operation of factors related to age or cohort or both. To partial out the effect of age, and thus test this idea, the model was assessed after regressing all nine manifest variables on age. In this model only the two significant regressions of slope on intercept (the regressions of the slope of processing efficiency and problem solving on their corresponding intercepts) and the three correlations between the intercepts were included.

The fit of this model was excellent: χ^2 (df = 31, N = 110) = 39.18, p < .15, RMSEA = .049.

Expectedly, the result of partialing out the effect of age was that all correlations between the three intercepts (see Table 8), although still significant, decreased extensively (the variance accounted for decreases from ~60% to ~30%). Moreover, the regression of the problem-solving slope on the corresponding intercept dropped drastically to nonsignificance although the regression of the processing efficiency slope on the corresponding intercept remained high and significant. Finally, all three latent variables slopes, in addition to the three intercepts, became significant. These results indicate clearly that the basic patterns of relations and development found by the model above are robust enough to stand up to the removal of the effects of age and cohort, although they become weaker as a result of this removal.

UNCOVERING DIFFERENT TYPES OF DEVELOPMENT

The above-described results are consistent with the assumption that developmental possibilities are differentially realized, and this justifies, in line with the fifth of the predictions stated in the Introduction, examining whether there are different types of developers in our sample. Mixture growth modeling was used to answer this question (Muthen & Muthen, 2001) because it enables specification of models in which one growth model applies to one subset of the data, and another growth model applies to another subset. The modeling here used a stepwise method—that is, the model already presented above was tested under the assumption that there are two, three, and four classes of subjects. The best fitting model was the one involving four classes. The means and variances of the intercept and slope of each of the three abilities across the four classes are shown in Table 9.

Appendix B shows that class 2 (52.7% of the total sample) was the largest. It can be considered as the class of developers because this class included the children who initially performed lowest in all three abilities but who showed the largest gains as a result of development in all three abilities. In fact, the majority of children in class 2 belonged to the two youngest age groups in our sample (45.8%, 39%, 13.6%, and 1.7% belonged to age cohorts 1, 2, 3, and 4, respectively).

Children in class 1 (10.7% of the total sample) were the fastest processors but their memory and problem-solving attainments were comparatively lower in both initial state and degree of change compared to children in classes 3 and 4. It is noted that 91.7% of these children belonged to the two older cohorts (0%, 8.3%, 50%, and 41.7% belonged to

TABLE 9
MEANS, VARIANCES, AND CORRELATIONS OF INTERCEPTS AND SLOPES OF THE FOUR CLASSES OF SUBJECTS GENERATED BY MIXTURE GROWTH MODELING

Variable	Class 1			Class 2			Class 3			Class 4		
	PrE	WM	PrS	PrE	WM	PrS	PrE	WM	PrS	PrE	WM	PrS
Mean of intercept	.83*	3.46*	3.98*	1.17*	2.99*	2.09*	.92*	4.05*	4.21*	.92*	3.66*	4.37*
Mean of slope	-.05*	.22*	.46*	-.10*	.43*	.81*	-.04*	.24*	.22*	-.06*	.38*	-.52*
Variance of intercept	.02*	.03	.02	.03*	.05*	.14	.03*	.01	.05	.02*	.04	.07
Variance of slope	.00	-.02	.00	.00*	-.01	.04	.00	-.09	-.09*	.00	-.02*	.10*
Correlation of slope and intercept	1.34*	—	7.68	-.70*	—	.35	1.23*	—	—	-1.58*	—	—

Note.—PrE = processing efficiency, WM = working memory, PrS = problem solving.

age cohorts 1, 2, 3, and 4, respectively), suggesting that they were already late in transforming their processing capabilities into actual problem-solving abilities.

Children in classes 3 (16.1% of the total sample; 0%, 11.1%, 44.4%, and 30.8% belonged to age cohorts 1, 2, 3, and 4, respectively) and 4 (20.5% of the total sample; 4.3%, 17.4%, 26.1%, and 52.2% belonged to age cohorts 1, 2, 3, and 4, respectively) were practically identical in processing efficiency but they differed in memory and problem solving. The children in class 3 were higher in memory and lower in problem solving than children in class 4; however, they developed less than children in class 4 in both memory and problem solving.

Appendix B presents percentage success on each of the items across the four classes and the three testing waves. Mean performance on speed of processing and the executive processes of memory are also shown, for indicative purposes. The pattern of performance shown in Appendix B helps refine the conclusions on development suggested by the results of the mixture growth modeling presented above. Specifically, regarding attainment age, children in class 4 developed faster than those in the other classes; they were able to solve the various tasks earlier than the children in all other classes by a period of 2 to 4 years. In turn, children in class 3 appeared to develop faster than those in class 1, which in turn was faster than those in class 2. Moreover, we note that it was basically the children in class 4 who were able to solve the most complex and elusive verbal and syllogistic reasoning items above chance and to preserve that attainment in time.

There were some other interesting differences among the four classes in addition to their rates of development. Specifically, there were differences in the stability of their problem-solving attainments. Growth in classes 2 and 4 was very stable, as indicated by the fact that performance improved and remained stable from one testing wave to the next across almost all items. In contrast, performance in classes 1 and 3 was rather unstable, especially in terms of the most difficult items, with a drop in performance from the second to the third wave of testing on many items. This drop was more pronounced in class 1.

The results presented here suggest that individuals differ in developmental efficiency and stability. *Developmental efficiency* may be defined as the transformation of the potentialities afforded by processing efficiency and available capacity into actual problem-solving abilities. *Developmental stability* may be defined as the preservation in time of the abilities constructed at a given phase of development. Based on these definitions and the patterns of performance revealed by the analyses above, the four classes may be ranked in developmental efficiency and stability as follows:

- Class 4 is clearly the most developmentally efficient because it developed faster than all other classes, reached the highest level possible under the conditions of this study, and was able to preserve its developmental gains.

- Class 2, although less developmentally efficient than class 4, was also very stable. Although this class was the lowest in processing efficiency and working memory, it exhibited the largest gains in problem-solving abilities from testing to testing. Moreover, it was able to preserve these gains from testing to testing.

- Class 1 was clearly the least developmentally efficient and stable. In this class, high processing efficiency was not actualized into correspondingly high memory capacity and problem-solving skills. Moreover, even the performance attained at a given testing wave was subject to regression at a subsequent wave.

- Class 3 was very similar to class 1, although performance in this class was generally higher and regressions were less frequent and pronounced.

How might one explain the instability of class 1 in contrast to the efficiency and stability of class 4? The answer to this question may lie in the relations between processing efficiency and working memory. Attention is drawn to the fact that class 1 was lower in working memory than classes 3 and 4, despite its high processing efficiency. In fact, working memory in class 1 was by and large the same as in class 2. This may suggest that high processing efficiency alone may allow for the construction of new problem-solving skills and operations, and this may indeed take place. However, a combination of a particular minimum level of working memory and processing efficiency is needed for this construction to be preserved and extended further. Obviously, this minimum combination was fully present in class 4. Under this assumption, one may argue that the relative lag in the development of working memory compared to processing efficiency in class 1 was responsible for its instability as related to the most cognitively demanding tasks.

What are the developmental and the individual differences dimensions that define the efficiency and capacity of the mind to construct new problem-solving skills? An answer to this question is provided by the pattern of processing efficiency and working memory attainment of the four classes as a function of age cohort. Specifically, it can be seen that there were systematic differences in processing efficiency both among the four classes, $F(3, 98) = 4.945$, $p < .003$, $\eta^2 = .13$, and the four age cohorts,

$F(3, 98) = 3.393$, $p < .02$, $\eta^2 = .09$. However, in the case of working memory, there were, naturally enough, large differences among classes, $F(3, 98) = 6921.268$, $p < .0001$, $\eta^2 = .30$, but no differences among age cohorts, $F(3, 98) = 1.953$, $p = .126$, $\eta^2 = .02$. The effect of testing wave was significant for both processing efficiency, $F(2, 97) = 24.966$, $p < .0001$, $\eta^2 = .34$, and working memory, $F(2, 97) = 46.726$, $p < 0001$, $\eta^2 = .49$. This pattern suggests that processing efficiency was the developmental factor and working memory was the individual differences factor. In other words, working memory was the main reason for differences between classes in problem solving, and processing efficiency was the main reason underlying developmental changes in both working memory and problem solving.

CONCLUSIONS

The pattern of findings presented above suggests several conclusions. First, the significant intercepts and intercept variances suggest that there are significant individual differences in attainment in each of the three aspects of mind investigated here. Second, the high correlations among the three intercepts suggest that there are strong interrelations among the initial conditions of all three aspects of the mind; however, development differently affects each of the three aspects of the mind as well as their interrelations. Third, the fact that the slope variable was significant only for processing efficiency suggests that development alters individual differences in processing efficiency but does not affect them with respect to working memory or problem solving.

Finally, particular attention is drawn to the fact that none of the regression effects of the slope variables on the intercept variables of another ability ever reached significance. This finding, if coupled with the fact that all intercept correlations were significant, appears strange. On the one hand, the high intercept correlations suggest that the state of one ability is related to the state of another at a given point in time. On the other hand, the lack of intercept-slope relations across abilities suggests, strangely enough, that *growth as such in each of the abilities is not affected by the state of the others at a given point in time.* This pattern of relations suggests the nonimplicative nature of developmental changes. That is, changes in cognitive functions, which are considered to function as drivers of change, such as processing efficiency, may simply open possibilities for growth in other abilities. In other words, changes in these functions may be necessary but not sufficient for changes in functions residing at other levels of the mental architecture. Therefore, the realization of these possibilities lies in agents external to these drivers (such as environmental opportunities, individual interests, self-regulatory processes, etc.). This realization occurs most of the time, at least to a certain extent. Moreover, this realization occurs differently and in varying degrees in different individuals, as suggested by mixture growth modeling. Differences in the realization of these possibilities are due to factors that must interfere if the potentials for the construction of new skills and concepts are to be transformed into actualities. The executive processes of working memory are probably the most powerful of these intervening factors. Thus, when only cross-sectional evidence is considered we frequently have the impression of necessary and sufficient relations between processes and abilities, when in fact the relations are actually only possible. That is, these relations may come into existence only if the relevant experiences are encountered by the developing person. The present study shows nicely that longitudinal evidence and converging methods of analyses are required to decipher necessary from possible relations and the different patterns of development.

VI. RESULTS: SPECIFYING PATTERNS OF CHANGE BY LOGISTIC EQUATIONS

Recently many of the ideas in the study of nonlinear dynamic systems have been introduced into developmental psychology (Ayers, 1997; Bogartz, 1994; Case & Okamoto, 1996; Eckstein & Koszhevnikov, 1997; Fischer & Bidell, 1998; Thelen & Smith, 1994; van Geert, 1991, 1994, 1997). The introduction of nonlinear systems to cognitive development provides a fresh perspective on the study of phenomena of cognitive growth which might reveal aspects unnoticed by the more traditional methods. Specifically, dynamic systems methods enable the researcher to specify the form of development of various cognitive processes and abilities more accurately than other more traditional methods. For example, based on May's (1976) conjecture that change in many phenomena involving living beings can be described by logistic equations, van Geert (1991) proposed the model of logistic growth as the general model of change intended to apply to all theories that "subscribe to the idea that cognitive growth occurs under limited resources" (p. 3).

In general, logistic growth is nonlinear and it follows an S-shaped pattern of changes. That is, change is rather slow at the beginning but gradually accelerates until it attains a certain momentum. When this momentum is attained, change becomes very fast and it remains so until it approaches the end state of the process or ability under consideration. After a certain point rather close to the end state, the rate of change decelerates continuously until it becomes difficult to notice. The general idea underlying this model is that change is autocatalytic and occurs under limited resources. That is, the change itself produces further change and in so doing it exhausts the resources fueling the process. Thus, change consumes the resources available for it, thereby slowing its rate after the remaining resources fall below a certain level. Obviously, this general model of change is worth examining because all the traditions of psychology reviewed here espouse the assumption that cognitive functioning and development occur under limited resources. Attention is drawn to the implications of logistic—therefore nonlinear—growth for the explanation of development. Specifically, the autocatalytic nature of change, with its varying rates of change that depend on the specific point of development reached at a particular moment in time, suggests that neither age nor time can be, in itself, an independent or explanatory factor of growth. The dynamic condition of the process or ability under consideration or its dynamic relations with other processes or abilities is part of the causation of growth.

Admittedly, logistic models, like all mathematical models, do not take into account important aspects of real change; however, they do capture other properties of growth and development that are impossible to capture otherwise (van Geert, 1994). The curves presented in the sections that follow try to abstract the overall shape of development from the real, short-term fluctuations in order to concentrate on particular aspects of the growth and developmental processes. Thus, our main aim in the present chapter is to apply the logistic model to our data in order to test whether it applies to processing efficiency, working memory, and problem solving, as anticipated in the fourth of the predictions stated in the Introduction. Moreover, we examine how the growth of each of these functions is related to the growth of the other functions. Specifically, through the application of logistic models, we tested models that would enable us to specify the following:

1. the form of development of working memory, processing efficiency, and problem solving

2. the contribution of processing efficiency and working memory to growth in problem solving

3. the reciprocal linkage that may exist in the growth of processing efficiency, working memory, and problem solving.

4. the possible differences among the four classes of children (uncovered by mixture growth modeling and presented in the previous chapter) in the form of development of each of the main abilities studied here and in their dynamic relations between these abilities.

The analyses presented in this chapter are complementary to those presented in the previous chapters, which were able to specify the dimensions involved in each of the main types of functions or abilities that concern us here, their organization, the general association of each of these dimensions with age, and even different types of developing individuals. However, those analyses fall short of specifying the exact form of development of each of the processes and abilities and uncovering both the internal dynamics of the development of each and the dynamics of their reciprocal interrelations. The methods discussed in this chapter do come close to satisfying this need.

We first present the essential features of the logistic model used throughout the study. Then we apply the model separately to the development of working memory, processing efficiency, and problem solving. In the next section, we test van Geert's model of cognitive growth on working memory and processing efficiency and also on the reciprocal relationships among all three types of cognitive functions. Then we apply the model separately to the different groups of developing individuals uncovered by mixture growth modeling. The chapter concludes with a discussion of the significance of the model and its implications.

THE GENERAL MODEL: MODELING WORKING MEMORY DEVELOPMENT

The basic constituents of memory, as measured in the present study, lead to a mathematical formulation of memory development. Ideally, the use of memory in its end state is complete and thus can be described by the highest score possible, meaning that the full use of memory is in equilibrium. Memory at any moment in time has a specific level or magnitude, M_t, and is growing from one state to the next until it reaches this equilibrium, which is equivalent to its carrying capacity—that is, its full capacity at its end state. We assume that development is partly time dependent and iterative: Present memory depends on previous memory levels. The rate or speed of change of the process depends on a growth rate r that influences memory at time t (M_t). The growth rate may be a fixed integer, which is individually defined only with reference to the process or ability under consideration. However, the growth rate may also be a composition of several factors, such as information processing or other processes or abilities, as will be shown in the next section. This last option is more realistic, since we assume that no process stands on its own. However, for the purposes of the present section, we assumed that working memory—and the other processes to be discussed later—develop without the contribution of other variables, external or internal to the individual. In other words, we assumed in this section that all variables except memory are constant in time. Thus, to express the memory development at time $t + \Delta t$ (i.e., at a time following a previous reference time), we used the following equation:

$$M_{t+\Delta t} = M_t (1 + r\Delta t \cdot (K - M_t)/K). \tag{3}$$

In this equation K is carrying capacity (i.e., the end state) and, practically, it is defined as the highest value of memory as measured at the last wave of testing. If we assume that Δ_t is equivalent to a standard period of time intervening between successive measurement points which is defined as equal to 1, the above equation can be simplified as follows:

$$M_{t+\Delta t} = M_t(1 + r - rM_t)/K. \qquad (4)$$

Equation (4) is the basic equation for logistic development. It describes how a later developmental level, at time $t + 1$, is associated to an earlier developmental level at time t, and to two additional parameters, r (the rate of change) and K (the carrying capacity at the end state), which are the driving forces in the sense that they cause the change in memory (Eckstein, 2000). (For a more detailed explanation see note 1 in Appendix C.) If applied iteratively, starting with t and proceeding to $t + 1$, $t + 2$, $t + 3$, etc., the equation generates a sequence of developmental levels that follow one another and form a developmental curve. Thus, Equation (4) allows memory to be calculated at a time later than t if we know the values of memory at time t. The term in the right-hand side of Equation (4) is the force that drives the memory change. van Geert (1994) called this form *autocatalytic* because it is understood as causing growth to feed on itself. That is, growth occurs as a result of its own momentum, in addition to other influences that may possibly be exerted by other factors. Equation (4) is a *nonlinear* differential equation and has an exact analytic solution, the logistic curve. The logistic curve is an S-shaped curve in which memory increases asymptotically to its carrying capacity K (i.e., slow at the beginning, increasingly faster in the middle, and increasingly slower at the end). In order to apply Equation (4), we assumed that memory cannot begin with zero since the right-hand side of the equation is autocatalytic, thus it would be impossible for change to start if there was nothing to change in the first place.

To test whether Equation (4) provides a good explanation for the development of memory, we applied it to the memory data of our present study. The reader is reminded that participants in this study were tested three times, with the tests separated by one-year intervals. By applying the equation to any pair of successive measurement points, we arrived at an estimation of the developmental rate r (which is approximately the average of the rs resulting from comparing each consecutive pair of measures; see note 2 in Appendix C). It is noted that the average of performance on the three tasks addressed to memory (the tasks addressed to phonological storage, visual storage, and working memory) was used in the present analysis. This was considered as a good index of the general state of working memory in our participants.

102

Since K is the size of carrying capacity (i.e., the upper limit of capacity available at the end state), it can take the highest number in the measures of the last testing wave to limit the growth to finite levels. In fact, when $K = M_t$, the autocatalytic force disappears. In other words, when the end state is reached there is no momentum for further change. If we enter the average rate r and the K values into Equation (4), we obtain the mathematical curve shown in Figure 13. To further understand the meaning of parameters r and K, it is useful to study graphs of the growth curves for different parameter values. Such graphs are given in Figure 13, where the horizontal axes are age in months and the vertical axes are the values of memory tasks.

In Figure 13a we used $r = 0.42$, which was the average of rs resulting from the computation of the first and second waves of data, and $K = 5.09$, which was the highest (mean) value in the memory tasks in the second wave of measures. In Figure 13b, we used $r = 0.16$, which represented the average rs as computed by the second and third waves of measures, and $K = 6$, which represented the highest (mean) value of memory tasks in the last wave of measures. This shows that the rate of development between the first and second waves of measures was higher than the rate between the second and third waves of measures, indicating that as the subjects grew older their memory development approached the asymptote of the curve.

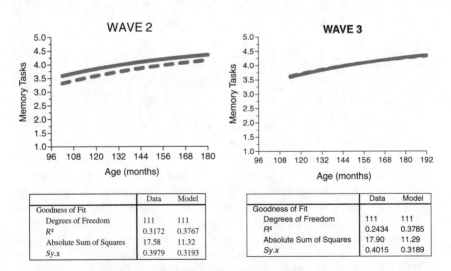

Goodness of Fit	Data	Model
Degrees of Freedom	111	111
R^2	0.3172	0.3767
Absolute Sum of Squares	17.58	11.32
$Sy.x$	0.3979	0.3193

Goodness of Fit	Data	Model
Degrees of Freedom	111	111
R^2	0.2434	0.3785
Absolute Sum of Squares	17.90	11.29
$Sy.x$	0.4015	0.3189

FIGURE 13.—Comparison between empirical data on memory tasks in the second and third waves of measures and the logistic model with parameters fitted onto these data

103

TABLE 10

COMPARISON OF R^2s Between Data and Logistic Models

	Logistic Model R^2	Data R^2	R^2 change	p-value ($df = 111$)
Memory	.38	.32	.06	.00
Phonological	.34	.18	.16	.00
Executive	.20	.15	.05	.01
Figural	.33	.14	.19	.00
Information processing	.45	.35	.06	.00
Speed	.48	.39	.09	.00
Control	.49	.38	.11	.00
Cognitive tasks	.57	.43	.14	.00
Categorical	.36	.36	.00	1
Spatial	.52	.23	.29	.00
Quantitative	.53	.43	.10	.00
Effects of memory and processing on cognition	.54	.45	.09	.00
Contribution of				
Memory to cognition	.54	.45	.10	.00
Processing to cognition	.49	.45	.04	.03
Joint memory-processing to cognition	.60	.45	.15	.00
Reciprocal relations				
Cognition on memory	.40	.34	.06	.00
Cognition on processing	.57	.49	.08	.00
Contribution of				
Memory to processing	.41	.50	−.09	.00
Processing to memory	.39	.34	.05	.01

The fit between the mathematical curve and the actual data in each wave of measures was very good, indicating strongly that memory development can be described very closely by this curve. Actually, the F changes between the data and the proposed logistic models for the second and third waves of measures were 10.74 ($p = .001$; see Table 10) and 26.68 ($p < 0.001$), respectively, indicating that logistic models explain much more variance than the models based on data, and provide better fits (see Figure 13), which means that logistic models can be used effectively to explain the growth of memory at different time intervals.

The fit of the mathematical curve and the empirical data could be improved by changing r, without considerable differences in the form of the curve. Indeed, the character of the curves in Figures 13a and 13b is similar. The slope of the memory growth curve in Figure 13a is slightly steeper than that in Figure 13b, reflecting a more rapid growth resulting from the larger value of r.

On closer inspection, memory growth on the two waves of measures appeared to consist of two main phases. The first phase was characterized by steady growth leading at about the age of 180 months (15 years) to the ceiling level of memory growth. It was immediately succeeded by a second phase that seemed to level off during the months following this age, at a growth level that represented the end state (about 5 points). This pattern of development was clearly in line with Pascual-Leone's and Case's models of working development, which maintain that working memory development levels off at about the age of 15 years, and in disagreement with Halford's model, which maintains that the maximum level of dimensionality is reached at the age of about 11 years.

The curves in Figure 13 also show that the rate of memory development was not the same during the two waves of measures. Specifically, the performance of participants on memory tasks in the age range of 120–180 months in the first wave of measures increased from 3.1 to 4.1, whereas in the second wave of measures the subjects' performance increased from 3.6 to 4.2 points, reflecting the deceleration of growth that results from approaching the end state.

Attention is drawn here to the difference between the form of development revealed by the logistic model and the form of development revealed by multivariate analysis of variance and shown in Figure 10. The form of development shown in Figure 10 simply shows how performance on the memory tasks is associated with age. Thus, although accurate from the point of view of a description of development at the surface, it ignores information about the moment-by-moment states and momentum for change. In addition to the age-memory association, the logistic model in Figure 13 shows what the development looks like at each successive point in time, when its internal dynamics is taken into account. Therefore, this model is more comprehensive and accurate as a description of development.

Development of the Components of Memory

The reader is reminded that our memory tasks addressed three components (see Chapter I), namely the phonological and visual storage and the central executive of working memory. The logistic models discussed so far have focused on the average performance on all memory tasks. In the following section, we depict the development of each memory component, and present the contribution of each component to the general curve of memory.

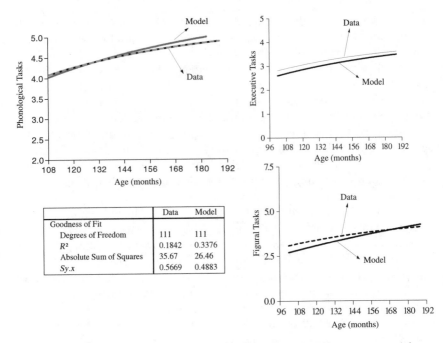

	Data	Model
Goodness of Fit		
Degrees of Freedom	111	111
R^2	0.1842	0.3376
Absolute Sum of Squares	35.67	26.46
$Sy.x$	0.5669	0.4883

FIGURE 14.—Comparison between empirical data on memory's components (phonological, executive, and visual) in the second wave of measures and the logistic model with parameters fitted onto these data

The logistic model described above also provides the basis for discussing the development of phonological (P), visual (V), and executive memory (E). We used the same kinds of equations and procedures as described above to compute the parameters of the logistic models for the three memory components (see Appendix C, note 3). Figure 14 shows the curves of the logistic model and the raw data for the second wave of measures. The fitting indices for all waves of measures did not show statistically significant disturbances between the proposed logistic models and the models estimated by real data, indicating that theoretical models can be used to represent the structure of the actual development. In all subsequent figures, the logistic model curves are shown in bold lines and the data curves are shown in dotted lines.

It is important to note that the theoretical models showed very good fits with the data. The F change between the data and the logistic models of phonological, executive, and visual tasks (see Table 10) was statistically significant (all p values $< .01$), indicating that logistic models provide better fits than the data. Furthermore, the overall shapes of the curves of memory components in each wave of measures were identical to the curves fitted to average performance on all memory tasks (see Figures 13 and 14), which indicates that each memory component develops in a similar manner to other components and general working memory ability. Specifically, in all cases the data and the theoretical models showed an increase in phonological, visual, and executive memory between the ages of 9 and 15 years (108 and 180 months). After the age of 15 years, the growth rate of memory in phonological, visual, and executive tasks slowed down until it approached the asymptotic levels as defined by the end states of each (i.e., the K value for each component; see Appendix C, note 3, Equations (5), (6), and (7)).

Modeling Information Processing and Problem Solving

The dynamic logistic model as described above for interpreting memory development is also used to study the development of processing efficiency. The form of the logistic model equation (see Appendix C, note 4, Equations (8) and (9)) used to fit the processing efficiency and problem-solving data (P, and Pr, respectively) is the same as in Equation (4), and all parameters were computed in the same manner (see notes 1 and 2 in Appendix C).

The autocatalytic coefficients in Figure 15 were computed following the same procedure described above. In Figure 15a, rs were negative ($r = -0.2$ showing the development between the first and second waves of measures, and $r = -0.29$ showing the development between the second and the third waves of measures), indicating that the lower the values in

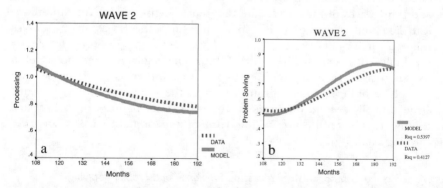

FIGURE 15.—Comparison between empirical data on processing efficiency and problem-solving tasks in the second wave of measures and the logistic model with parameters fitted onto these data

processing efficiency, the more efficiently individuals process information. The Ks used for predicting the second and the third waves of measures was 1.36, since the same value represented the participant's highest performance on both measures.

Figures 15a and 15b show the fitting of the logistic model and the data on processing efficiency and problem solving, respectively, for the second wave of measures. Figure 15a shows that processing efficiency grew during the age range of 9 to 14 years, and that rate of growth tended to level off at age 15. In other words, in all three waves of measures the rate of development of processing efficiency was maximal at the beginning of the curves, at ages 9 to 14, and the rate decreased as it approached its asymptote at age 15. These results indicate that processing efficiency approximates ceiling rather earlier than working memory (at about ages 14 and 15 years, respectively). After this point, major improvements in processing efficiency cannot be expected unless special practice is provided (Case & Okamoto, 1996).

The logistic model, which fitted the data of the second wave of measures, explained 45% of the variance in processing efficiency tasks (see Figure 15a and Table 10). Age explained about the same amount of the variance in the data set, indicating that the logistic model provides a good means for predicting the information processing performance of individuals, since the F change was 20.18, which is statistically significant ($p < .0001$).

Figure 15b illustrates the development of problem solving across the second wave of measures. The curve, which is also representative of the development of cognitive tasks in the third wave of measures, has an initial value of 0.25, representing the lowest value in the data set in the first wave of measures. It also has a growth rate of .94 and a carrying capacity of $K = 0.91$, representing the maximal value in the data set of the second and third waves of measures. The theoretical logistic curve fits the empirical data well, illustrating that in all measures the forms of the curves follow a similar pattern ($R^2_{\text{model}} = .57$, $R^2_{\text{data}} = .43$, $F_{\text{change}} = 36.14$, $p < .0001$; see Table 10). As shown in Figure 15b, problem solving seems to develop in two phases, in quite a different way than processing efficiency. The first phase of development primarily covers the age range of 9 to 14 years. Growth in the second phase seems to level off during ages 14 to 15 years, leading to the temporary ceiling level of the predefined K value (the carrying capacity).

Modeling the Components of Processing Efficiency and Problem Solving

In the present study, speed (Sp) and control (C) of processing are considered as the main constituents of processing in general. Verbal reasoning (VP), quantitative reasoning (QR), and spatial reasoning (SI) are the main three components of problem solving (see Chapter 2). Our aim in this section is to model each of the components in processing and cognition in order to examine the character of their curves and compare them to the curve shapes of general processing efficiency and problem solving.

The same logistic equation was computed to produce the curves for the components of processing and problem solving. Figure 16 shows the curves for the processing components as formed by parameters fitted onto the data set of the second wave of measures (rs and Ks were computed in the same way as explained above). It is shown that the curve shapes for both the speed and control tasks develop in the same way as the curve of general processing efficiency, and reflect the same pattern of change. Specifically, both control and speed grew at a higher logistic rate than the rate of data at ages 9 to 12 years, logistic growth developed at a rate lower than that of the data after age 12, and at age 15 development leveled off to approach the asymptote of the curve. This pattern suggests that growth in speed and growth in control tasks reach their highest growth at the same time as processing efficiency. Table 10 shows that the logistic models for speed and control of processing are better than their respective data models, since the F change in both cases was statistically significant ($p < .00001$, $a = 0.5$). The same pattern of development was also observed in the third wave of measures.

Figure 17 shows the development of the problem-solving abilities. First, we observe that all logistically computed curves fit the data in a satisfactory manner (see Table 10). Specifically, the logistic models for spatial

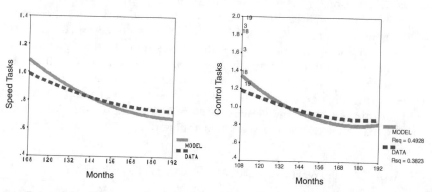

FIGURE 16.—Comparison between empirical data on the components of processing efficiency (speed and control) of the second wave of measures and the logistic model with parameters fitted onto these data

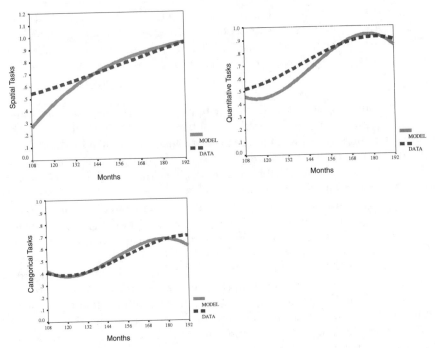

FIGURE 17.—Comparison between empirical data on problem-solving components in the second wave of measures and the logistic model with parameters fitted onto these data

and quantitative reasoning explained more variance than the data set; in the case of verbal reasoning both the logistic and the data models explained 36% of the variance. Second, the shapes of the curves of quantitative and reasoning tasks follow the sigmoid character of the general cognition curve, whereas the spatial tasks curve detours from the shape of the general cognition curve and tends to follow a quadratic form. Both the sigmoid and quadratic forms of the curves indicate the developmental nature of quantitative, reasoning, and spatial tasks. Third, in all curves we observe that the rate of development of the mathematical curves was lower during the age range of 9 to 12 years (108 to 144 months). Moreover, in this age range individuals developed problem-solving skills more rapidly than they did in the years that followed.

THE RELATIONS BETWEEN MEMORY AND PROCESSING EFFICIENCY

Results presented in the previous chapters showed that the functioning and development of the various aspects of memory depend, to a con-

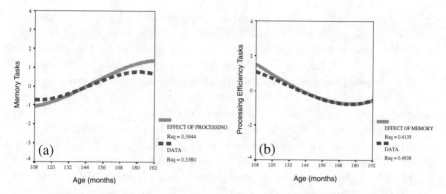

FIGURE 18.—The effects of processing efficiency on memory tasks and the effects of memory on processing tasks

siderable extent, on processing efficiency. In this section, we will attempt to model the effect of processing efficiency on memory development, and vice versa, using the same logistic procedures.

Figure 18a shows the effect of processing efficiency on memory, and Figure 18b represents the effect of memory on processing efficiency (the curves result from Equations (10) and (11) in Appendix C, note 5). The curve in Figure 18a fits the data in a much better manner than the curve depicted in Figure 13, indicating that development of memory depends not only on its autocatalytic effects but also on the contribution and development of processing efficiency. In contrast, the curve depicted in Figure 18b does not provide a better fit to the data than the curve depicted in Figure 15a, indicating that development of processing efficiency does not depend on memory development. This is also shown in Table 10, where the logistic model failed to adequately predict the data. The data set explained 50% of the variance, but the logistic model explained only 41%, and the F change, favoring the data set, was statistically significant at the 0.5 level ($p < .0001$). These findings suggest that the dynamic relations among the fundamental components of the human processing system are *not* symmetrical. That is, processing efficiency affects the development of memory but memory does not affect the development of processing efficiency.

The Effect of Memory and Processing on Problem-Solving Development

The purpose of this section is to examine the role of memory and processing efficiency in the development of problem solving. To examine whether these factors have an impact on problem-solving development, we use the basic logistic equation developed above and extend it to reflect the assumption that the development of problem solving receives a contribution from both memory and information processing variables.

Specifically, we assumed that problem solving, memory, and processing efficiency can each be modeled with its own logistic curve, as we showed in the previous section. The equation for each specific curve would be a simple specific function with its own initial value, growth rate, and carrying capacity. Thus, the equation for the development of problem solving (Pr) that reflects the effects of memory and processing can be expressed in the same way as in Equation (4) with the addition of the effects of memory and processing efficiency (see Appendix C, note 6, for the respective equation). This would result in a new curve of problem-solving development rising to a new level, one above the level specified by the original carrying capacity, due to the extra influx of memory and processing efficiency received each year from these two latter sources. Problem solving is not elastic enough to permit this sort of artificial enlargement beyond certain limits. In addition, as we have already indicated (see Figures 13 and 15), memory and processing efficiency have certain limits. Thus, in order to model the situation in realistic terms, we needed to add a damping parameter, to allow problem-solving development to deteriorate in the specified carrying capacity (Case & Okamoto, 1996). The damping parameter, which is expressed as a ratio (see note 6 in Appendix C), indicates that growth in problem solving can be terminated only when the size of problem-solving performance reaches the carrying capacity. Equation (12), in Appendix C, note 6, means that the additional quantity of problem solving that is added each year as a result of problem-solving development itself (autocatalytic process), and as a result of the memory and processing efficiency influence, is compounded in each subsequent year because it becomes a part of problem solving and thus cannot be distinguished from it. This situation is illustrated in Figure 19, which shows that the new curve with the effects of memory and processing efficiency grows considerably faster than the curve of the problem-solving model and the data curve. However, the new curve (effect curve) now reaches asymptotic level at about the same absolute level of 7 (see Figure 19). This may be taken to imply that making use of changes in processing efficiency and working memory for the sake of the development of problem solving does not lead problem solving to its end state earlier but it does makes its development more robust.

The effect curve has the same characteristics as the model curve of the autocatalytic growth shown in Figure 15b but it fits the data in a much better way (see Table 10; $F_{\text{change}} = 21.72$, $p < .00001$ at $\alpha = 0.5$). We propose that in the latter model both memory and processing efficiency

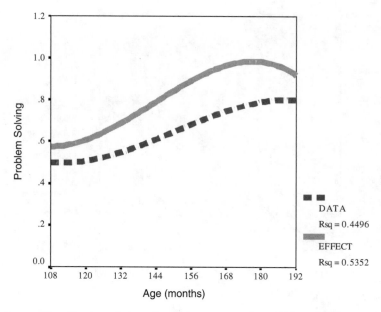

FIGURE 19.—The cumulative effects of memory and processing efficiency on problem solving

make a contribution to the growth of problem solving. Through the proposed model, we were able to assess the contribution of each of the two variables by plotting both the problem-solving autocatalytic curve and the curves indicating the contribution of memory and processing efficiency (see note 7 in Appendix C). As may be seen in Figure 20, the memory effect curve increased slightly more rapidly than the processing efficiency curve. Even though they both have the same sigmoid shape, their contribution to the growth of problem solving is somewhat different due to the difference in the rate of growth. Thus, the memory curve started at a problem-solving point level of 0.5 and reached its asymptote at 0.75, while the processing efficiency curve began at point 0.4 and resulted in the curve asymptote at 0.5. (Figure 20 involves standardized values to avoid problems of different measuring scales in the memory and processing efficiency tasks.) That is, the contribution of processing efficiency to problem solving started earlier and ended earlier than the contribution of working memory. In light of the findings regarding the role of these two potentiation factors, this pattern of effects is perfectly understandable. It indicates that the primary developmental factor in processing efficiency and working memory is an intervening factor vis-à-vis the development of problem solving.

113

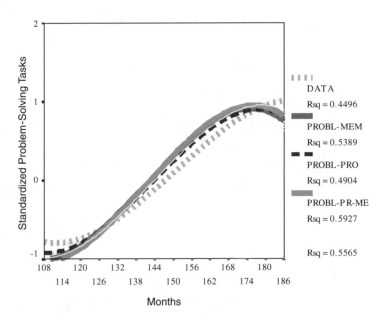

FIGURE 20.—The effects of memory and processing on problem solving (standardized solution). (PROBL-MEM = the effect of memory on cognitive tasks, PROBL-PRO = the effect of processing on cognitive tasks, PROBL-PR-ME = the accumulative effects of memory and processing on cognitive tasks.)

RECIPROCAL RELATION BETWEEN THE DEVELOPMENT OF PROCESSING EFFICIENCY, WORKING MEMORY, AND PROBLEM SOLVING

The proposed model (see Figure 17) does not provide evidence to indicate whether problem solving, in turn, makes a contribution to memory or processing efficiency. To test the hypothesis of reciprocal linkage between growth in problem solving and growth in general capacity dimensions such as memory and processing efficiency, another set of equations was needed (see note 8 in Appendix C).

Figure 21 shows the growth curves that would result from the reciprocal contribution of problem-solving growth to memory and processing efficiency. It is important to note the difference between this figure and Figure 20. The two major differences indicating the effects of the reciprocal linkage are that (a) the development of memory and processing efficiency curves (Figure 21a and Figure 21b, respectively) is accelerated due to the fact that these variables receive additional input from problem-solving growth, and (b) the specific curves are more closely tied to their respective models (shown with dotted lines) and provide better fits than

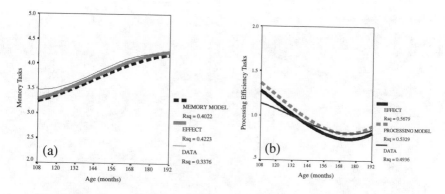

FIGURE 21.—Modeling the reciprocal relation of problem-solving growth, memory, and processing efficiency variables

the observed data (shown with thin lines). This means that problem-solving growth functions as a mediator for improving memory and processing efficiency, at least up to the point of the asymptote.

DIFFERENTIATION OF DEVELOPMENT AMONG SUBCLASSES OF INDIVIDUALS

In this section, we examine the extent to which theoretical logistic curves can describe the actual development of memory, processing efficiency, and problem solving as well as their dynamic interrelationships in terms of different developers in our sample. Specifically, we examine the type of development of the four subclasses identified in Chapter V. Class 1 involved individuals who were fast processors but their memory and problem-solving abilities were lower than individuals in other classes. Class 2 included children whose memory, processing efficiency, and problem-solving attainments were the lowest in the sample. Children in Class 3 were similar to those in Class 1 in processing efficiency and working memory but were slightly more stable in the development of problem solving. Finally, Class 4 included children who were lower in memory but higher in problem solving than children in Class 3. For the sake of the analysis to be presented below, we pulled together Classes 1 and 3 due their many similarities. This manipulation was necessary because each of these classes involved a rather small number of participants. This combined group is called Class 1 in the analyses that follow.

Figure 22 presents the developmental curves of children in the three classes on processing efficiency, working memory, and problem solving. These curves reaffirm most of the class characteristics extracted by growth

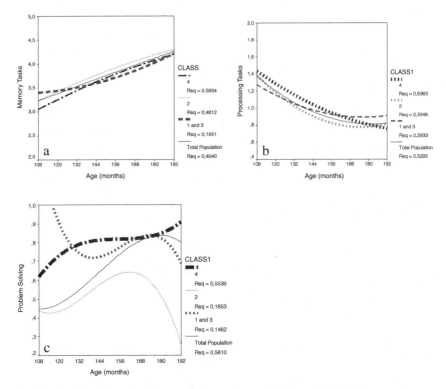

FIGURE 22.—The developmental curves for each class of individuals on memory, processing efficiency, and problem solving

analysis (see Chapter IV). The logistic curves provide the frame for under-standing the pattern of development in each class. It can be seen that the growth in working memory and processing efficiency in Classes 2 and 4 was very stable, since their curves have the same shape as that of the total sample. In contrast, growth in Class 1 was to some extent unstable, as indicated by the fact that the variance accounted for in Class 1 was 20% but the variances in Classes 2 and 4 were 48% and 55%, respectively. Moreover, the curves in Classes 2 and 4 follow the same pattern as the pattern of the total population, whereas the shape of the Class 1 curve follows a quite different pattern of development. It needs to be empha-sized that the differences between the three classes with regard to prob-lem solving were much more pronounced—the differences in r^2 were all significant. The performance of Class 4 children in problem solving was systematically higher than the performance of the sample, while the per-formance of Class 2 children was lower. Class 1 was again unstable in

116

problem-solving tasks; the performance of children aged from 9 to 12 was higher than the performance of the sample, while that of children aged 12 to 13 was lower.

The results for the children in different classes is more easily interpreted by the curves indicating the interactions among working memory, processing efficiency, and problem solving. Figure 23a presents the effects of processing efficiency on memory. These effects for Class 4 are similar to the effects in the sample; the effects for Classes 1 and 2 are quite different. This means that the contribution of processing efficiency to memory was greater in Class 4, and that this was not the case for other classes ($r^2 = .33$). Figure 23b shows that the effects of memory on processing efficiency were greater in Class 2 than in other classes ($r^2 = .32$). Figure 23c shows that the effects of memory and processing efficiency on

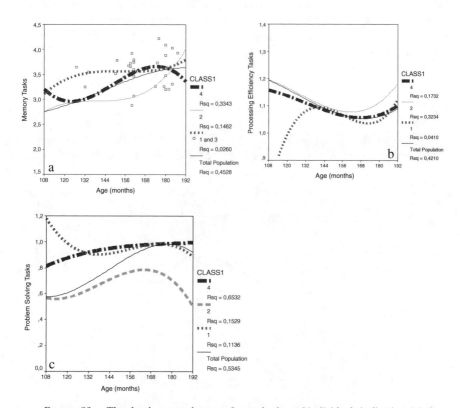

FIGURE 23.—The developmental curves for each class of individuals indicating (a) the effects of processing efficiency on memory, (b) the effects of memory on processing, and (c) the effects of memory and processing efficiency on problem solving

117

problem solving were much larger in Class 4 ($r^2 = .65$) than in the other classes. The same pattern appears in Figure 24, which depicts the reciprocal effects in each class of problem solving on memory and processing efficiency. Problem solving in Class 4 contributed more to the reciprocal relation; that is, problem solving improved memory and processing efficiency ($r^2 = .33$).

In summary, the logistic curves in this section revealed some interesting differences among the three classes. Class 1 was the most unstable of the three and the developmental pattern of children in this class cannot be easily predicted from the behavior of the sample. Class 2, in most cases, followed the developmental pattern exhibited by the sample of the study, but it was less developmentally efficient than Class 4. Class 4 was the most developmentally efficient and followed the behavior indicated by the development of the sample of the study. In fact, it seems that the interactions between processes and abilities were stronger in this class than in the other classes. As a result, development in this class was more robust and powerful because each system of processes and abilities capitalized more fully on the momentum of development that existed in other systems.

CONCLUSIONS

The psychological issue is how to model the various relationships in the development of problem solving, memory, and processing efficiency

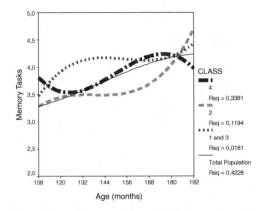

FIGURE 24.—The developmental curves for each class of individuals indicating the reciprocal relation of problem-solving growth, memory, and processing efficiency

118

for the age span 8 to 16 years. We have proposed that logistic models offer an approach to the study of developmental growth, and provide a method of predicting the problem-solving, memory, and processing capabilities of individuals which is complementary to the methods used in the previous chapters. We examined the extent to which theoretical logistic curves can accurately describe the actual development of the processes investigated here as well as their dynamic interrelationships. This method aims at providing criteria for the study of discontinuities, and embraces the concept of nonlinearity. Nonlinear models have proven to be fruitful in (developmental) psychology, and are mostly based on dynamic systems models and dynamic systems theory.

The reason for using dynamic systems models is that they can describe behavior that does not follow smooth paths along the time continuum. In fact, every behavior that has a time component and every behavior that cannot be explained by standard linear theories may profit from a nonlinear approach. For example, in Chapter V it was shown by means of structural equations modeling that the third wave of measures did not follow a linear pattern and that there was a discontinuity in the data. However, through the use of logistic models it proved possible to determine the exact form of change in the development of the various systems at the various periods of time represented in this study.

In the present chapter, we have illustrated that logistic models can appropriately fit the empirical data in models developed in the previous chapters. There is disagreement among researchers concerning the values of the parameters that should be selected to plug into the mathematical models. In the context of neo-Piagetian theory, the end state (i.e., the carrying capacity) of a developing system is identified with its processing efficiency capacity, which in turn is presumed to be estimable from the size of its working memory (Case & Okamoto, 1996). In the present study, the carrying capacity K for the growth models was set at the maximum observed value of the empirical data. The latter solution was used extensively by van Geert (1994) in his study of grammar growth, and it does not differ substantially from the solution proposed by Case and Okamoto (1996). According to Case and Okamoto (1996), the working memory of individuals is well described by a curve with a carrying capacity of 1 at age 4 years and 3.7 at age 10 years. In this study, we used the capacity value K of 4 in the developing model from the first to the second wave of measures, and the value of 5 for estimating the model from the second to the third wave of measures. Both values represent the maximum observed values and they do not differ substantially from those proposed by Case and Okamoto (1996) or Baddeley (1990). Although the proposed K values are more conservative, they have the advantage of being supported by the empirical data of the study.

119

The match between theory and data results from the choice of growth rates. In the present study all rates of growth were calculated from the data of the three waves of measures. It is encouraging that the general shape and spread of the theoretical growth, which resulted from the application of the logistic models, are similar to those obtained empirically.

The first aim of the present study was to study the development of problem solving, memory, and processing efficiency. In all cases, the logistic models successfully predicted the empirical data and in most cases provided evidence that more effectively explained the observed variance (see Table 10). It was shown that the components of working memory, processing efficiency, and problem solving behave in a manner consistent with their respective general models. Specifically, logistic models provide evidence that (a) performance in memory, processing efficiency, and problem solving improves from one testing wave to the next and their growth decelerates as they approach the corresponding asymptotes; (b) the components of memory, processing efficiency, and problem solving improve systematically with age; and (c) the rates of growth are lower in older individuals.

The second aim of the study was to examine the effects of memory and processing efficiency on problem solving. Our results are in agreement with neo-Piagetian theorists, according to whom working memory and processing efficiency play a strong role in facilitating the changes that occur at the level of the environment system of the mind (Case, 1985; Demetriou et al., 1993; Halford, 1982; Pascual-Leone, 1994). That is, we have shown, in line with the analyses presented in the previous chapters, that processing efficiency has a strong effect on working memory and that working memory, in turn, exerts an influence on the rate of development in problem solving. At the same time, however, we also demonstrated in this chapter, through exploring the reciprocal relations between processing efficiency, working memory, and problem solving, that there are top-down influences as well. That is, changes in problem solving are beneficially associated with changes in working memory and processing efficiency. This finding is in line with the model of cognitive change summarized in the Introduction and also with that of conceptual change assuming that changes in higher order cognitive processes may affect more fundamental cognitive processes such as memory (Chi, 1976; Schneider, in press; Schneider & Bjorklund, 1998).

Finally, it should be noted that the combination of mixture growth modeling and dynamic systems modeling presented here provides some promise for the integration of the study of individual growth with the study of growth based on group analyses. According to some scholars, it is not possible to infer growth curves and processes from group analyses (van der Maas & Molenaar, 1992). The approach adopted here makes it clear that it is possible to distinguish between different types of developers by one type of method (mixture growth modeling) and then specify the growth curve of each type (logistic modeling). Normally, one would expect that the growth curves of each group would approach the growth curve of each individual in the group much more than the growth curves specified in reference to the whole population. This is an interesting question that may be answered by future study.

VII. TOWARD AN OVERARCHING THEORY

Which tradition or theory discussed in this *Monograph* is supported by this study? Literally speaking, our findings do not support, in their entirety, any of the basic positions in psychometric theorizing concerning the role of the fundamental components of processing in the functioning of thinking. Moreover, our results deviate considerably from many of the positions of the developmental models discussed earlier. However, our findings do point to how the three traditions can be integrated. Thus, the results presented in the previous chapters justify several far-reaching conclusions concerning the structure of developing intellect and the dynamic relations intertwining the various processes and functions during development. In the pages following we will elaborate on these conclusions, focusing first on the architecture of the mind and then on its development. The aim of this discussion is to show how the concepts from the three traditions discussed in the Introduction (the cognitive, the differential, and the developmental traditions) can be integrated into a comprehensive model that answers the questions stated in the Introduction: How are the various functions and abilities organized? How do they develop from middle childhood to middle adolescence? How are change and individual differences in each of them associated with change and individual differences in all of the others? Is there one pattern of development or many in this dynamic system?

IMPLICATIONS FOR THE ARCHITECTURE OF THE MIND

In line with the first of the predictions stated in the Introduction, the developing intellect appears to be a multilevel and multisystem structure. This structure includes four basic constellations of processes and abilities: processing efficiency, working memory, thinking and problem solving, and self-awareness and self-regulation. The present study was directly concerned with the first three of these constellations and, thus, only these will be discussed here. Reference to the fourth will be made only when it is obviously implied by the tasks addressed to the other constellations.

Each of these constellations comprises a series of specialized processes or functions. Processing efficiency refers to the capacity of the thinker to focus on goal-relevant information and make use of available mental resources as efficiently as possible. The present study demonstrates that processing efficiency can clearly be specified with reference to two dimensions. The first is speed of processing, which indicates the ability of the thinker to encode and give meaning to information quickly and correctly, thereby conserving mental resources. The second is control of processing, which indicates the ability of the thinker to protect processing from the interference of irrelevant information, if needed. Working memory includes executive processes and two modality-specific stores, namely a phonological and a visual store. Thinking and problem-solving processes are organized in domain-specific systems, which are differentiated on the basis of the types of relations they represent and on the process and the symbol systems to which they are biased.

These systems are interconnected by a network of complex relations. Technically speaking, these relations may be conceived of and specified in a number of alternative ways. The simpler way is to conceive of them as a higher order factor to which the three systems above are related. This is the third-order factor of the common model shown in Figure 6 in Chapter III. This factor may be interpreted in two ways. The first is a minimal interpretation, which specifies a common denominator for all intellectual processes and functions. We would suggest, for reasons to be explained later, that this denominator is directed attention or executive control. This, and not storage capacity or any kind of inference, seems to run through all the tasks used here, from the speed of processing to the SCS-specific tasks. Thus, this factor may be taken to stand for the part of working hypercognition that is responsible for ensuring that processing remains focused on goal throughout a task, even when performance is fast enough to evade awareness, as in the Stroop-like tasks.

The second interpretation is a dynamic one. According to this interpretation, the common denominator noted above simply indicates the fact that the processes and functions involved in the various systems or levels of the mind interact in order to attain the mental goals that direct adaptive functioning in the environment. This interaction occurs, by definition, within the field of directed attention or executive control. Thus, the minimal and the dynamic interpretation of the general factor of intelligence are two faces of the same coin. That is, these processes and functions interact dynamically with each other as they are brought to bear on the same mental task, under the constraints of the person's

123

field of concentration. Thus, the general factor may be conceived of as a network of dynamic relations rather than as a single entity, possibility, or ability.

The structural model shown in Figure 8 (in Chapter III) and the dynamic models shown in Figures 13–21 (Chapter VI) are complementary manifestations of this reality. Specifically, the structural model indicates, in agreement with the cascade model put forward in the Introduction (in the second prediction), that more fundamental processes are part and parcel of more complex processes. Thus, speed of processing is the most important aspect of processing efficiency and it fully determines the condition of the other aspect of processing efficiency, namely control of processing. In fact, the absorption of control of processing measures by speed of processing measures indicates that the more efficient an individual is in stimulus encoding and identification, the more efficient the individual is in the control of interference. Therefore, this finding indicates that measures addressed to speed of processing require as much control as is required by measures directly addressed to control. In other words, both types of measures require the participant to keep processing focused on the stimulus of interest. Thus, our speed of processing measures may be considered more as measures of attentional and executive control rather than sheer speed. This pattern of results is consistent with recent findings of Band, van der Molen, Overtoom, and Verbaten (2000) which strongly indicate that there is a general response activation mechanism that underlies both speed of responding tasks and tasks requiring inhibition. In line with these findings, Stancov and Roberts (1997) found that the importance of speed of processing is not due to speed itself but to the fact that speeded tasks require selective attention.

In turn, so defined, processing efficiency extensively explains the condition of executive processes in working memory, and those processes in turn explain the condition of the two modality-specific stores (phonological and visual). Finally, problem solving, which has been the main explanant of theories of intelligence, is itself explained by both processing efficiency and working memory, and in particular by the executive processes of the latter. What does this imply in terms of the nature of the various processes?

Regarding memory, the strong association between speed, on the one hand, and all components of working memory, on the other hand, indicates that processing efficiency is an important component of both the central executive processes and the specialized storage processes involved in working memory. This concurs with current models of working memory (e.g., Engle, Kane, & Tuholski, 1999; Towse, Hitch, & Hutton, 1998). Moreover, attention is drawn to the fact that the relation between processing efficiency and executive processes was generally stronger than the relation between processing efficiency and storage buffers. This indicates that efficiency is more important for the control and selection processes involved in the central executive than for storage. One might assume here that efficiency in the memory buffers is related to the renewal of the memory traces of the items to be held in storage. Efficiency in the central executive is related to the selection and orchestration of information and the operations to be performed on it. This latter process is by definition more demanding, thereby explaining its higher demands in terms of processing efficiency.

Regarding the involvement of speed and working memory in problem solving, the results were very clear. Speed contributes directly and about equally (a respectable 40% of the variance) to the functioning of all three SCSs investigated here. The executive part of working memory also contributes systematically to performance in all of these SCSs, in addition to what is contributed by speed. However, the size of this contribution varies across SCSs. It is very high in the case of the quantitative SCSs (53% of the variance) and moderate in the cases of the spatial SCS (17% of the variance) and the verbal propositional SCS (29% of the variance). The contribution of storage was much lower, in fact it was appreciable only in the case of the spatial SCS (11% of the variance) and practically null in the other two SCSs. In total, the speed and the memory components accounted for 96% (quantitative), 65% (spatial), and 66% (verbal) of the variance of the three SCSs. Thus, it is clear that both efficiency and working memory (as executive control and storage) are needed to account for problem solving. Technically speaking, storage is needed to represent the information involved in a problem and efficiency is needed to operate on and combine the information represented for the sake of the current goal. It is interesting that storage was more important for the spatial rather than for the two other SCSs. This implies that representation of information, as contrasted to operation on information, is more important for this SCS.

These findings about the relations between speed of processing and working memory, on the one hand, and the three SCS, on the other hand, are fully consistent with recent studies of the relations between fluid intelligence and working memory (Engle et al., 1999; Engle, Tuholski, Laughlin, & Conway, 1999; Kyllonen, 2002). Fluid intelligence is defined as the general inferential and reasoning ability (Carroll, 1993; Jensen, 1998) underlying thinking and problem solving under novel situations. It is contrasted with crystallized intelligence, which refers to the knowledge possessed. According to these studies, fluid intelligence, which seems to be identical to g (Gustafsson & Undheim, 1996), is closely associated with processing efficiency and working memory. In is noted that the tasks used here to address the three SCSs are, from the psychometric point of view, good measures of fluid intelligence because they require deductive and inductive reasoning (Case et al., 2001).

Of course, a considerable amount of variance (approximately .3) remained unexplained in two of the three SCSs. This variance is obviously related to the inferential, symbolic, semantic, and operational skills (as well as special interests) that are specific to each SCS. This complex of skills and processes underlies their differentiation as separate factors. The reader may be reminded here that our recent study with Case (Case et al., 2001) showed that these very same factors emanate from analysis of performance on tasks drawn from the work of Case (1992a), the work of Demetriou (Demetriou, Efklides, & Platsidou, 1993), and the WISC-R. Thus, these factors are robust and independent of tradition or theory. Obviously, analysis focusing on what is involved in processing capacity is not enough to model the variance that is specific to these SCSs. More semantically laden analyses, such as Case's (Case, 1992a; Case & Okamoto, 1996) semantic analysis of central conceptual structures and Kargopoulos and Demetriou's (1998) analysis of the logical particularities of each SCS, may be more useful to capture this aspect of the SCSs. Also, the analyses developed by experimental psychologists of the various domains of thinking, such as spatial (Kosslyn, 1983) and propositional reasoning (Rips, 1994), are relevant here.

Where is awareness in this system? Executive processes and controlled attention are found to be central in the organization of the mind and these processes are effortful and, as such, do generate awareness (Demetriou, 2000; Engle et al., 1999). Thus, it can be expected that there must be self-awareness reflecting the functioning and condition of these processes. In fact, the construct of long-term hypercognition posed by our theory is based on this assumption. The present study did not involve any direct measures of self-awareness in regard to the processes investigated. In another study, however, we showed (Demetriou & Kazi, 2001) that the condition of processing efficiency and reasoning is indeed projected into the person's cognitive self-image. In that study, subjects were tested for their performance on tasks measuring speed of processing and deductive and inductive reasoning. Based on their performance on these tasks, four groups of subjects were formed: (a) slow processors and low reasoners, (b) slow processors and high reasoners, (c) fast processors and low reasoners, and (d) fast processors and high reasoners. The four groups were examined by a self-representation inventory addressed to, among other items, their self-concept about their learning and reasoning ability. We found that there was a very close relation between actual processing efficiency and reasoning ability and these two aspects of their cognitive self-concept. That is, the faster in processing and the higher on reasoning tasks the subjects were, the better they considered themselves to be in reasoning and learning ability. Moreover, in another study (Demetriou & Kazi, submitted), we found that there were clear differences between subjects belonging to the four classes of developers revealed by mixture growth modeling and their evaluation of actual performance on cognitive tasks. That is, the subjects of Class 2 in that study, who were rather slow in developmental rate, tended to be more conservative in their evaluations of their solutions as compared to the other groups. This finding suggests that the hypercognitive system does register and represent the condition of the processing system and the environment-oriented reasoning processes and may itself be a force in the dynamics of development of these processes. It is noticeable that all these processes—that is, executive control, working memory, fluid intelligence, and self-awareness—were found to be associated with the functioning of the prefrontal cortex of the brain (Kane & Engle, in press). Further research is needed to uncover and specify these dynamics.

In conclusion, the present study suggests that processing efficiency is indeed a crucial factor, as Jensen (1998) maintained, but it is not the only one. Similarly, working memory is another crucial factor, as Kyllonen (Kyllonen, 2002; Kyllonen & Christal, 1990) maintained, but the strong claim that this factor is g is not supported. Finally, it may indeed be true that working memory functions as an interface between processing efficiency and thinking, as Conway et al. (in press) maintain, but processing efficiency is also directly connected to thinking. Moreover, a considerable amount of variance in different domains of thinking remains unexplained by these general factors and, thus, any theory of intelligence must be able to account for the organization and functioning of these domains. In fact, even the state of the general factors, at any given moment, is partially affected by domain-specific factors, such as the symbol system concerned. On top of everything, self-awareness and self-regulation may participate and contribute to the relations between all other processes and abilities.

IMPLICATIONS FOR THE DEVELOPMENT OF MIND

A number of strong developmental chains were uncovered by this study. Changes in speed of processing precede and seem to be directly related to changes in the central executive and the storage buffers. Moreover, these changes, together with the changes that occur in working memory, seem to be directly related to changes in the SCSs. Interestingly, changes in memory are not in any way related to changes in processing efficiency, but changes in thinking seem to be related to changes in both speed and memory. This implies that speed and memory provide the means for thought, so when they are altered thinking will, by definition, operate differently. Memory does not have an effect on speed because the sheer volume of information that can be remembered does not necessarily affect how fast the units of information involved can be processed. However, development in thinking offers strategies that may be useful for the organization of processing activity or for the storage of information. Thus, changes in thinking may occur as a result of changes in processing efficiency and working memory and then, in their turn, changes in thinking may contribute to further changes in processing efficiency and working memory. In short, we found, in line with the third of our predictions, that the various processes interact dynamically during development, so that change in each process is shaped both by its own internal dynamics and contributions originating from other processes.

What are the implications of these findings for the theories of development discussed here? Although our findings do not provide full support to any one of these theories, they do highlight constructs in each of them that seem accurate as descriptions of some aspects of development. First of all, we found that processing efficiency as defined above (i.e., response activation and directed attention or executive control) is an important predictor of changes in working memory and thinking. The reader is reminded that purifying the relation between processing efficiency and working memory or thinking from the possible influences of age resulted in a large decrease in the strength of this relation (see Figure 8), indicating that growth as such is a strong component underlying this relation. This finding is consistent with the models emphasizing the role of processing efficiency in cognitive development (Kail, 1991; Salthouse, 1991). That is, age-related intra-individual differences in thinking derive from changes in the ability to focus processing on a goal and derive meaning from goal-relevant information with the minimum use of the mental resources available.

The situation is much more complicated with respect to the implications of our findings for the neo-Piagetian models regarding the role of working memory in cognitive development. The reader is reminded that a fundamental assumption of each of the three models discussed is that working memory is considered to be the main factor in the development of thinking and problem solving. Our findings suggest that this is clearly not the case. We found that the association between processing efficiency and thinking is much stronger than the association between working memory and thinking. Moreover, taking out the effect of age on these relations extensively affects the association between processing efficiency and thinking but does not affect the association between working memory and thinking. In fact, of the two main types of processes in working memory (executive processes as such and short-term storage), the executive processes were found not to be associated with age; yet it is these age-

128

independent processes and not the age-dependent storage which are associated with thinking. These findings are totally unexpected from the point of view of neo-Piagetian theories and indicate that working memory is not *the* causal factor of cognitive development. However, it is a factor that is associated with individual differences in cognitive performance within the same age group of persons.

One might wonder why the neo-Piagetian theories considered working memory as a developmental rather than an individual differences factor in regard to the development of thinking. The reason for this interpretation is both technical and substantive. Technically speaking, the neo-Piagetian researchers did not systematically manipulate, experimentally or statistically, the two supposedly causal factors (i.e., processing efficiency and working memory) by methods that would allow them to specify separately the association of each with the development of thinking. They focused only on the association between changes in working memory and changes in thinking. These changes are indeed related but the relation is due to changes in processing efficiency, which is related to both changes in working memory and thinking. That is, the developmental role of working memory with respect to thinking comes from its association with processing efficiency rather than from itself. When this association with processing efficiency is not controlled and only working memory and thinking are observed, one remains with the fallacious impression that changes in working memory cause changes in thinking; yet the changes in working memory simply reflect, to a large extent, the condition of processing efficiency, which is the actual causal agent of development in both working memory and thinking.

It is to be stressed that the role of working memory in the functioning of thinking and problem solving, although different from how it is conceived by neo-Piagetian theories, remains strong: It is one of the main factors underlying individual differences in thinking and problem solving. That is, working memory is a mechanism for the implementation of the processing potential of a given age into actual thinking and problem solving skills and abilities. Therefore, differences between individuals in the condition or the use of this mechanism result in differences in how fully they can transform their processing potentials into actual thinking and problem-solving skills and abilities. Of course, it is recognized that these differences between individuals may, to a large extent, depend on social and cultural opportunities, such as education, the complexity of the social environment in which the individual develops, and so forth.

The discussion above seems to have far-reaching implications for the general theory of intelligence and intellectual development. That is, it leads to the conclusion that differences in mental age are associated with differences in processing efficiency, both within and across individuals.

129

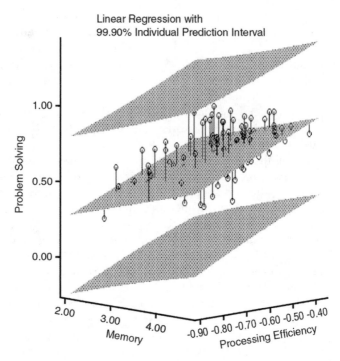

Linear Regression with
99.90% Individual Prediction Interval

FIGURE 25.—The model showing the developmental relations between processing efficiency, working memory, and thinking

Differences in IQ are associated with differences in the executive (i.e., the management) processes of working memory. The model shown in Figure 25 depicts graphically the relations between processing efficiency, working memory, and thinking, highlighting what is the developmental factor and what is the individual differences factor. It can be seen in this model that for each higher level of processing efficiency there is a correspondingly higher range of working memory capacity. The condition of thinking and problem solving is associated with both of these potentiation factors, such that the higher the state of working memory (within the range associated with each level of processing potentials), the higher the thinking and problem-solving abilities are going to be.

In the section above we emphasized the role of self-awareness as part of the architecture of the mind. Similar comments may be made concerning the role of self-awareness and self-control in the development of the mind. That is, we argued above that executive control generates self-awareness and that this is part of the organization of the mind. With respect to development, Zelazo (1998) suggests that many of the infant's

achievements during the second year of life (such as means-end coordination, symbolic play, and even walking) are due to the fact that at this
phase the infant becomes able to place at least two units of information
(sensations, feelings, movements, objects, etc.) in mental focus or working hypercognition. In turn, this is possible because processing has become efficient enough to allow the infant to bring into mental focus a
new unit before the unit previously in focus fades away. Moreover, recent
research has shown that the child's theory of mind, which refers to awareness about one's own and others' mental states, is related to executive
control (Perner et al., 2002). Finally, Rothbart's theory of temperamental
control (Rothbart & Bates, 1998) moves along the same lines. According
to this theory, the ability to monitor and inhibit inappropriate impulses
and tendencies depends on development of attentional networks, as these
enable the individual to corepresent internal tendencies and external stimuli. These findings make it clear that we need research that will decipher
how changes in processing efficiency and working memory generate
changes in self-awareness and self-regulation and how these changes, in
their turn, influence the further course of development of processing
efficiency, working memory, and thinking.

Regarding the nature of development, our findings suggest, in line
with the fourth of the predictions stated in the Introduction, that development seems like a series of overlapping waves or cycles of change (Fischer
& Bidell, 1998; Siegler, 1996). In this series, the processes and functions
of the various levels and systems of the mind may be at differing points
in their own cycle of development. However, when one of them reaches a
certain point in its own cycle of development (e.g., processing efficiency),
it opens the possibility for another process or function to move to a different point in its cycle (e.g., working memory or problem solving). Moreover, movement in these later processes may bounce back and alter the
movement of the first process in its cycle.

On top of all this, two more things must be remembered. First, the
wavelength or, more literally, the rate of change, is not uniform across
successive phases of development. It is logistic as anticipated by dynamic
systems theory (Fischer & Bidell, 1998; van Geert, 1994). Second, the
phases of the logistic development of the various abilities do not coincide. For instance, processing efficiency approaches asymptote before
working memory and this approaches its own asymptote before the various domains of thinking and problem solving. These differences in the
developmental behavior of the various processes reflects their functional
relations as revealed by both the structural equations and dynamic systems models tested here.

Therefore, fully symmetrical models of developmental sequences, in
which durations and complexities at different phases of development either

131

within or across cycles are equal (such as the stages of development described by Piaget and by some of the neo-Piagetians, especially Pascual-Leone), can hold under one very relaxing assumption—that is, when analysis is limited to one level of the mind, such as working memory or problem solving and when changes are not associated with the progression of age. If different levels of the mind are to be coupled or if change in a given level is to be coupled with age, developmental distances and complexities tend to blur and vary across levels or age phases. For example, the results of the present study suggested that successive levels of complexity in working memory do not have a one-to-one correspondence to supposedly equivalent levels in problem solving. The reader is reminded that the four levels of difficulty in the numerical operations task (each defined by 1 to 4 unknown operations) are not equally spaced in terms of attainment age. In fact, the crucial difference is between levels 1 and 2, the rest being equivalent in difficulty with level 2. This lends support to Halford's conception, which emphasizes the relational complexity of concepts and problems rather than their composition in terms of goal stacks or number of schemes involved (see Andrews & Halford, in press). However, the present study suggests that working memory alone is not sufficient as a yardstick for specifying differences between concepts or problems. The structural and the logistic models discussed here are a first step in the direction of constructing this yardstick on the basis of both the dimensions involved in working memory and in processing efficiency.

It is also important that we differentiate between developmental sequences in different domains of thought, such as the various SCSs, and the rate of progression along them. That is, all domains may develop along a sequence of levels which, according to a given formal language—such as Fischer's system of skill levels (1980), Case's executive control structures (1985), or Commons, Trudeau, Stein, Richards, and Krause's (1998) model of hierarchical complexity—may be specified in the same terms. However, formal equivalence in the hierarchies across domains does not necessarily imply that the rate of transition along the hierarchy in two or more domains or the ultimate attainment on it must be the same. We have seen here that there may be large differences in this regard between domains. One may contrast here the development of the spatial and the propositional domain. The reader is reminded that the dynamic models tested on the three SCSs suggested that even the form of change in the spatial SCS is different from the other two SCSs. These differences are obviously due to how each domain may be affected by a change in the underlying potentiation factors, such as processing efficiency or executive control. It may be that a change in a given magnitude m in these potentiation factors is able to alter the possibility for changes in one domain more than in another. For instance, the patterns of changes observed here suggest that changes in the potentiation factors of intellectual development accelerate the development of spatial thought more than the development of propositional thought. In fact, the domains may even differ in their relative dependencies on the various potentiation factors. For instance, we found that the spatial domain depends on the visual storage buffer more than the other domains depend on the phonological buffer. Thus, a change in visual storage may accelerate changes in spatial thought whereas a change in the phonological buffer does not initiate an equivalent change in quantitative or propositional thought.

Another feature of development to be noted is that mixture growth modeling indicated that, in line with the fifth of our predictions, there were four classes of developers, and dynamic systems modeling indicated that the dynamics and coherence of development in each of these groups were markedly different. That is, the four groups differed in how fully and efficiently they transformed the potentialities afforded by processing efficiency into executive efficiency and actual problem-solving abilities and how stable they were in their acquisitions. In fact, only one of the four classes of developers (Class 4) was able to attain and steadily preserve the most advanced levels of propositional and analogical reasoning. This indicates that if the necessary combination among the potentiation factors (and probably others not studied here) is not present, then the highest levels of a given sequence cannot be attained. Thus, the attainment of these levels—which, from a given point of view, indicates more an ability to conceive of the counterintuitive and semantically intriguing rather than just an ability to reason logically—becomes more a matter of individual rather than developmental differences because it depends extensively on factors responsible for individual rather than for developmental differences.

In conclusion, we suggest that the present study shows how the specification of developmental sequences, which has been the main task of the developmental tradition, and the specification of differences, which has been the main task of the differential tradition, can be integrated into a unified model. Executive control in its various faces seems to be the backbone of classic information processing models of thinking, classic psychometric models of general intelligence, and developmental models of thinking. Changes in some dimensions, such as efficiency in focusing on and processing information, underlie developmental differentiation, and differences in certain other dimensions, such as management strategies of information, underlie inter-individual differentiation. Thus, we need to develop models for both kinds of factors and developments. It is hoped that the present *Monograph* will be a stepping-stone in our attempt to move in this direction and that it has raised more questions than the answers it provided, thereby opening the way for more and better answers in the future.

CORRELATION MATRIX BETWEEN VARIABLES OF PROCESSING SYSTEM, PROBLEM SOLVING, AND WORKING MEMORY

	AGE	MVWCI	MNLCI	MFLCI	MVGII	MNSII	MFSII	NUM11	NUM12	VER11	VER12	FIG1	POS1	ORIEN1	PROD1	OPER1	DED1	IND1	ROT1	REFE1
MVWCI	-.538*	1.000																		
MNLCI	-.619*	.665*	1.000																	
MFLCI	-.645*	.670*	.703*	1.000																
MVGII	-.444*	.591*	.507*	.582*	1.000															
MNSII	-.643*	.589*	.841*	.674*	.533*	1.000														
MFSII	-.657*	.614*	.650*	.743*	.586*	.623*	1.000													
NUM11	.411*	-.321*	-.464*	-.393*	-.386*	-.431*	-.460*	1.000												
NUM12	.497*	-.249*	-.394*	-.442*	-.248*	-.406*	-.471*	.415*	1.000											
VER11	.426*	-.210*	-.330*	-.395*	-.298*	-.283*	-.353*	.460*	.386*	1.000										
VER12	.471*	-.265*	-.449*	-.444*	-.228*	-.373*	-.483*	.462*	.536*	.510*	1.000									
FIG1	.468*	-.335*	-.466*	-.396*	-.384*	-.481*	-.426*	.375*	.249*	.344*	.233*	1.000								
POS1	.394*	-.302*	-.432*	-.331*	-.264*	-.355*	-.401*	.285*	.290*	.289*	.309*	.297*	1.000							
ORIEN1	.462*	-.267*	-.319*	-.371*	-.256*	-.303*	-.407*	.275*	.317*	.279*	.263*	.458*	.436*	1.000						
PROD1	.634*	-.348*	-.372*	-.416*	-.280*	-.389*	-.403*	.234*	.381*	.226*	.365*	.271*	.072	.358*	1.000					
OPER1	.633*	-.372*	-.495*	-.525*	-.362*	-.483*	-.549*	.327*	.451*	.330*	.433*	.317*	.313*	.380*	.562*	1.000				
DED1	.228*	-.142	-.120	-.278*	-.089	-.127	-.180	.120	.184*	.257*	.226*	.133	.053	.240*	.206*	.228*	1.000			
IND1	.568*	-.414*	-.288*	-.413*	-.268*	-.425*	-.425*	.262*	.314*	.255*	.293*	.194*	.145	.331*	.455*	.489*	.175	1.000		
ROT1	.601*	-.477*	-.552*	-.557*	-.444*	-.569*	-.559*	.324*	.424*	.320*	.471*	.315*	.374*	.448*	.525*	.588*	.305*	.431*	1.000	
REFE1	.614*	-.333*	-.428*	-.441*	-.268*	-.395*	-.378*	.222*	.325*	.276*	.321*	.384*	.390*	.403*	.429*	.400*	.212*	.345*	.446*	1.000
MVWC2	-.477*	.620*	.544*	.650*	.539*	.548*	.584*	-.358*	-.246*	-.309*	-.274*	-.341*	-.191*	-.231*	-.325*	-.413*	-.139	-.274*	-.372*	-.317*
MNLC2	-.554*	.625*	.688*	.648*	.542*	.599*	.620*	-.412*	-.446*	-.274*	-.299*	-.362*	-.377*	-.250*	-.349*	-.515*	-.170	-.418*	-.530*	-.402*
MFLC2	-.626*	.519*	.544*	.646*	.549*	.563*	.641*	-.354*	-.420*	-.187*	-.416*	-.356*	-.325*	-.319*	-.442*	-.509*	-.187*	-.341*	-.514*	-.496*
MVGI2	-.460*	.415*	.479*	.528*	.538*	.501*	.564*	-.282*	-.288*	-.183	-.268*	-.280*	-.161	-.179	-.415*	-.409*	-.189*	-.209*	-.394*	-.282
MNSI2	-.650*	.613*	.630*	.688*	.539*	.622*	.659*	-.374*	-.480*	-.283*	-.289*	-.425*	-.314*	-.398*	-.517*	-.545*	-.173	-.433*	-.527*	-.409*
MFSI2	-.550*	.494*	.579*	.640*	.480*	.568*	.610*	-.359*	-.356*	-.261*	-.301*	-.273*	-.289*	-.255*	-.352*	-.526*	-.093	-.263*	-.458*	-.337*
NUM21	.414*	-.146	-.282*	-.274*	-.223*	-.216*	-.377*	.392*	.467*	.377*	.418*	.286*	.294*	.250*	.257*	.378*	.086	.292*	.314*	.301*
NUM22	.325*	-.148	-.251*	-.333*	-.265*	-.183	-.417*	.298*	.455*	.353*	.486*	.127	.211*	.234*	.295*	.425*	.150	.264*	.245*	.233*
VER21	.335*	-.160	-.202*	-.270*	-.211*	-.133	-.337*	.344*	.402*	.437*	.328*	.137	.149	.227*	.228*	.285*	.231*	.358*	.260*	.177

VER22	.272*	-.060	-.208*	-.262*	-.182	-.185	-.307*	.361*	.365*	.339*	.428*	.144	.202*	.250*	.181	.290*	.046	.247*	.148	.109
FIG2	.308*	-.280*	-.279*	-.374*	-.293*	-.159	-.279*	.254*	.258*	.160	.268*	.193*	.163	.312*	.282*	.331*	.118	.382*	.326*	.276*
POS2	.304*	-.216*	-.390*	-.425*	-.279*	-.328	-.240*	.202*	.137	.137	.156	.242*	.214*	.307*	.217*	.275*	-.031	.139	.341*	.331*
ORIEN2	.309*	-.224*	-.257*	-.288*	-.238*	-.114	-.188*	.116	.154	.153	.089	.212*	.159	.313*	.271*	.267*	.048	.350*	.264*	.347*
PROD2	.657*	-.416*	-.446*	-.498*	-.394	-.457	-.508*	.279*	.472*	.306*	.315*	.212*	.296*	.438*	.587*	.552*	.217*	.528*	.519*	.511*
OPER2	.440*	-.357*	-.416*	-.444*	-.290*	-.451*	-.421*	.218*	.381*	.204*	.367*	.258*	.264*	.253*	.288*	.492*	.218*	.310	.483	.327
DED2	.347*	-.254*	-.172	-.283*	-.122	-.233*	-.239*	.230*	.141	.238*	.183	.163	.204*	.216*	.185	.320*	.063	.374	.230	.224
IND2	.549*	-.309*	-.439*	-.382*	-.207*	-.428*	-.355*	.341*	.407*	.257*	.285*	.323*	.124	.256*	.500*	.530*	.199*	.403*	.418*	.306*
ROT2	.368*	-.171	-.351*	-.384*	-.172	-.366*	-.258*	.268*	.426*	.255*	.441*	.291*	.277*	.298*	.345*	.388*	.307*	.222*	.513*	.458*
REFE2	.439*	-.323*	-.473*	-.442*	-.293*	-.497*	-.313*	.180	.235*	.116	.250*	.295*	.295*	.226*	.360*	.359*	.181	.146	.443*	.576*
MVWC3	-.452*	.585*	.526*	.543*	.532*	.472*	.509*	-.199*	-.273*	-.178	-.116	-.305*	-.146	-.237*	-.285*	-.359*	-.070	-.296*	-.318*	-.198*
MNLC3	-.557*	.460*	.590*	.521*	.402*	.515*	.565*	-.373*	-.399*	-.244*	-.283*	-.317*	-.281*	-.252*	-.423*	-.550*	-.217*	-.323*	-.422*	-.409*
MFLC3	-.524*	.451*	.529*	.523*	.350*	.499*	.515*	-.329*	-.437*	-.244*	-.398*	-.205*	-.204*	-.175	-.379*	-.438*	-.162	-.304*	-.350*	-.275*
MVCI3	-.430*	.473*	.476*	.588*	.536*	.418*	.545*	-.263*	-.224*	-.218*	-.320*	-.181	-.241*	-.191*	-.361*	-.365*	-.261*	-.250*	-.437*	-.340*
MNSI3	-.530*	.465*	.582*	.574*	.571*	.576*	.578*	-.395*	-.386*	-.295*	-.276*	-.325*	-.325*	-.353*	-.383*	-.419*	-.085	-.295*	-.421*	-.258*
MFSI3	-.526*	.449*	.518*	.524*	.369*	.497*	.665*	-.384*	-.323*	-.311*	-.394*	-.260*	-.195*	-.246*	-.349*	-.429*	-.156	-.262*	-.374*	-.285*
NUM31	.294*	-.118	-.222*	-.300*	-.183	-.203*	-.415*	.390*	.554*	.413*	.364*	.209*	.263*	.270*	.245*	.374*	.227*	.244*	.314*	.150
NUM32	.200*	-.111	-.139	-.180	-.088	-.059	-.276*	.332*	.286*	.289*	.340*	.083	.126	.168	.291*	.223*	.102	.230*	.237*	.121
VER31	.358*	-.119	-.325*	-.192*	-.271*	-.222*	-.426*	.501*	.465*	.427*	.560*	.256*	.344*	.351*	.288*	.359*	.180	.301*	.436*	.241*
VER32	.188*	-.074	-.183	-.263*	-.180	-.086	-.269*	.294*	.330*	.283*	.345*	.081	.074	.155	.249*	.238*	.147	.237*	.213*	.176
FIG3	.354*	-.258*	-.286*	-.263*	-.176	-.231*	-.277*	.093	.142	.100	.163	.152	.393*	.198*	.238*	.348*	.119	.186	.396*	.346*
POS3	.174	-.135	-.141	-.182	-.059	-.113	-.200*	-.036	.076	-.030	.092	.157	.198*	.095	.181	.200*	.072	.101	.303*	.170
ORIEN3	.174	-.181	-.290*	-.214*	-.114	-.178	-.182	-.032	.125	.060	.047	.107	.241*	.130	.125	.178	-.105	.096	.238*	.235*
PROD3	.465*	-.304*	-.407*	-.456*	-.346*	-.450*	-.341*	.260*	.403*	.188*	.261*	.311*	.288*	.275*	.510*	.515*	.270*	.314*	.490*	.389*
OPER3	.230*	-.161	-.304*	-.382*	-.182	-.278*	-.322*	.246*	.372*	.240*	.372*	.126	.178	.129	.312*	.447*	.108	.291*	.261*	.115
DED3	.241*	-.216*	-.219*	-.265*	-.030	-.154	-.254*	.165	.195*	.178	.109	.146	.077	.230*	.270*	.297*	.161	.231*	.345*	.252*
IND3	.454*	-.155	-.319*	-.317*	-.060	-.301*	-.213*	.156	.429*	.258*	.170	.202*	.097	.221*	.356*	.453*	.163	.229*	.320*	.217*
ROT3	.305*	-.286*	-.300*	-.358*	-.270*	-.275*	-.335*	.193*	.203*	.336*	.313*	.227*	.276*	.213*	.311*	.306*	.239*	.217*	.502*	.330*
REFE3	.303*	-.231*	-.314*	-.253*	-.144	-.268*	-.192*	.044	.180	.132	.108	.213*	.140	.221*	.294*	.361*	.194*	.283*	.287*	.252*

continued

	MVWC2	MNLC2	MFLC2	MVCI2	MNSI2	MFSI2	NUM21	NUM22	VER21	VER22	FIG2	POS2	ORIEN2	PROD2	OPER2	DED2	IND2	ROT2
MVWC2	1.000																	
MNLC2	.675*	1.000																
MFLC2	.649*	.678*	1.000															
MVCI2	.590*	.552*	.604*	1.000														
MNSI2	.704*	.781*	.694*	.590*	1.000													
MFSI2	.624*	.623*	.643*	.574*	.637*	1.000												
NUM21	-.156	-.328*	-.319*	-.237*	-.295*	-.177	1.000											
NUM22	-.293*	-.319*	-.425*	-.339*	-.363*	-.315*	.470*	1.000										
VER21	-.067	-.184	-.191*	-.154	-.210*	-.106	.472*	.315*	1.000									
VER22	-.162	-.155	-.266*	-.153	-.217*	-.131	.394*	.483*	.417*	1.000								
FIG2	-.174	-.285*	-.322*	-.125	-.343*	-.199*	.239*	.207*	.267*	.100	1.000							
POS2	-.271*	-.275*	-.293*	-.069	-.382*	-.280*	.081	.080	.078	.076	.472*	1.000						
ORIEN2	-.112	-.241*	-.235*	-.360*	-.301*	-.223*	.059	.096	.112	-.021	.539*	.427*	1.000					
PROD2	-.400*	-.465*	-.570*	-.203*	-.559*	-.411*	.358*	.391*	.296*	.256*	.361*	.337*	.433*	1.000				
OPER2	-.328*	-.399*	-.378*	-.174	-.360*	-.380*	.167	.269*	.045	.157	.201*	.303*	.224*	.497*	1.000			
DED2	-.296*	-.246*	-.214*	-.275*	-.245*	-.253*	.104	.139	.136	.171	.159	.149	.111	.355*	.380*	1.000		
IND2	-.299*	-.377*	-.399*	-.221*	-.412*	-.330*	.349*	.252*	.208*	.251*	.232*	.157	.184	.524*	.285*	.310*	1.000	
ROT2	-.215*	-.338*	-.406*	-.314*	-.374*	-.186	.224*	.281*	.276*	.225*	.354*	.461*	.201*	.386*	.317*	.263*	.285*	1.000
REFE2	-.337*	-.353*	-.402*	-.314*	-.361*	-.297*	.084	.050	.046	-.001	.233*	.280*	.233*	.377*	.499*	.243*	.229*	.417*
MVWC3	.585*	.648*	.566*	.442*	.573*	.527*	-.273*	-.284*	-.241*	-.133	-.209*	-.191*	-.208*	-.332*	-.239*	-.076	-.276*	-.084
MNLC3	.597*	.682*	.590*	.500*	.631*	.635*	-.214*	-.391*	-.175	-.170	-.275*	-.283*	-.205*	-.452*	-.399*	-.205*	-.277*	-.269*
MFLC3	.493*	.567*	.587*	.466*	.576*	.582*	-.288*	-.429*	-.247*	-.192*	-.260*	-.126	-.189*	-.383*	-.245*	-.149	-.364*	-.205*
MVCI3	.537*	.616*	.630*	.606*	.525*	.510*	-.258*	-.365*	-.181	-.134	-.342*	-.315*	-.199*	-.344*	-.301*	-.114	-.193*	-.364*
MNSI3	.573*	.620*	.573*	.443*	.631*	.494*	-.270*	-.244*	-.197*	-.187	-.294*	-.313*	-.206*	-.346*	-.254*	-.133	-.229*	-.201*
MFSI3	.508*	.575*	.620*	.464*	.608*	.569*	-.239*	-.387*	-.144	-.288*	-.205*	-.172	-.118	-.312*	-.295*	-.070	-.195*	-.211*
NUM31	-.212*	-.327*	-.304*	-.225*	-.405*	-.277*	.527*	.525*	.338*	.478*	.154	.083	.016	.310*	.156	.134	.332*	.265*
NUM32	-.194*	-.191*	-.246*	-.111	-.203*	-.119	.370*	.479*	.311*	.300*	.212*	.069	-.111	.262*	.054	.125	.315*	.203*
VER31	-.185	-.272*	-.316*	-.283*	-.323*	-.310*	.476*	.347*	.470*	.375*	.265*	.147	.102	.370*	.245*	.120	.220*	.334*
VER32	-.177	-.200*	-.183	-.083	-.261*	-.177	.333*	.336*	.329*	.490*	.159	.131	.021	.288*	.207*	.107	.145	.214*
FIG3	-.126	-.246*	-.289*	-.181	-.157	-.270*	.186	.203*	.126	-.061	.287*	.266*	.277*	.310*	.211*	.056	.150	.201*
POS3	-.091	-.169	-.285*	-.159	-.225*	-.203*	.088	.134	.013	-.085	.203*	.272*	.219*	.180	.047	-.093	.062	.274*
ORIEN3	-.180	-.269*	-.274*	-.139	-.252*	-.216*	.102	.175	.023	-.051	.216*	.315*	.175	.220*	.153	.048	.107	.225*
PROD3	-.273*	-.409*	-.432*	-.303*	-.464*	-.381*	.255*	.261*	.158	.232*	.143	.191*	.197*	.584*	.457*	.202*	.375*	.350*
OPER3	-.251*	-.293*	-.301*	-.198*	-.300*	-.328*	.246*	.445*	.209*	.389*	.301*	.245*	.160	.372*	.478*	.200*	.309*	.340*
DED3	-.213*	-.242*	-.090	-.095	-.269*	-.261*	.032	.151	.074	.050	.084	.025	.094	.108	.297*	.227*	.262*	.127
IND3	-.253*	-.285*	-.286*	-.209*	-.338*	-.254*	.182	.250*	.128	.114	.146	.222*	.179	.439*	.335*	.302*	.510*	.475*
ROT3	-.201*	-.236*	-.307*	-.217*	-.286*	-.316*	.168	.159	.237*	.042	.375*	.296*	.198*	.320*	.282*	.321*	.217*	.442*
REFE3	-.348*	-.387*	-.276*	-.287*	-.373*	-.278*	.042	.158	-.007	.023	.281*	.204*	.183	.354*	.427*	.343*	.303*	.283*

	REFE2	MVWC3	MNLC3	MFLC3	MVCI3	MNSI3	MFSI3	NUM31	NUM32	VER31	VER32	FIG3	POS3	ORIEN3	PROD3	OPER3	DED3	IND3	ROT3
REFE2	1.000																		
MVWC3	-.147	1.000																	
MNLC3	-.314*	.590*	1.000																
MFLC3	-.153	.561*	.596*	1.000															
MVCI3	-.345*	.533*	.498*	.487*	1.000														
MNSI3	-.227*	.664*	.569*	.493*	.547*	1.000													
MFSI3	-.101	.535*	.580*	.610*	.553*	.608*	1.000												
NUM31	-.034	-.196*	-.320*	-.352*	-.170	-.243*	-.338*	1.000											
NUM32	-.052	-.182	-.176	-.212*	-.155	-.285*	-.258*	.475*	1.000										
VER31	.203*	-.140	-.298*	-.264*	-.277*	-.303*	-.262*	.527*	.424*	1.000									
VER32	.072	-.065	-.241*	-.128	-.167	-.124	-.240*	.377*	.347*	.563*	1.000								
FIG3	.245*	-.124	-.256*	-.161	-.238*	-.185	-.197*	.050	.164	.117	-.129	1.000							
POS3	.117	-.115	-.230*	-.166	-.193*	-.065	-.226*	.057	.044	.057	-.014	.686*	1.000						
ORIEN3	.225*	-.102	-.252*	-.222*	-.265*	-.107	-.170	.015	.037	-.032	-.031	.456*	.498*	1.000					
PROD3	.376*	-.335*	-.441*	-.285*	-.238*	-.368*	-.277*	.248*	.186	.309*	.245*	.224*	.152	.069	1.000				
OPER3	.193*	-.175	-.296	-.242	-.298	-.212	-.239	.371	.275	.280	.309	.205	.164	.204	.396	1.000			
DED3	.193*	-.292	-.255	-.226	-.157	-.173	-.179	.139	.141	.122	.129	.009	.030	.017	.218	.213	1.000		
IND3	.296*	-.190	-.293	-.285	-.208	-.188	-.171	.225	.148	.181	.118	.113	.135	.154	.353	.270	.256	1.000	
ROT3	.380*	-.090	-.208	-.163	-.327	-.217	-.217	.230	.266	.357	.141	.261	.198	.204	.358	.233	.177	.220	1.000
REFE3	.490*	-.224	-.330	-.206	-.292	-.158	-.148	.075	.051	.193	.152	.075	.037	.145	.269	.244	.235	.437	.350

*Correlation is significant at the .05 level (two-tailed).

Notes:

1. The models shown in Figures 6–8 are based on the correlations included in this table.

2. In each name referring to a processing efficiency variable, M stands for mean; the second letter identifies the symbol system (V, N, and F for verbal, numerical, and figural, respectively); the third letter is the aspect of the stimulus to be attended to (W, C, L, and S for word, color, large, and small, respectively); and the fourth letter is the condition (C and I for compatible and incompatible, respectively). NUM and VER stand for the numerical and the verbal stimuli addressed to phonological memory; FIG, POS, and ORIEN stand for the conditions of recalling the identity of a figure, its position, and its orientation in the task addressed to visual memory; PROD and OPER refer to the proportionality and the numerical operations tasks addressed to quantitative thought; DED and IND refer to the syllogistic reasoning and the verbal analogies tasks addressed to verbal reasoning; ROT and REFE stand for the mental rotation and the tilted bottles tasks addressed to spatial reasoning, respectively. The first number attached to each symbol stands for the testing wave and the second for the item number.

APPENDIX B
PERCENTAGES SUCCESS ON THE COGNITIVE TASKS ACROSS THE FOUR CLASSES GENERATED BY MIXTURE GROWTH MODELING AND ACROSS THE THREE TESTING WAVES

Tasks	Testing Waves	Class	8	9	10	11	12	13	14	15	16
Spatial 1	1	1			100		16.7		40		
		2		7.4		21.7	25				
		3			100		37.5		75		
		4	100			50		66.7		75	
	2	1				100		50		40	
		2		37		43.5		25			
		3				100		50		100	
		4		100		100		83.3		91.7	
	3	1					100		100		100
		2			100		73.9		87.5		100
		3					100		100		100
		4			100		100		100		100
Spatial 2	1	1					66.7		40		
		2		14.8		21.7	50				
		3			50		62.5		87.5		
		4	100		75		50		66.7		
	2	1				100		33.3		60	
		2		29.6		30.4		12.5			
		3						75		100	
		4		100		100		83.3		66.7	
	3	1					100		50		100
		2				48.1		47.8		50	100
		3					100		37.5		100
		4				100		75		83.3	100
Spatial 3	1	1			100		100		80		
		2		14.8		56.5	62.5		100		
		3			50		75		100		
		4			100		66.7		100		
	2	1				100		100		100	
		2		77.8		87		100		100	
		3				100		100		100	
		4		100		100		100		100	
	3	1					100		83.3		100
		2				70.4		78.3		62.5	
		3					100		100		87.5
		4				100		100		100	100

continued

Tasks	Testing Waves	Class	Age (in years)								
			8	9	10	11	12	13	14	15	16
Spatial 4	1	1					100		100		
		2	33.3		52.2		62.5		100		
		3			100		87.5		100		
		4	100		75		100		100		
	2	1				100		100		100	
		2		63		73.9		87.5		100	
		3				100		100		100	
		4		100		100		100		100	
	3	1					100		100		100
		2			88.9		73.9		87.5		100
		3					100		100		100
		4			100		100		100		100
Spatial 5	1	1					66.7		100		
		2	14.8		43.5		62.5				
		3			100		87.5		87.5		
		4	100		75		100		91.7		
	2	1				100		83.3		100	
		2		48.1		65.2		75		100	
		3				100		75		100	
		4		100		100		100		91.7	
	3	1					100		100		100
		2			77.8		69.6		75		100
		3					100		100		100
		4			100		100		100		100
Qualitative 1	1	1			100		100		80		
		2	63		56.5		100		100		
		3			100		100		87.5		
		4			100		100		100		
	2	1				100		100		100	
		2		92.6		100		100		100	
		3				100		100		100	
		4		100		100		100		100	
	3	1					100		100		100
		2			92.6		69.6		87.5		100
		3					100		100		100
		4			100		100		100		100
Qualitative 2	1	1					50		20		
		2			13		25				
		3			100		37.5		50		
		4			50		66.7		50		
	2	1				100		100		100	
		2		55.6		87		100		100	
		3				100		87.5		100	
		4		100		100		100		100	
	3	1					100		66.7		100
		2			59.3		52.2		37.5		
		3					100		50		100
		4			100		100		83.3		91.7

continued

139

Tasks	Testing Waves	Class	8	9	10	11	12	13	14	15	16
Qualitative 3	1	1					16.7		20		
		2	11.1		8.7		12.5				
		3					12.5		25		
		4			25		33.3		58.3		
	2	1						50		60	
		2				4.3		12.5			
		3				50		50		75	
		4				75		66.7		91.7	
	3	1					100		33.3		60
		2			11.1		17.4		37.5		100
		3							50		50
		4			100		100		66.7		75
Qualitative 4	1	1					83.3		80		
		2	7.4		13		12.5		100		
		3			50		50		75		
		4			75		100		91.7		
	2	1				100		100		100	
		2		66.7		82.6		87.5		100	
		3				100		100		87.5	
		4		100		100		100		100	
	3	1					100		83.3		100
		2			59.3		60.9		75		100
		3					100		87.5		75
		4			100		100		100		100
Qualitative 5	1	1					50		80		
		2	7.4		13		12.5				
		3					12.5		37.5		
		4			25		50		91.7		
	2	1				100		83.3		60	
		2		22.2		26.1		25		100	
		3				50		87.5		62.5	
		4				100		100		91.7	
	3	1					100		66.7		80
		2			22.2		52.2		50		100
		3					50		75		37.5
		4			100		100		100		100
Qualitative 6	1	1					33.3		41.7		
		2	3.7		8.7				5.1		
		3					12.5		22.2		
		4	100		50		33.3		56.5		
	2	1				100		50		60	
		2				8.7		12.5			
		3				50		37.5		75	
		4		100		100		66.7		91.7	
	3	1					100		33.3		60
		2			7.4		17.4		25		100
		3							37.5		62.5
		4			100		100		66.7		83.3

continued

Tasks	Testing Waves	Class	8	9	10	11	12	13	14	15	16
Qualitative 7	1	1			100		100		100		
		2	77.8		65.2		87.5				
		3			100		100		100		
		4	100		75		100		100		
	2	1				100		100		100	
		2		100		100		100		100	
		3				100		100		100	
		4		100		100		100		100	
	3	1					100		100		100
		2			100		91.3		100		100
		3					100		87.5		100
		4			100		100		100		100
Qualitative 8	1	1			100		100		80		
		2	48.1		30.4		87.5				
		3			50		100		87.5		
		4			100		100		91.7		
	2	1				100		100		100	
		2		85.2		78.3		87.5		100	
		3				100		100		100	
		4		100		100		100		91.7	
	3	1					100		100		100
		2			88.9		82.6		87.5		100
		3					100		100		100
		4			100		100		100		100
Qualitative 9	1	1			100		100		100		
		2	25.9		21.7		75		100		
		3			100		87.5		100		
		4	100		100		100		91.7		
	2	1				100		100		100	
		2		51.9		65.2		87.5		100	
		3				100		100		87.5	
		4		100		100		100		100	
	3	1					100		83.3		100
		2			88.9		73.9		37.5		100
		3					100		87.5		100
		4			100		100		100		100
Qualitative 10	1	1			100		100		80		
		2	7.4		13		37.5		100		
		3			100		100		75		
		4	100		100		100		91.7		
	2	1				100		83.3		80	
		2		37		52.2		87.5		100	
		3				100		100		75	
		4		100		100		100		100	
	3	1					100		66.7		100
		2			59.3		47.8		50		100
		3					100		75		75
		4			100		100		100		100

continued

141

Tasks	Testing Waves	Class	8	9	10	11	12	13	14	15	16
							Age (in years)				
Verbal 1	1	1			100		100		20		
		2	33.3		30.4						
		3			50		50		75		
		4			50		66.7		75		
	2	1				100		83.3		80	
		2		66.7		56.5		37.5		100	
		3				50		87.5		87.5	
		4		100		100		100		91.7	
	3	1					100		100		100
		2			55.6		47.8		50		100
		3					50		87.5		87.5
		4			100		100		100		91.7
Verbal 2	1	1			100		100		100		
		2	85.2		87		75		100		
		3			100		87.5		100		
		4	100		100		100		83.3		
	2	1				100		100		100	
		2		88.9		87		100		100	
		3				100		100		87.5	
		4		100		100		100		100	
	3	1					100		100		100
		2			88.9		69.6		75		100
		3					50		87.5		87.5
		4			100		75		100		91.7
Verbal 3	1	1									
		2	11.1		21.7		50				
		3					25				
		4									
	2	1								20	
		2		25.9		13		12.5			
		3								25	
		4								8.3	
	3	1							16.7		
		2			14.8		13				
		3									
		4									8.3
Verbal 4	1	1									
		2	3.7				25				
		3					12.5		12.5		
		4			50				33.3		
	2	1				100		50		100	
		2		18.5		8.7		37.5		100	
		3				50		37.5		62.5	
		4				50		50		50	
	3	1							16.7		40
		2			14.8		26.1		12.5		100
		3					50		25		12.5
		4			100				33.3		41.7

continued

Tasks	Testing Waves	Class	8	9	10	11	12	13	14	15	16
Verbal 5	1	1			100		50		100		
		2	14.8		4.3		37.5		100		
		3					62.5		75		
		4			25		66.7		75		
	2	1				100		83.3		60	
		2		44.4		30.4		50			
		3						62.5		100	
		4				75		83.3		91.7	
	3	1					100		66.7		80
		2			51.9		34.8		62.5		
		3					50		87.5		100
		4			100		100		83.3		91.7
Verbal 6	1	1					83.3		100		
		2	55.6		34.8		62.5		100		
		3			100		87.5		100		
		4			100		83.3		91.7		
	2	1				100		100		80	
		2		63		78.3		50		100	
		3				100		100		87.5	
		4		100		100		100		100	
	3	1					100		66.7		80
		2			66.7		73.9		62.5		100
		3					50		100		100
		4			100		100		83.3		100
Verbal 7	1	1					16.7				
		2	18.5		13		25				
		3			50		37.5		25		
		4					33.3		41.7		
	2	1								40	
		2		14.8		4.3		25			
		3									
		4				25		16.7		25	
	3	1					100				40
		2			3.7		26.1		25		
		3					50		37.5		
		4					25		33.3		25
Verbal 8	1	1					16.7		20		
		2	3.7				12.5				
		3			50		12.5		50		
		4					16.7		16.7		
	2	1		7.4				83.3		60	
		2				13		37.5		100	
		3				50		50		75	
		4				50		66.7		75	
	3	1							50		60
		2			7.4		8.7		12.5		
		3							37.5		25
		4			100		25		33.3		100

1. Memory at any moment in time has a specific level or magnitude, M_t, M_{t+m}, M_{t+n}, and so forth. The relationship between successive points is expressed in the form of a ratio:

$$M_t/M_{t+m} = R_{t+m}, \qquad M_{t+m}/M_{t+n} = R_{t+n,\dots},\text{ where } n > m.$$

Thus, to express the memory development at time $t + \Delta t$, we use the equation

$$M_{t+\Delta t} = M_t + \Delta t \cdot M_t \cdot R \quad \text{or} \quad M_{t+\Delta t} = M_t\,(1 + \Delta t \cdot R).$$

The ratio R is actually proportional to the remaining unutilized capacity for memory development (van Geert, 1994). The utilized capacity of memory is the ratio of the current capacity (i.e., the capacity during the first wave of measures of memory tasks) to the size at the time of the last measure—that is, M_t/K. Therefore, the unutilized memory capacity is what remains: $(K - M_t)/K$. Making R proportional (r) to remaining unutilized capacity means that the level of development increases over a time period Δ_t, and thus the above equation takes the following form:

$$M_{t+\Delta t} = M_t(1 + r\Delta t \cdot (K - M_t)/K).$$

2. The developmental rate r (or the coefficient of the autocatalytic force) can be computed for any two successive data points in the following way:

$$r = (M_{t+\Delta t}/M_t - 1)/(1 - M_t/K).$$

3. $P_{t+\Delta t} = P_t(1 + r - rP_t)/K.$ (5)

$V_{t+\Delta t} = V_t(1 + r - rV_t)/K.$ (6)

$E_{t+\Delta t} = E_t(1 + r - rE_t)/K.$ (7)

The rates of change (the autocatalytic coefficients, r) in Equations (5), (6), and (7) for the second wave of measures were 0.28, 0.55, and 0.35, respectively, and the Ks were 6.15, 5.1, and 4.76, respectively.

4. $P_{t+\Delta t} = P_t(1 + r - rP_t)/K.$ (8)

$Pr_{t+\Delta t} = Pr_t(1 + r - rPr_t)/K.$ (9)

5. $M_{t+\Delta t} = +M_t \cdot r_1 - (r_1 M_t \cdot M_t/K + P_t \cdot r - r \cdot P_t P_t/K).$ (10)

$P_{t+\Delta t} = +P_t \cdot r_2 - (r_2 P_t \cdot P_t/K + M_t \cdot r - r \cdot M_t M_t/K).$ (11)

6. $Pr_{t+\Delta t} = Pr_t(1 + r - rPr_t)/K + M_t \cdot r_1 - (r_1 M_t \cdot Pr_t/K)$

$\qquad + P_t \cdot r_2 - (r_2 \cdot P_t Pr_t/K).$ (12)

The first term of Equation (12) is identical to Equation (4). The second and third terms have two components. The first term in each line indicates the value of memory (M_t) and processing efficiency (P_t) at the beginning of the time interval multiplied by their respective rates of growth (indicating the amount of value that is to be taken), and added to problem solving during each growth interval. In this manner, the terms $(r_1 M_t \cdot Pr_t/K)$ and $(r_1 P_t \cdot Pr_t/K)$ subtract a quantity equal to the previous term multiplied by the first measure of cognitive tasks divided by K. The term Pr_t/K is the damping effect.

7. The situation is illustrated by Equations (13) and (14), which comprise parts of Equation (16).

$Pr_{t+\Delta t} = Pr_t(1 + r - rPr_t)/K + M_t \cdot r_1 - (r_1 M_t \cdot Pr_t/K).$ (13)

$Pr_{t+\Delta t} = pr_t(1 + r - rPr_t)/K + P_t \cdot r_2 - (r_2 \cdot P_t Pr_t/K).$ (14)

145

8. $Pr_{t+\Delta t} = Pr_t(1 + r - rPr_t)/K + M_t \cdot r_1 - (r_1 M_t \cdot Pr_t/K)$

$$+ P_t \cdot r_2 - (r_2 \cdot P_t Pr_t/K) \tag{15}$$

$$M_{t+\Delta t} = +M_t \cdot r_1 - [r_1 M_t \cdot M_t/K) + Pr_t \cdot r - [r \cdot Pr_t M_t/K). \tag{16}$$

$$P_{t+\Delta t} = +P_t \cdot r_2 - [r_2 P_t \cdot P_t/K) + Pr_t \cdot r - [r \cdot C_t P_t/K). \tag{17}$$

Equation (15) is the same as Equation (12), while Equations (16) and (17) represent the effects of problem-solving growth on memory and processing, respectively.

REFERENCES

Adey, P., & Shayer, M. (1994). *Really raising standards: Cognitive intervention and academic achievement.* London: Routledge.

Andrews, G., & Halford, G. S. (in press). A cognitive complexity metric applied to cognitive development. *Cognitive Psychology.*

Ayers, S. (1997). The application of chaos theory to psychology. *Theory and Psychology,* **7,** 373–398.

Baddeley, A. D. (1990). *Human memory: Theory and practice.* Hillsdale, NJ: Erlbaum.

Baddeley, A. D. (1993). Working memory or working attention? In A. D. Baddeley & L. Weiskrantz (Eds.), *Attention, selection, awareness, and control. A tribute to Donald Broadbent* (pp. 152–170). Oxford: Clarendon Press.

Baddeley, A. D., & Hitch, G. H. (2000). Development of working memory: Should the Pascual-Leone and the Baddeley and Hitch models be merged? *Journal of Experimental and Child Psychology,* **77,** 128–137.

Baltes, P. B. (1991). The many faces of human aging: Toward a psychological culture of old age. *Psychological Medicine,* **21,** 837–854.

Baltes, P. B., Lindenberger, U., & Staudinger, U. M. (1998). Life-span theory in developmental psychology. In W. Damon & R. M. Lerner (Eds.), *Handbook of child psychology. Vol. 1: Theoretical models of human development* (5th ed., pp. 1027–1143). New York: Wiley.

Band, G., P. H., van der Molen, M. W., Overtoom, C. C. E., & Verbaten, M. N. (2000). The ability to activate and inhibit speeded responses: Separate developmental trends. *Experimental Child Psychology,* **75,** 263–290.

Bjorklund, D. F., & Harnishfeger, K. K. (1995). The evolution of inhibition mechanisms and their role in human cognition and behavior. In F. N. Dempster & C. J. Brainerd (Eds.), *Interference and Inhibition in Cognition* (pp. 141–173). New York: Academic Press.

Bogartz, R. S. (1994). The future of dynamic systems models in developmental psychology in the light of the past. *Journal of Experimental Child Psychology,* **58,** 289–319.

Bors, D. A., MacLeod, M. C., & Forrin, B. (1993). Eliminating the IQ-RT correlation by eliminating an experimental confound. *Intelligence,* **17,** 475–500.

Broadbent, D. E. (1958). *Perception and communication.* London: Pergamon Press.

Broadbent, D. E. (1971). *Decision and stress.* New York: Academic Press.

Caplan, D., & Waters, G. S. (1999). Verbal working memory and sentence comprehension. *Brain and Behavioral Science,* **22,** 77–126.

Carroll, J. B. (1993). *Human cognitive abilities: A survey of factor-analytic studies.* New York: Cambridge University Press.

Case, R. (1985). *Intellectual development. Birth to adulthood.* New York: Academic Press.

Case, R. (1992a). *The mind's staircase: Exploring the conceptual underpinnings of children's thought and knowledge*. Hillsdale, NJ: Erlbaum.

Case, R. (1992b). The role of the frontal lobes in the regulation of cognitive development. *Brain and Cognition*, **20**, 51–73.

Case, R., Demetriou, A., Platsidou, M., & Kazi, S. (2001). Integrating concepts and tests of intelligence from the differential and the developmental traditions. *Intelligence*, **29**, 307–336.

Case, R., Kurland, M., & Goldberg, J. (1982). Operational efficiency and the growth of short-term memory. *Journal of Experimental Child Psychology*, **33**, 386–404.

Case, R., & Okamoto, Y. (1996). The role of conceptual structures in the development of children's thought. *Monographs of the Society for Research in Child Development*, **61** (Serial No. 246).

Chi, M. T. H. (1976). Short-term memory limitations in children: Capacity or processing deficits? *Memory and Cognition*, **23**, 266–281.

Comalli, P. E. Jr., Wapner, S., & Werner, H. (1962). Interference effects of Stroop color-word test in childhood, adulthood, and aging. *The Journal of Genetic Psychology*, **100**, 47–53.

Commons, M. L., Trudeau, E. J., Stein, S. A., Richards, F. A., & Krause, S. R. (1998). Hierarchical complexity of tasks shows the existence of developmental stages. *Developmental Review*, **18**, 237–278.

Conway, A. R. A., Cowan, N., Burting, M. F., Therriault, D. J., & Minkoff, S. R. B. (in press). A latent variable analysis of working memory capacity, short-term memory capacity, processing speed, and general fluid intelligence. *Intelligence*.

Cowan, N. (1999). An embedded-processes model of working memory. In A. Miyake & P. Shah (Eds.), *Models of working memory: Mechanisms of active maintenance and executive control* (pp. 62–101). Cambridge, UK: Cambridge University Press.

Cowan, N. (2001). The magical number 4 in short-term memory: A reconsideration of mental storage capacity. *Brain and Behavioral Sciences*, **24**, 87–114.

Davidson, J. E., & Downing, C. L. (2000). Contemporary models of intelligence. In R. J. Sternberg (Ed.), *Handbook of Intelligence* (pp. 34–49). Cambridge, UK: Cambridge University Press.

Deary, I. J. (2000). Simple information processing and intelligence. In R. J. Sternberg (Ed.), *Handbook of intelligence* (pp. 267–284). Cambridge, UK: Cambridge University Press.

Demetriou, A. (1998a). Nooplasis: 10 + 1 Postulates about the formation of mind. *Learning and Instruction: The Journal of the European Association for Research on Learning and Instruction*, **8**, 271–287.

Demetriou, A. (1998b). Cognitive development. In A. Demetriou, W. Doise, & K. F. M. van Lieshout (Eds.), *Life-span developmental psychology* (pp. 179–269). London: Wiley.

Demetriou, A. (2000). Organization and development of self-understanding and self-regulation. In M. Boekaerts, P. R., Pintrich, & M. Zeidner (Eds.), *Handbook of self-regulation* (pp. 209–251). New York: Academic Press.

Demetriou, A., & Efklides, A. (1985). Structure and sequence of formal and postformal thought: General patterns and individual differences. *Child Development*, **56**, 1062–1091.

Demetriou, A., & Efklides, A. (1987). Towards a determination of the dimensions and domains of individual differences in cognitive development. In E. De Corte, H. Lodewijks, R. Parmentier, & P. Span (Eds.), *Learning and Instruction: European research in an international context* (Vol. 1). Oxford: Leuven University Press and Pergamon Press.

Demetriou, A., & Efklides, A. (1988). Experiential structuralism and neo-Piagetian theories: Toward an integrated model. In A. Demetriou (Ed.), *The neo-Piagetian theories of cognitive development: Toward an integration* (pp. 173–222). Amsterdam: North-Holland.

Demetriou, A., & Efklides, A. (1989). The person's conception of the structures of developing intellect: Early adolescence to middle age. *Genetic, Social, and General Psychology Monographs,* **115,** 371–423.

Demetriou, A., Efklides, E., Papadaki, M., Papantoniou, A., & Economou, A. (1993). The structure and development of causal-experimental thought. *Developmental Psychology,* **29,** 480–497.

Demetriou, A., Efklides, A., & Platsidou, M. (1993). The architecture and dynamics of developing mind: Experiential structuralism as a frame for unifying cognitive developmental theories. *Monographs of the Society for Research in Child Development,* **58** (5–6, Serial No. 234).

Demetriou, A., & Kazi, S. (2001). *Unity and modularity in the mind and the self: Studies on the relationships between self-awareness, personality, and intellectual development from childhood to adolescence.* London: Routledge.

Demetriou, A., & Kazi, S. (submitted). Cognitive self-evaluation and cognitive attainment: The inter-play of developmental and differential dynamics.

Demetriou, A., Kazi, S., & Georgiou, S. (1999). The emerging self: The convergence of mind, self, and thinking styles. *Developmental Science,* **2**(4), 387–409.

Demetriou, A., Pachaury, A., Metallidou, Y., & Kazi. S. (1996). Universal and specificities in the structure and development of quantitative-relational thought: A cross-cultural study in Greece and India. *International Journal of Behavioral Development,* **19,** 255–290.

Demetriou, A., Platsidou, M., Efklides A., Metallidou, Y., & Shayer, M. (1991). Structure and sequence of the quantitative-relational abilities and processing potential from childhood and adolescence. *Learning and Instruction: The Journal of the European Association for Research on Learning and Instruction,* **1,** 19–44.

Demetriou, A., & Raftopoulos, A. (1999). Modeling the developing mind: From structure to change. *Developmental Review,* **19,** 319–368.

Demetriou, A., Raftopoulos, A., & Kargopoulos, P. (1999). Interactions, computations, and experience: Interleaved springboards of cognitive emergence. *Developmental Review,* **19,** 389–414.

Demetriou, A., & Valanides, N. (1998). A three level of theory of the developing mind: Basic principles and implications for instruction and assessment. In R. J. Sternberg & W. M. Williams (Eds.), *Intelligence, instruction, and assessment* (pp. 149–199). Hillsdale, NJ: Lawrence Erlbaum.

Dempster, F. N. (1991). Inhibitory processes: A neglected dimension of intelligence. *Intelligence,* **15,** 157–173.

Dempster, F. N. (1992). The rise and fall of the inhibitory mechanism: Toward a unified theory of cognitive development and aging. *Developmental Review,* **12,** 45–75.

Dempster, F. N. (1993). Resistance to interference: Developmental changes in a basic processing mechanism. In M. L. Howe & R. Pasnak (Eds.), *Emerging themes in cognitive development. Vol 1, Foundations* (pp. 3–27). New York: Springer-Verlag.

Eckstein, S. G. (2000). Growth of cognitive abilities: Dynamic models and scaling. *Developmental Review,* **20,** 1–28.

Eckstein, S. G., & Koszhevnikov, M. (1997). Parallelism in the development of children's ideas and the historical development of projectile motion theories. *International Journal of Science Education,* **19,** 1057–1073.

Efklides, A., Demetriou, A., & Metallidou, A. (1994). The structure and development of propositional reasoning ability. In A. Demetriou and A. Efklides (Eds.), *Mind, intelligence, and reasoning: Structure and development* (pp. 151–172). Amsterdam: Elsevier.

Embretson, S. E. (1995). The role of working capacity and general processes in intelligence. *Intelligence, 20,* 169–189.

Engle, R. W. (2002). Working memory capacity as executive attention. *Current Directions in Psychological Science, 11,* 19–23.

Engle, R. W., Kane, M. J., & Tuholski, S. W. (1999). Individual differences in working memory capacity and what they tell us about controlled attention, general fluid intelligence, and functions of the prefrontal cortex. In A. Miyake & P. Shah (Eds.), *Models of working memory* (pp. 103–134). Cambridge, UK: Cambridge University Press.

Engle, R. W., Tuholski, S. W., Laughlin, J. E., & Conway, A. R. A. (1999). Working memory, short-term memory, and general fluid intelligence: A latent variable approach. *Journal of Experimental Psychology: General, 128,* 309–331.

Fabricius, W. V., & Schwanenflugel, P. J. (1994). The older child's theory of mind. In A. Demetriou & A. Efklides (Eds.), *Intelligence, mind, and reasoning: Structure and development* (pp. 111–132). Amsterdam: North-Holland.

Fischbach, G. D. (1993). Mind and brain. In *Mind and brain: Readings from Scientific American Magazine* (pp. 1–14). New York: Freeman & Company.

Fischer, K. W. (1980). A theory of cognitive development: The control and construction of hierarchies of skills. *Psychological Review, 87,* 477–531.

Fischer, K. W., & Bidell, T. R. (1998). Dynamic development of psychological structures in action and thought. In R. M. Lerner (Ed.) & W. Damon (Series Ed.), *Handbook of child psychology.* Vol. 1, *Theoretical models of human development* (5th ed., pp. 467–561). New York: Wiley.

Flavell, J. H., Green, F. L., & Flavell, E. R. (1995). Young children's knowledge about thinking. *Monographs of the Society for Research in Child Development, 60* (1, serial No. 243).

Flavell, J. H., Miller, P. H., & Miller, S. A. (2001). *Cognitive development* (4th ed.). Englewood Cliffs, NJ: Prentice Hall.

Fry, A. F., & Hale, S. (1996). Processing speed, working memory, and fluid intelligence: Evidence for a developmental cascade. *Psychological Science, 7,* 237–241.

Gathercole, S. E. (1998). The development of memory. *Journal of Child Psychology and Psychiatry, 39,* 2–27.

Griffin, S. A. (1994). *Working memory capacity and the acquisition of mathematical knowledge: Implications for learning and development.* Paper presented at the meeting of the International Society for the Study of Behavioral Development, Amsterdam.

Gustafsson, J-E., & Stahl, P. A. (2000). *STREAMS user's guide. Version 2.1 for Windows.* Molndal, Sweden: Multivariate Ware.

Gustafsson, J. E., & Undheim, J. O. (1996). Individual differences in cognitive functions. In D. C. Berliner & R. C. Calfee (Eds.), *Handbook of educational psychology* (pp. 186–242). New York: Macmillan.

Halford, G. S. (1982). *The development of thought.* Hillsdale, NJ: Erlbaum.

Halford, G. S. (1993). *Children's understanding: The development of mental models.* Hillsdale, NJ: Erlbaum.

Halford, G. S., Mayberry, M. T., O'Hare, A. W., & Grant, P. (1994). The development of memory and processing capacity. *Child Development, 65,* 1330–1348.

Halford, G. S., Wilson, W. H., & Phillips, S. (1998). Processing capacity defined by relational complexity: Implications for comparative, developmental, and cognitive psychology. *Behavioral and Brain Sciences, 21,* 803–864.

Harnishfeger, K. K. (1995). The development of cognitive inhibition: Theories, definitions, and research evidence. In F. N. Dempster & C. J. Brainerd (Eds.), *Interference and inhibition in cognition* (pp. 175–204). New York: Academic Press.

Harter, S. (1990). Causes, correlates, and the functional role of global self-worth: A life-span perspective. In R. J. Sternberg and J. Kolligian, Jr. (Eds.), *Competence considered* (pp. 67–97). New Haven: Yale University Press.

Inhelder, B., & Piaget, J. (1958). *The growth of logical thinking from childhood to adolescence.* London: Routledge.

Jensen, A. R. (1998). *The G factor: The science of mental ability.* New York: Praeger.

Jensen, A. R., & Rohwer, W. D. (1966). The Stroop color-word test: A review. *Acta Psychologica*, **25**, 36–93.

Johnson, J., Pascual-Leone, J., & Agostino, A. (2001). *Solving multiplication word problems: The role of mental attention.* Presented at the meeting of the Society for Research in Child Development, Minneapolis.

Just, M. A., & Carpenter, P. A. (1992). A capacity theory for comprehension: Individual differences in working memory. *Psychological Review*, **99**, 122–149.

Kail, R. (1991). Developmental functions for speed of processing during childhood and adolescence. *Psychological Bulletin*, **109**, 490–501.

Kail, R. (2000). Speed of information processing: Developmental change and links to intelligence. *Journal of School Psychology*, **38**, 51–61.

Kail, R., & Park, Y. (1994). Processing time, articulation time and memory span. *Journal of Experimental Child Psychology*, **57**, 281–291.

Kail, R., & Salthouse, T. A. (1994). Processing speed as a mental capacity. *Acta Psychologica*, **86**, 199–225.

Kane, M., J., & Engle, R. W. (in press). The role of prefrontal cortex in working memory capacity, executive attention, and general fluid intelligence: An individual-differences perspective. *Psychonomic Bulletin and Review.*

Kargopoulos, P., & Demetriou, A. (1998). What, why, and whence logic? A response to the commentators. *New Ideas in Psychology*, **16**, 125–139.

Kaufman, A. S. (2000). Tests of intelligence. In R. J. Sternberg (Ed.), *Handbook of Intelligence* (pp. 445–476). Cambridge, UK: Cambridge University Press.

Kazi, S. (2002). *Structure and development of cognitive and hypercognitive abilities from 3 to 8 years of age.* Unpublished doctoral dissertation, Aristotle University of Thessaloniki.

Kemps, E., De Rammelaere, S., & Desmet, T. (2000). The development of working memory: Exploring the complementarily of two models. *Journals of Experimental Child Psychology*, **77**, 89–109.

Kosslyn, S. M. (1983). *Ghosts in the mind's machine.* New York: Norton.

Kuhn, D., Garcia-Mila, M., Zohar, A., & Anderson, C. (1995). Strategies of knowledge acquisition. *Monographs of the Society for Research in Child Development*, **60**, (Serial No. 245).

Kyllonen, P. (2002). "g": Knowledge, speed, strategies, or working memory capacity? A systems perspective. In R. J. Sternberg & E. L. Grigorenko (Eds.), *The general factor of intelligence: How general is it* (pp. 415–445). Mahwah, NJ: Lawrence Erlbaum Associates.

Kyllonen, P., & Christal, R. E. (1990). Reasoning ability is (little more than) working-memory capacity? *Intelligence*, **14**, 389–433.

Lamon, S. (1994). Ratio and proportion: Cognitive foundations in unitizing and norming. In G. Harel, & J. Confrey (Eds.), *Multiplicative reasoning* (pp. 89–122). Albany: State University of New York Press.

Lesh, R., Post, T., & Behr, M. (1988). Proportional reasoning. In J. Hiebert & M. Behr (Eds.), *Number concepts and operations in the middle grades*. Reston, VA: National Council of Teachers of Mathematics.

Lohman, D. F. (2000). Complex information processing and intelligence. In R. J. Sternberg (Ed.), *Handbook of intelligence* (pp. 285–340). Cambridge, UK: Cambridge University Press.

151

Mackintosh, N.J. (2000). *IQ and human intelligence.* Oxford: Oxford University Press.

MacLeod, C. M. (1991). Half a century of research on the Stroop effect: An integrative review. *Psychological Bulletin,* **109,** 163–203.

May, R. M. (1976). Simple mathematical models with very complicated dynamics. *Nature,* **261,** 459–467.

McLaughlin, G. H. (1963). Psycho-logic: A possible alternative to Piaget's formulation. *British Journal of Educational Psychology,* **33,** 61–67.

Miller, G. A. (1956). The magical number seven, plus or minus two: Some limits on our capacity for processing information. *Psychological Review,* **63,** 81–97.

Miller, L. T., & Vernon, P. A. (1992). The general factor in short-term memory, intelligence, and reaction time, *Intelligence,* **16,** 5–29.

Morra, S. (2000). A new model of verbal short-term memory. *Journal of Experimental Child Psychology,* **75,** 191–227.

Moshman, D. (1990). The development of metalogical understanding. In W. F. Overton (Ed.), *Reasoning, necessity, and logic: Developmental perspectives* (pp. 205–225). Hillsdale, NJ: Erlbaum.

Moshman, D. (1994). Reasoning, metareasoning and the promotion of rationality. In A. Demetriou & A. Efklides (Eds.), *Mind, intelligence, and reasoning: Structure and development* (pp. 135–150). Amsterdam: Elsevier.

Moshman, D. (1995). Reasoning as self-constrained thinking. *Human Development,* **38,** 53–64.

Muthen, L. K., & Muthen, B. O. (2001). *Mplus: The comprehensive modelling program for applied researchers. User's guide.* Los Angeles: Muthen & Muthen.

Navon, D. (1977). Forest before trees: The precedence of global features in visual perception. *Cognitive Psychology,* **9,** 353–383.

Neill, W. T., Valdes, L. A., & Terry, K. M. (1995). Selective attention and the inhibitory control of cognition. In F. N. Dempster & C. J. Brainerd (Eds.), *Interference and Inhibition in cognition* (pp. 207–261). New York: Academic Press.

Nesselroade, J. R., & Featherman, D. L. (1991). Intraindividual variability in older adults' depression scores: Some implications for developmental theory and longitudinal research. In Magnusson, L. Berman, G. Rudinger, & Y. B. Torestad (Eds.), *Problems and methods in longitudinal research: Stability and change* (pp. 47–66). London: Cambridge University Press.

Neubauer, A. C., & Busik, V. (1996). The mental speed-IQ relationship: Unitary or modular. *Intelligence,* **22,** 23–48.

Newell, A., & Simon, H. (1972). *Human problem solving.* Englewood Cliffs, NJ: Prentice-Hall.

Pascual-Leone, J. (1970). A mathematical model for the transition rule in Piaget's developmental stages. *Acta Psychologica,* **32,** 301–345.

Pascual-Leone, J. (1988). Organismic processes for neo-Piagetian theories: A dialectical causal account of cognitive development. In A. Demetriou (Ed.), *The neo-Piagetian theories of cognitive development: Toward an integration* (pp. 25–64). Amsterdam: North-Holland.

Pascual-Leone, J. (1994). An experimentalist's understanding of children. *Human Development,* **37,** 370–385.

Pascual-Leone, J. (2000). Reflections on working memory: Are the two models complementary? *Journal of Experimental and Child Psychology,* **77,** 138–154.

Pascual-Leone, J., & Baillargeon, R. (1994). Developmental measurement of mental attention. *International Journal of Behavioral Development,* **17,** 161–200.

Pascual-Leone, J., & Goodman, D. R. (1979). Intelligence and experience: A neo-Piagetian approach. *Instructional Science,* **8,** 301–367.

Pascual-Leone, J., & Morra, S. (1991). Horizontality of water level: A neo-Piagetian developmental review. *Advances in Child Development and Behavior,* **23,** 231–275.

Passolunghi, M. C., & Siegel, L. S. (2001). Short-term memory, working memory, and inhibitory control in children with difficulties in arithmetic problem solving. *Journal of Experimental Child Psychology,* **80,** 44–57.

Perner, J., Lang, B., & Kloo, D. (2002). Theory of mind and self-control: More than a common problem of implication. *Child Development,* **73,** 752–767,

Piaget, J. (1970). Piaget's theory. In P. H. Mussen (Ed.), *Carmichael's handbook ofchild development* (pp. 703–732). New York: Wiley.

Piaget, J. (2001). *Studies in reflecting abstraction.* London: Psychology Press.

Piaget, J., & Inhelder, B. (1967). *The child's conception of space.* New York: Norton.

Posner, M. I., & Raicle, M. E. (1997). *Images of mind.* New York: Scientific American Library.

Ribaupierre, A. de (1993). Structural invariants and individual differences: On the difficulty of dissociating developmental and differential processes. In R. Case & W. Edelstein (Eds.),*The new structuralism in cognitive development: Theory and research on individual pathways* (pp. 11–33). Basel: S. Karger.

Ribaupierre, A. de, & Bailleux, C. (1994). Developmental change in a spatial task of attentional capacity: An essay toward an integration of two working memory models. *International Journal of Behavioral Development,* **17,** 5–35.

Ribaupierre, A. de, & Bailleux, C. (1995). Development of attentional capacity in childhood: A longitudinal study. In F. E. Weinert & W. Schneider (Eds.), *Memory performance and competencies: Issues in growth and development* (pp. 45–70). Hillsdale, NJ: Erlbaum.

Ribaupierre, A. de, & Bailleux, C. (2000). The development of working memory: Further note on the comparability of two models of working memory. *Journal of Experimental Child Psychology,* **77,** 110–127.

Ribaupierre, A. de, & Pascual-Leone, J. (1984). Pour une intégration des methods en psychologie: Approaches expérimentale, psycho-génétique et différentielle. *L'Année Psychologique,* **84,** 227–250.

Rips, L. J. (1994). *The psychology of proof: Deductive reasoning in human thinking.* Cambridge, MA: The MIT Press.

Rothbart, M. K., & Bates, J. E. (1998). Temperament. In N. Eisenberg (Vol. Ed.) & W. Damon (Series Ed.), *Handbook of child psychology: Vol. 3. Social, emotional, and personality development* (5th ed., pp. 105–176). New York: Wiley.

Salthouse, T. A. (1991). *Theoretical perspectives on cognitive aging.* Hillsdale, NJ: Erlbaum.

Salthouse, T. A. (1996). The processing-speed theory of adult age differences in cognition. *Psychological Review,* **103,** 403–428.

Schaie, K. W., Willis, S. L., Jay, G., & Chipuer, H. (1989). Structural invariance of cognitive abilities across the adult life span: A cross-sectional study. *Developmental Psychology,* **25,** 652–662.

Schneider, W. (in press). Memory development in childhood. In U. Goswami (Ed.), *Blackwell handbook of childhood cognitive development.* London, UK: Blackwell.

Schneider, W., & Bjorklund, D., F. (1998). Memory. In D. Kuhn & R. S. Siegler, (Eds.) & W. Damon (Series Ed.), *Handbook of child psychology: Vol. 2. Cognition, perception, and language* (5th ed., pp. 467–521). New York: Wiley.

Shah, P., & Miyake, A. (1996). The separability of working memory resources for spatial thinking and language processing: An individual differences approach. *Journal of Experimental Psychology: General,* **125,** 4–27.

Shayer, M., Demetriou, A., & Pervez, M. (1988). The structure and scaling of concrete operational thought: Three studies in four countries. *Genetic, Social, and General Psychology Monographs,* **114,** 307–376.

Shepard, R. N., & Cooper, L. A. (1982). *Mental images and their transformations.* Cambridge, MA: MIT Press.

Siegler, R. S. (1996). *Emerging minds: The process of change in children's thinking*. Oxford, UK: Oxford University Press.

Spearman, C. (1904). "General intelligence" objectively determined and measured. *American Journal of Psychology*, **15**, 201–293.

Stankov, L. (2002). A diminutive general. In R. S. Sternberg & E. L. Grigorenko (Eds.), *The general factor of intelligence: How general is it?* (pp. 19–38). Mahwah, NJ: Lawrence Erlbaum.

Stankov, L., & Roberts, R. (1997). Mental speed is not the 'basic' process of intelligence. *Personality and Individual Differences*, **22**, 69–84.

Sternberg, R. J. (1985). *Beyond IQ. A triarchic theory of human intelligence*. New York: Cambridge University Press.

Sternberg, R. J., Conway, B. E., Ketron, J. L., & Berstein, M. (1981). People's conceptions of intelligence. *Journal of Personality and Social Psychology*, **41**, 37–55.

Sternberg, S. (1975). Memory scanning: New findings and controversies. *Quarterly Journal of Experimental Psychology*, **27**, 1–32.

Stewart, L., & Pascual-Leone, J. (1992). Mental capacity constraints and the development of moral reasoning. *Journal of Experimental Child Psychology*, **54**, 251–287.

Stroop, J. R. (1935). Studies of interference in serial verbal reactions. *Journal of Experimental Psychology*, **18**, 643–662.

Swanson, L. H., & Sachse-Lee, C. (2001). Mathematical problem solving and working memory in children with learning disabilities: Both executive and phonological processes are important. *Journal of Experimental Child Psychology*, **79**, 294–321.

Thatcher, R. W. (1994). Cyclic cortical reorganization: Origins of human cognitive development. In G. Dawson and K. W. Fischer (Eds.), *Human behavior and the developing brain* (pp. 232–266). New York: Guilford.

Thelen, E., & Smith, L. B. (1994). *A dynamic systems approach to the development of perception and action*. Cambridge, MA: MIT Press.

Thomas, H., & Lohaus, A. (1993). Modeling growth and individual differences in spatial tasks. *Monographs of the Society for Research in Child Development*, **58** (9, Serial No. 237).

Towse, J. N., Hitch, G., & Hutton, U. (1998). A reevaluation of working memory capacity in children. *Journal of Memory and Language*, **39**, 195–217.

van der Maas, H., & Molenaar, P. (1992). A catastrophe-theoretical approach to cognitive development. *Psychological Review*, **99**, 395–417.

van Geert, P. (1991). A dynamic systems model of cognitive and language growth. *Psychological Review*, **99**, 395–417.

van Geert, P. (1994). *Dynamic systems development: Change between complexity and chaos*. Hemel Hempstead: Harvester Wheatsheaf.

van Geert, P. (1997). Time and theory in social psychology. *Psychological Inquiry*, **8**, 143–151.

Wechsler, D. (1991). *Manual for the Wechsler Intelligence Scale for Children—Third Edition (WISC-III)*. San Antonio, TX: The Psychological Corporation.

Wellman, H. M (1990). *The child's theory of mind*. Cambridge, MA: MIT Press

Zelazo, P. R. (1998). McGraw and the development of unaided walking. *Developmental Review*, **18**, 449–471.

154

ACKNOWLEDGMENTS

The research reported in this *Monograph* was supported by a grant (87EΔ178) provided by the Greek Directorate of Research and Technology to A. Demetriou, when he was a professor at the Aristotle University of Thessaloniki, Greece. All of the studies presented in the *Monograph* were conducted at the Aristotle University of Thessaloniki but the analysis of the results and the writing of the *Monograph* was done at the University of Cyprus. Thanks are due to Kiriaki Sirmali for her contribution to the testing of participants and the preparation of the electronic data files. Special thanks are due to Professor Jan-Eric Gustafsson, University of Gothenburg, Sweden, for his contribution to the application of growth modeling to our data. We are also grateful to Andy Conway, Theo Dawson, Kurt Fischer, Juan Pascual-Leone, Bill Overton, and two anonymous reviewers for constructive suggestions and advice that were very beneficial in raising the *Monograph* to its present form.

For correspondence, contact Andreas Demetriou, Department of Educational Sciences, University of Cyprus, P. O. Box 537, 1678 Nicosia, Cyprus (ademetriou@ucy.ac.cy) phone: +357 22892045; fax: +357 22750297.

A NEW KIND OF DEVELOPMENTAL SCIENCE:
USING MODELS TO INTEGRATE THEORY AND RESEARCH

Kurt W. Fischer and Theo L. Dawson

This *Monograph* heralds a new era in developmental research. New tools make it possible to build more powerful, grounded assessments and to use them to test complex developmental models empirically, potentially producing a quantum leap in developmental research. For more than a hundred years, psychology has been marked by grand, elaborate theories of developmental process and structure, such as those of Baldwin (1894), Bruner, Goodnow, and Austin (1956), Freud (1909/1955), Hebb (1949), Piaget (1936/1952, 1983), Vygotsky (1978), and Werner (1948), but research methods have not been up to the task of testing these sophisticated theories.

The situation has changed radically in recent years, as advances in developmental scaling and model testing, along with powerful computers, have made it possible to embody complex theories in explicit models and to test them with carefully scaled assessments (Dawson, 2002; Fischer & Bidell, 1998; Lerner, 1998; van Geert, 1991, 1998; Willett, 1997). Experimental and theoretical work now can be integrated in a way that was difficult or impossible twenty years ago. With these new tools, most of the perennial debates in developmental science can emerge from the endless, irresolvable arguments that amount to little more than asserting differing positions. For example, the stage debate, which has vacillated between "Development occurs in stages" and "Development is continuous," has been transformed by the building of explicit models capable of being tested empirically. A model now specifies how and when development shows staged growth patterns and how and when it shows continuous patterns (Dawson, Commons, & Wilson, under review; Fischer & Kennedy, 1997). In many such cases, the debates can be resolved by integration of apparently opposing explanations into a model of relations between complementary processes of development.

Relating Efficiency, Memory, and Structure

In this *Monograph* Demetriou, Christou, Spanoudis, and Platsidou have produced one of the most ambitious efforts to realize this emerging paradigm, using some of the new tools to connect constructs from different frameworks for cognitive development. The primary debates addressed involve relations between processing efficiency, working memory, and cognitive structure (which the authors often call *problem solving*). Instead of treating these processes as opposing explanations, the authors combine them in a single study in order to unpack how the processes relate to one another in development of 8- to 14-year-old children.

Demetriou and his colleagues have done an exciting, important service for developmental science, setting forth a complex, multidimensional, hierarchical model of the "architecture of the mind" that integrates three distinct perspectives (information processing, differential psychology, and neo-Piagetian developmental theory) in a combined cross-sectional, longitudinal design. This project shows how developmental scientists can assess concepts from multiple frameworks and relate them through explicit modeling and targeted research. In this way researchers can begin to build explanations that are powerfully grounded in the best combination of data and theory.

This ambitious study links measures from each tradition and analyzes those measures with sophisticated modeling tools to empirically assess the relations among the constructs from the models. The results demonstrate the usefulness of the sophisticated combination of psychometric assessment with explicit mathematical modeling to build a new generation of tools for developmental science. They illustrate how the new tools for modeling and assessment can bring together previously disparate branches of development, making possible the new kind of approach that several scholars have been calling for (Fischer & Bidell, 1998; Gottlieb, Wahlsten, & Lickliter, 1998; Lerner, 1998; Overton, 1998; van Geert, 1998). The three different processes relate to one another, each contributing to growth patterns in distinctive ways.

Developmental Rulers

As in any new enterprise, there are challenges in using new tools. To employ the new assessment and modeling tools most effectively in advancing understanding of development requires careful construction of scales to measure concepts and careful specification of models in relation to the processes being tested. We are not convinced of specific conclusions in this *Monograph* because of important issues about the design of the developmental scales and the use of models.

To measure length, a ruler needs to be carefully constructed, with regular intervals demarcated and measurement procedures standardized. In measuring volume, the multidimensionality (three dimensions multiplied together) makes the accuracy of the ruler and the exactness of the procedures even more important. A major factor that has limited the use of new modeling tools in developmental research has been the absence of well-constructed rulers for cognitive processes (Rose & Fischer, 1998). Without common, well-constructed measures, it is not even possible to know whether two researchers studying, say, memory development, are even talking about the same thing. Researchers know how to measure speed and location of movement, which provide good standards for examination of motor development (Thelen, 1995). For constructs such as working memory, processing efficiency, and cognitive structure, no such easy measures exist. Researchers need to carefully construct rulers to be able to measure these constructs, test their growth functions, and use the models of the new paradigm. This issue of constructing rulers pervades the study that is the subject of this *Monograph*.

Creation of a ruler to measure a developmental construct requires meticulously devising and testing items and administration procedures and testing scale properties. Only after such careful work can a scale be used effectively in a study to test a multidimensional model. Until recently, the idea of developing rulers for measuring developmental constructs appeared unrealistic because such constructs can be conceptually slippery, complex, multidimensional, and subject to contextual biases (Fischer, Rotenberg, Bullock, & Raya, 1993). That is why there are not yet any universally recognized and accepted developmental measures. This problem, which is common in the early development of any scientific discipline, is magnified by the psychological nature of concepts such as working memory and cognitive structure, which are based not on physical characteristics of action but on higher order descriptions of the organization of action.

The situation is reminiscent of the measurement of length, size, temperature, and time prior to the establishment of universally agreed-upon units and procedures. People agreed that temperature was a useful construct, and that there were broad general criteria that could be used in its assessment, such as freezing water and melting ice, boiling water, feeling hot or cold, and so forth. Measurement began with the most consistent observable referents, such as the melting of ice and the boiling of water, and was extended to referents that showed some consistency, such as when people feel cold, when they feel hot, when they shiver, when they sweat profusely. But these events delineate relatively large units of temperature and so mark only a beginning for measurement. Until researchers agreed on the units and procedures for measuring temperature, they had no satisfactory means of coordinating their observations in various locations and positions.

The same situation applies in developmental measurement. People recognize that development is a useful construct and that there are important differences in the thinking of infants, children, adolescents, and adults. At the same time, there has been no agreement about the units of development and no satisfactory way of coordinating observations of development across domains and contexts. Researchers can potentially agree on a few observable referents. Development begins with birth and ends with death, and interspersed along the way there are developmental "milestones," such as walking, speaking sentences, puberty, and having children. Though these points, like melting point, boiling point, feeling cold, and feeling hot, represent relatively large units that are limited in their utility, they can form the basis for beginning to build a developmental ruler.

Recent advances in psychometrics in general and developmental assessment in particular have allowed developmentalists to move beyond this beginning to build better rulers for measuring important developmental constructs. One such ruler relevant to this *Monograph* examines cognitive-developmental complexity as marked by discontinuities in growth (fits and starts, jumps and gaps). Cognitive performances can be usefully characterized in terms of a limited number of developmental levels marked by discontinuities that show considerable consistency across tasks, contexts, and children (Dawson, 2002; Dawson et al., under review; Fischer & Bidell, 1998; Fischer, Rotenberg, et al., 1993). The levels of activities vary under some conditions, just as water freezes at different temperatures when it has mud in it, when it is mixed with alcohol, when it is under increased or decreased atmospheric pressure, and so forth. When assessed with consistent procedures and especially under conditions designed to stabilize and optimize performance, however, development shows a systematic series of discontinuities, which we call levels or stages.

These levels provide fine calibration for a developmental ruler that measures cognitive development, defining subunits on the ruler—the degrees of development. This kind of ruler was not used in the current study, although the authors did perform an intuitive analysis of their tasks and suggest relations to this scale. The specific levels and the grain of coding have not been tested in scale construction, and they seem to vary with different items and scales. Variations in levels assessed and grain of

159

coding have important effects on findings, especially in a multidimensional model.

Another kind of ruler that has been finely developed in prior research is that for working memory. Case, Baddeley, Halford, and others have done extensive research constructing rulers to measure working memory, some of which has focused on development (Case, 1991; Case, 1992; Halford, Wilson, & Phillips, 1998) and some on variation in performance in adults (Baddeley, 1990). Scales vary with different content and assessment conditions, and items must be carefully tested to ensure a good ruler. For the most part, Demetriou and colleagues did not use these research-based rulers to assess working memory.

What are the important properties of a good measure or ruler? A consensual definition is that a measure must (a) address a single trait, (b) apply to multiple samples, (c) produce reliable assessments that are independent of the particular items in one instrument, and (d) have interval units, not merely ordinal ones (Bond & Fox, 2001; Fisher, 1994; Luce & Tukey, 1964; Masters, 1988; Michell, 1999; Narens & Luce, 1993; Wang, Wilson, & Adams, 1996). Measures with these qualities are necessary to meaningfully model developmental processes.

Researchers can rely on the rulers established in prior scaling research, or they can build their own rulers by using the new methods that facilitate such construction. First, researchers must carefully define a construct or dimension and its assessment context. Second, tasks and items must be tested to determine how people perform them and whether performance is consistent. Highly variable performance can be interesting in its own right, but analyzing it requires a different approach, focusing on the cognitive dynamics (see Fischer & Bidell, 1998; Fischer, Knight, & Van Parys, 1993; Siegler, 1994). Third, classical Guttman scaling tests the sequentiality of tasks to determine which tasks form linear orderings (Fischer, Knight, et al., 1993; Guttman, 1944; Wohlwill, 1970). Factor analysis and related techniques test whether tasks form a coherent domain or divide into different domains. Fourth, Rasch analysis tests the specific scaling of items (and people) in a domain, assessing the intervals between items, gaps in the scale (demarking levels), and other scale properties (Bond & Fox, 2001; Rasch, 1980).

In practice, these four steps do not form a simple linear pattern but involve a discursive process. Based on theoretical notions researchers produce a tentative definition of a domain or construct. They then collect empirical evidence about performance within the domain, including specification of the strategies that individuals actually use to perform the tasks. For example, in developmental assessment, an item should not be solvable with a strategy that is less developmentally advanced than the targeted strategy or skill. To build a good ruler, all new items must undergo extensive testing. Procedures are helpful that ask older children and adults to think aloud as they perform a task. Items can be identified through observation and scaling assessment that can be solved with multiple strategies or that are performed differently from what was intended. Once identified, these items can be refined with further research to determine whether they can be improved or whether they show something interesting or important.

This kind of scale development is especially important in a study like the present one where each battery is of necessity made up of very few items. Under these conditions, every single item must be a good indicator of the construct. The iterative test design process advances theory in two ways. First, it provides accurate, reliable measures that can be widely employed to test constructs. Second, it aids in refinement of constructs through assessment of dimensionality. Does a ruler measure one dimension, or does it measure several combined dimensions? Recent projects employing the Rasch model to validate developmental assessments present a rigorous approach to the construction of developmental measures (Bond & Fox, 2001; Dawson, 2002; Fisher, 1994). Because the computer programs employed to conduct Rasch analyses provide highly detailed information about item, person, and scale functioning, they are ideally suited for this application.

As a discipline, cognitive developmental science now has the tools to establish agreed-upon scales for major constructs—the construction of reliable and accurate developmental assessments and, eventually, of genuine developmental rulers. Good measurement has an enormous impact on theory development, for it is only when we can measure a construct reliably, accurately, and repeatedly that we can rigorously examine models and explanations. The importance of good measurement is even greater in research with models because the multidimensionality of models like those in this *Monograph* increases error. Typically, error increases exponentially as the number of dimensions increases. A small error in the calculation of length, for example, magnifies into a large error in the determination of volume. Because of the enormous increase in the effects of error in studies that use models to test relations among constructs, the requirement for good measures increases greatly.

Using Models of Development

In the new kind of developmental science, methods and theories are integrated through the use of good rulers for multiple constructs in appropriately complex developmental models. Research does not stop with one model, however. Most developmental theory requires several kinds of models for a thorough test of constructs. Demetriou and colleagues provide

161

a strong example of this process by using structural equation modeling, linear growth modeling, and a simple form of dynamic growth modeling to examine processing efficiency, working memory, and cognitive structure in development. Complex dynamic systems models are a fourth kind that is important for the new developmental science. Different kinds of models can answer different questions about the nature of cognitive development.

First, structural equation modeling has become the most widely used form of explicit model testing in developmental science (Kaplan, 2000). Based on linear regression, it is a valuable tool for comparing different models of linear relations among measures and/or constructs. Demetriou and his colleagues use it appropriately to test their model of linear relations among processing efficiency, working memory, and cognitive complexity. They find that their model is supported. From their analyses they report many interesting findings, such as that processing efficiency apparently predicts long-term development of cognitive structure (problem solving) better than does working memory.

Along with its strengths, the *Monograph* illustrates two of the difficulties that investigators encounter in multidimensional modeling. The first difficulty is that sketchily defined rulers obscure the interpretation of findings. For example, the finding that processing efficiency predicts long-term development best, and apparently accounts for cognitive structure statistically, is interesting and potentially important. However, the finding may result entirely from the difference in the quality of the rulers for processing efficiency, working memory, and cognitive structure. Based on the statistical properties of the measures and their grounding in prior measurement research, the best ruler seems to be processing efficiency, the next best seems to be working memory, and the fuzziest seems to be cognitive structure (because these rulers were not pretested and scaled and were based only loosely on prior research).

The second difficulty is that complex multidimensional modeling demands relatively large sample sizes. Structural equation modeling optimizes effect sizes; consequently, low sample sizes (low power) can produce unreliable path estimates. That means that low sample sizes can produce inappropriate matches with a model, rejecting the null hypothesis when it should be accepted. The result is that models are "confirmed" because of small sample sizes.

Happily, there is a straightforward solution to the need for larger sample sizes: The difficulties and expenses of obtaining large samples can be overcome by use of the same sound measures across studies (Dawson, 2002). Then researchers can pool data from independently conducted studies to obtain large sample sizes and facilitate testing of multidimensional models.

Structural equation models are not optimal for asking many developmental questions because of their linear assumptions and their lack of focus on patterns of change. Fortunately, other powerful new tools are available that are specifically designed for developmental research (Singer & Willett, in press; Willett, 1997). The simplest developmental tool is the linear growth model, including latent growth models, which are structural equation models modified to apply to questions of growth (Duncan, Duncan, Strycker, & Li, 1999). Growth models use the growth function of each person as a unit in analysis, as illustrated by Demetriou et al.'s analysis of children's different types of growth curves (Chapter V). The authors use latent growth models to test the linear growth properties of their major measures, and other researchers should follow their lead. Growth analysis should be a basic part of developmental research.

The third kind of model used in this study moves away from the assumption of linear growth, recognizing that most development involves nonlinear change arising from the dynamics of growth (Fischer & Bidell, 1998; Overton, 1998; Siegler, 1994; van Geert, 1994). Logistic growth analysis takes a first step toward nonlinear growth analysis by starting with logistic growth rather than linear growth (van Geert, 1991). Logistic growth is based on the standard equation for growth used in the biological sciences, in which the basic curve is S-shaped rather than linear. The logistic function is fundamental and represents growth more accurately than linear growth, especially for individual as opposed to group curves. Using logistic growth models, the authors can examine curvilinear growth functions, as is evident in the logistic curves in Figures 22, 23, and 24. They thus move their models closer to the basic form of growth and begin the process of analyzing the complex growth functions of individual students.

Logistic growth points to a fourth set of powerful tools for developmental research: dynamic growth modeling. Like most specific models of development, Demetriou et al.'s models for cognitive development make clear predictions not only about group means but also about individual growth. Demetriou et al.'s statistical tools focus on group patterns, but growth modeling moves the analyses toward individual growth by taking each person's growth curve as the basic unit.

Individual growth typically shows complex, dynamic change, often even more complex than in Figures 22, 23, and 24. When complex individual growth curves are averaged across many children, a smooth curve typically results, but that curve does not accurately represent the patterns of individual growth (Estes, 1956; van der Maas & Molenaar, 1992). Dynamic growth models eliminate the linear assumption of most statistical analyses and allow growth patterns to take complex forms. The spurts and plateaus of the development of cognitive complexity illustrate the complexities of dynamic growth, and they are generally more striking and obvious

163

in individual growth curves than in group curves (Fischer & Bidell, 1998). The complexity of those forms provide rich data to explicate the processes of growth and to test complex growth models (Rose & Fischer, 1998; van Geert, 1994). An important research paradigm for the new developmental science is dense collection of longitudinal data on individuals over short time periods to assess developmental processes in individual growth (Yan & Fischer, 2002). In their next study, perhaps Demetriou, Christou, Spanoudis, and Platsidou can add the rich tools of dynamic modeling to the new form of developmental science that they are helping to pioneer.

Conclusion

In this important study Demetriou and colleagues point the way to a new era in developmental research in which models and data are combined to build explanations worthy of the rich traditions of developmental theory. The requirements for this new kind of research include large-scale data sets with a longitudinal component and explicit mathematical models of important developmental constructs. The large-scale data sets can be collected in several ways: (a) through ambitious studies like the present one that combine longitudinal and cross-sectional data, (b) by combining data from different studies that use common methods and scales (Dawson, 2002), or (c) from densely collected longitudinal data on individuals that allow multidimensional modeling of development and learning in individuals (van Geert, 1991; Yan & Fischer, 2002).

The use of explicit mathematical models to ground and test developmental theory is greatly facilitated by new computer-based tools for multidimensional modeling: structural equation modeling, individual growth modeling, and dynamic systems modeling (including logistic growth). Effective research with these models requires carefully constructed rulers for the developmental constructs. Creation of such rulers involves testing of items and scale properties before collecting data to test models. Guttman (1944) scaling and Rasch (1980) scaling provide valuable tools to facilitate the construction of sound rulers and avoid difficulties with interpretation of findings, which are magnified by scaling problems in multidimensional models.

With these new tools for scaling and modeling, developmental science can move beyond arguments pitting complementary perspectives against each other and build a more powerful, effective field grounded in strong data and explicit theory that is appropriately complex for representing the processes of development. Instead of arguing for processing efficiency, working memory, or cognitive complexity as alternative explanations of cognitive development, we can examine all three constructs in the same models and analyze how they influence each other and contribute to development, as Demetriou and his colleagues have done. Instead of arguing about whether development occurs in stages or continuous functions, we can examine when growth has stage characteristics and when it is continuous (Fischer & Bidell, 1998). Instead of arguing about whether development follows Piaget's (1975/1985) individual equilibration process or Vygotsky's (1978) social support process, we can combine the two processes in a model that specifies how both individual learning and social support shape development (van Geert, 1998). What an exciting future we face as we join data with models to build the new developmental science!

References

Baddeley, A. D. (1990). *Human memory: Theory and practice.* Hillsdale, NJ: Erlbaum.

Baldwin, J. M. (1894). *Mental development in the child and the race.* New York: MacMillan.

Bond, T. G., & Fox, C. M. (2001). *Applying the Rasch model: Fundamental measurement in the human sciences.* Mahwah, NJ: Erlbaum.

Bruner, J. S., Goodnow, J. J., & Austin, G. (1956). *A study of thinking.* New York: Wiley.

Case, R. (Ed.). (1991). *The mind's staircase: Exploring the conceptual underpinnings of children's thought and knowledge.* Hillsdale, NJ: Erlbaum.

Case, R. (1992). The role of the frontal lobes in the regulation of cognitive development. *Brain & Cognition,* **20**(1), 51–73.

Dawson, T. L. (2002). New tools, new insights: Kohlberg's moral reasoning stages revisited. *International Journal of Behavior Development,* **26**, 154–166.

Dawson, T. L., Commons, M. L., & Wilson, M. (under review). The shape of development.

Duncan, T. E., Duncan, S. C., Strycker, L. A., & Li, F. (1999). *An introduction to latent variable growth curve modeling: Concepts, issues, and applications.* Mahwah, NJ: Erlbaum.

Estes, W. K. (1956). The problem of inference from curves based on group data. *Psychological Review,* **53**, 134–140.

Fischer, K. W., & Bidell, T. R. (1998). Dynamic development of psychological structures in action and thought. In R. M. Lerner (Ed.) & W. Damon (Series Ed.), *Handbook of child psychology: Vol. 1. Theoretical models of human development* (5th ed., pp. 467–561). New York: Wiley.

Fischer, K. W., & Kennedy, B. (1997). Tools for analyzing the many shapes of development: The case of self-in-relationships in Korea. In E. Amsel & K. A. Renninger (Eds.), *Change and development: Issues of theory, method, and application* (pp. 117–152). Mahwah, NJ: Erlbaum.

Fischer, K. W., Knight, C. C., & Van Parys, M. (1993). Analyzing diversity in developmental pathways: Methods and concepts. In W. Edelstein & R. Case (Ed.), *Constructivist approaches to development. Contributions to human development* (Vol. 23, pp. 33–56). Basel: S. Karger.

Fischer, K. W., Rotenberg, E. J., Bullock, D. H., & Raya, P. (1993). The dynamics of competence: How context contributes directly to skill. In R. H. Wozniak & K. W. Fischer (Eds.), *Development in context: Acting and thinking in specific environments. The Jean Piaget symposium series* (pp. 93–117). Hillsdale, NJ: Erlbaum.

Fisher, W. P., Jr. (1994). The Rasch debate: Validity and revolution in educational measurement. In M. Wilson (Ed.), *Objective measurement* (pp. 36–72). Norwood, NJ: Ablex Publishing.

Freud, S. (1955). Analysis of a phobia in a five-year-old boy. In J. Strachey (Ed. and Trans.), *Standard edition of the complete psychological works of Sigmund Freud* (Vol. 10, pp. 3–152). London: Hogarth. (Originally published, 1909)

Gottlieb, G., Wahlsten, D., & Lickliter, R. (1998). The significance of biology for human development: A developmental psychobiological systems view. In R. M. Lerner (Ed.) & W. Damon (Series Ed.), *Handbook of child psychology: Vol. 1. Theoretical models of human development* (5th ed., pp. 233–274). New York: Wiley.

Guttman, L. (1944). A basis for scaling qualitative data. *American Sociological Review*, **9**, 139–150.

Halford, G. S., Wilson, W. H., & Phillips, S. (1998). Processing capacity defined by relational complexity: Implications for comparative, developmental, and cognitive psychology. *Behavioral and Brain Sciences*, **21**, 803–864.

Hebb, D. O. (1949). *The organization of behavior*. New York: Wiley.

Kaplan, D. (2000). *Structural equation modeling: Foundations and extensions*. Thousand Oaks, CA: Sage.

Lerner, R. M. (Ed.). (1998). *Theoretical models of human development*. In W. Damon (Ed.), *Handbook of child psychology (Vol. 1*, 5th ed.). New York: Wiley.

Luce, R. D., & Tukey, J. W. (1964). Simultaneous conjoint measurement: A new kind of fundamental measurement. *Journal of Mathematical Psychology*, **1**, 1–27.

Masters, G. N. (1988). Measurement models for ordered response categories. In R. Langeheine & J. Rost (Eds.), *Latent trait and latent class models* (pp. 11–29). New York: Plenum.

Michell, J. (1999). *Measurement in psychology: A critical history of a methodological concept*. New York: Cambridge University Press.

Narens, L., & Luce, R. D. (1993). Further comments on the "nonrevolution" arising from axiomatic measurement theory. *Psychological Science*, **4**, 127–130.

Overton, W. (1998). Developmental psychology: Philosophy, concepts, and methodology. In R. M. Lerner (Ed.) & W. Damon (Series Ed.), *Handbook of child psychology: Vol. 1. Theoretical models of human development* (5th ed., pp. 107–188). New York: Wiley.

Piaget, J. (1952). *The origins of intelligence in children* (M. Cook, Trans.). New York: International Universities Press. (Originally published, 1936)

Piaget, J. (1985). *The equilibration of cognitive structures: The central problem of cognitive development* (T. Brown & K. J. Thampy, Trans.). Chicago: University of Chicago Press. (Originally published, 1975)

Piaget, J. (1983). Piaget's theory. In W. Kessen (Ed.) & P. H. Mussen (Series Ed.), *Handbook of child psychology: Vol. 1. History, theory, and methods* (pp. 103–126). New York: Wiley.

Rasch, G. (1980). *Probabilistic model for some intelligence and attainment tests*. Chicago: University of Chicago Press.

Rose, S. P., & Fischer, K. W. (1998). Models and rulers in dynamical development. *British Journal of Developmental Psychology*, **16**(*Pt 1*), 123–131.

Siegler, R. S. (1994). Cognitive variability: A key to understanding cognitive development. *Current Directions in Psychological Science*, **3**, 1–5.

Singer, J. D., & Willett, J. B. (in press). *Analyzing longitudinal data*. New York: Oxford University Press.

Thelen, E. (1995). Motor development: A new synthesis. *American Psychologist*, **50**, 79–95.

van der Maas, H., & Molenaar, P. (1992). A catastrophe-theoretical approach to cognitive development. *Psychological Review*, **99**, 395–417.

van Geert, P. (1991). A dynamic systems model of cognitive and language growth. *Psychological Review*, **98**, 3–53.

van Geert, P. (1994). *Dynamic systems of development: Change between complexity and chaos.* London: Harvester Wheatsheaf.

van Geert, P. (1998). A dynamic systems model of basic developmental mechanisms: Piaget, Vygotsky, and beyond. *Psychological Review, 105,* 634–677.

Vygotsky, L. (1978). *Mind in society: The development of higher psychological processes* (M. Cole, V. John-Steiner, S. Scribner, & E. Souberman, Trans.). Cambridge, MA: Harvard University Press.

Wang, W.-C., Wilson, M., & Adams, R. J. (1996). Rasch models for multidimensionality between items and within items. In M. Wilson, G. Englehard, & K. Draney (Eds.), *Objective measurement IV: Theory into practice.* Norwood, NJ: Ablex.

Werner, H. (1948). *Comparative psychology of mental development.* New York: Science Editions.

Willett, J. B. (1997). Measuring change: What individual growth modeling buys you. In E. Amsel & K. A. Renninger (Eds.), *Change and development: Issues of theory, research, and application* (pp. 213–243). Mahwah, NJ: Erlbaum.

Wohlwill, J. F. (1970). Methodology and research strategy in the study of developmental change. In L. R. Goulet & P. B. Baltes (Eds.), *Life-span developmental psychology: Research and theory* (pp. 149–191). New York: Academic.

Yan, Z., & Fischer, K. W. (2002). Always under construction: Dynamic variations in adult cognitive development. *Human Development, 45,* 141–160.

Acknowledgment

Preparation of this paper was supported by grants from Frederick P. Rose and Sandra P. Rose, the Harvard Graduate School of Education, and the Spencer Foundation.

Andreas Demetriou (Ph.D., 1983, Aristotle University of Thessaloniki, Greece) is professor of psychology and the Vice-Rector of the University of Cyprus. He is a member of the governing boards of several national institutions, including the Research Promotion Foundation and the Cyprus Scholarship Authority. He sits on the editorial board of several journals, including *Developmental Science* and *Learning and Instruction: The Journal of the European Association for Research on Learning and Instruction*. His research focuses on life-span cognitive development. Currently he studies the relationships between intellectual, self, and personality development. He is the author or coauthor of more than 120 publications, including "The Architecture and Dynamics of Developing Mind" in the *Monographs of the Society for Research in Child Development* (1993, Serial No. 234, with A. Efklides and M. Platsidou), *Life-Span Developmental Psychology* (1998, Wiley, with W. Doise, and C. F. M. van Lieashout), and *Unity and Modularity in the Mind and the Self* (2001, Routledge, with S. Kazi).

Constantinos Christou (Ph.D., 1993, University of Toledo, Ohio, USA) is associate professor of mathematics education at the University of Cyprus and the vice-chairman of the Department of Education. His research focuses on the cognitive development of mathematical concepts. Currently he studies the effects of memory and information processing on the development of students' abilities in problem solving. His the author or coauthor of 70 publications and is in the editorial board of the *Mediterranean Journal of Mathematics Education*.

George Spanoudis (M.A., 1996, Aristotle University of Thessaloniki, Greece) is a tutor and doctoral student at the University of Cyprus. His research focuses on the development of the child's theory of mind and the development of processing capacity.

Maria Platsidou (Ph.D., 1993, Aristotle University of Thessaloniki, Greece) is an assistant professor of psychology at the University of Macedonia, Greece. Her research focuses on moral and intellectual development. She published a number of articles in scholarly journals, including "The Architecture and Dynamics of Developing Mind" in the *Monographs of the Society for Research in Child Development* (1993, Serial No. 234, with A. Demetriou and A. Efklides).

Kurt W. Fischer (Ph.D., 1971, Harvard University) is Charles Bigelow Professor of Education and Human Development and Director of Mind, Brain, and Education at the Harvard Graduate School of Education. His research combines modeling and measurement to understand how change and variation produce diverse pathways of development and learning. Primary research directions include dynamic growth modeling of change processes, measurement of cognitive and emotional development, microdevelopmental change in real-life learning situations, development in diverse cultures, pathways to psychopathology, brain bases of cognitive change, and pedagogical implications of knowledge about development of cognition, emotion, and brain. Fischer is the author of numerous books, monographs, and scientific articles.

Theo L. Dawson (Ph.D., 1998, University of California, Berkeley) is the director of the Developmental Assessment Project in the Graduate School of Education at the University of California, Berkeley. In 1999 she received the APA Division 7 Outstanding Dissertation Award. Her research centers on life-span cognitive development, and she has special interests in the problem of measurement in developmental science, and in methods for modeling complex developmental processes.

STATEMENT OF EDITORIAL POLICY

The *Monographs* series is devoted to publishing developmental research that generates authoritative new findings and uses these to foster fresh, better integrated, or more coherent perspectives on major developmental issues, problems, and controversies. The significance of the work in extending developmental theory and contributing definitive empirical information in support of a major conceptual advance is the most critical editorial consideration. Along with advancing knowledge on specialized topics, the series aims to enhance cross-fertilization among developmental disciplines and developmental sub fields. Therefore, clarity of the links between the specific issues under study and questions relating to general developmental processes is important. These links, as well as the manuscript as a whole, must be as clear to the general reader as to the specialist. The selection of manuscripts for editorial consideration, and the shaping of manuscripts through reviews-and-revisions, are processes dedicated to actualizing these ideals as closely as possible.

Typically *Monographs* entail programmatic large-scale investigations; sets of programmatic interlocking studies; or—in some cases—smaller studies with highly definitive and theoretically significant empirical findings. Multi-authored sets of studies that center on the same underlying question can also be appropriate; a critical requirement here is that all studies address common issues, and that the contribution arising from the set as a whole be unique, substantial, and well integrated. The needs of integration preclude having individual chapters identified by individual authors. In general, irrespective of how it may be framed, any work that is judged to significantly extend developmental thinking will be taken under editorial consideration.

To be considered, submissions should meet the editorial goals of *Monographs* and should be no briefer than a minimum of 80 pages (including references and tables). There is an upper limit of 175–200 pages. In exceptional circumstances this upper limit may be modified. (please submit four copies). Because a *Monograph* is inevitable lengthy and usually substantively complex, it is particularly important that the text be well organized and written in clear, precise, and literate English. Note, however, that authors from non-English speaking countries should not be put off by this stricture. In accordance with the general aims of SRCD, this series is actively interested in promoting international exchange of developmental research. Neither membership in the Society nor affiliation with the academic discipline of psychology are relevant in considering a *Monographs* submission.

The corresponding author for any manuscript must, in the submission letter, warrant that all coauthors are in agreement with the content of the manuscript. The corresponding author also is responsible for informing all coauthors, in a timely manner, of manuscript submission, editorial decisions, reviews received, and any revisions recommended. Before publication, the corresponding author also must warrant in the submission letter that the study has been conducted according to the ethical guidelines of the Society for Research in Child Development.

Potential authors who may be unsure whether the manuscript they are planning would make an appropriate submission are invited to draft an outline of what they propose, and send it to the Editor for assessment. This mechanism, as well as a more detailed description of all editorial policies, evaluation processes, and format requirements can be found at the Editorial Office web site (http://astro.temple.edu/~overton/monosrcd.html) or by contacting the Editor, Willis F. Overton, Temple University-Psychology, 1701 North 13th St. – Rm 567, Philadelphia, PA 19122-6085 (e-mail: monosrcd@blue.temple.edu) (telephone: 1-215-204-7360).

Monographs of the Society for Research in Child Development (ISSN 0037-976X), one of three publications of the Society for Research in Child Development, is published four times a year by Blackwell Publishers, Inc., with offices at 350 Main Street, Malden, MA 02148, USA, and 108 Cowley Road, Oxford OX4 1JF, UK. Call US 1-800-835-6770, fax: (781) 388-8232, or e-mail: subscrip@ blackwellpub.com. A subscription to *Monographs of the SRCD* comes with a subscription to *Child Development* (published six times a year in February, April, June, August, October, and December). A combined package rate is also available with the third SRCD publication, *Child Development Abstracts and Bibliography*, published three times a year.

INFORMATION FOR SUBSCRIBERS   For new orders, renewals, sample copy requests, claims, change of address, and all other subscription correspondence, please contact the Journals Subscription Department at the publisher's Malden office.

INSTITUTIONAL SUBSCRIPTION RATES FOR MONOGRAPHS OF THE SRCD/CHILD DEVELOPMENT 2002   The Americas $293, Rest of World £192. All orders must be paid by credit card, business check, or money order. Checks and money orders should be made payable to Blackwell Publishers. Canadian residents please add 7% GST.

INSTITUTIONAL SUBSCRIPTION RATES FOR MONOGRAPHS OF THE SRCD/CHILD DEVELOPMENT 2002   The Americas $328, Rest of World £232. All orders must be paid by credit card, business check, or money order. Checks and money orders should be made payable to Blackwell Publishers. Canadian residents please add 7% GST.

BACK ISSUES   Back issues are available from the publisher's Malden office.

MICROFORM   The journal is available on microfilm. For microfilm service, address inquiries to ProQuest Information and Learning, 300 North Zeeb Road, Ann Arbor, MI 48106-1346, USA. Bell and Howell Serials Customer Service Department: 1-800-521-0600 ×2873.

POSTMASTER   Periodicals class postage paid at Boston, MA, and additional offices. Send address changes to Blackwell Publishers, 350 Main Street, Malden, MA 02148, USA.

FORTHCOMING

The Developmental Course of Gender Differentiation: Conceptualizing, Measuring and Evaluating Constructs and Pathways—*Lynn S. Liben and Rebecca S. Bigler* (SERIAL NO. 269, 2002)

CURRENT

The Development of Mental Processing: Efficiency, Working Memory, and Thinking—*Andreas Demetriou, Constantinos Christou, George Spanoudis, and Maria Platsidou* (SERIAL NO. 268, 2002)

The Intentionality Model and Language Acquisition: Engagement, Effort, and the Essential Tension in Development—*Lois Bloom and Erin Tinker* (SERIAL NO. 267, 2001)

Children with Disabilities: A Longitudinal Study of Child Development and Parent Well-being—*Penny Hauser-Cram, Marji Erickson Warfield, Jack P. Shonkoff, and Marty Wyngaarden Krauss* (SERIAL NO. 266, 2001)

Rhythms of Dialogue in Infancy: Coordinated Timing in Development—*Joseph Jaffe, Beatrice Beebe, Stanley Feldstein, Cynthia L. Crown, and Michael D. Jasnow* (SERIAL NO. 265, 2001)

Early Television Viewing and Adolescent Behavior: The Recontact Study—*Daniel R. Anderson, Aletha C. Huston, Kelly Schmitt, Deborah Linebarger, and John C. Wright* (SERIAL NO. 264, 2001)

Parameters of Remembering and Forgetting in the Transition from Infancy to Early Childhood—*P. J. Bauer, J. A. Wenner, P. L. Dropik, and S. S. Wewerka* (SERIAL NO. 263, 2000)

Breaking the Language Barrier: An Emergentist Coalition Model for the Origins of Word Learning—*George J. Hollich, Kathy Hirsh-Pasek, Roberta Michnick Golinkoff* (SERIAL NO. 262, 2000)

Across the Great Divide: Bridging the Gap Between Understanding of Toddlers' and Other Children's Thinking—*Zhe Chen and Robert Siegler* (SERIAL NO. 261, 2000)

Making the Most of Summer School: A Meta-Analytic and Narrative Review—*Harris Cooper, Kelly Charlton, Jeff C. Valentine, and Laura Muhlenbruck* (SERIAL NO. 260, 2000)

Adolescent Siblings in Stepfamilies: Family Functioning and Adolescent Adjustment—*E. Mavis Hetherington, Sandra H. Henderson, and David Reiss* (SERIAL NO. 259, 1999)

Atypical Attachment in Infancy and Early Childhood Among Children at Developmental Risk—*Joan I. Vondra and Douglas Barnett* (SERIAL NO. 258, 1999)